BEYOND INTIMACY

McGill-Queen's Iberian and Latin American Cultures Series
Series editor: Nicolás Fernández-Medina

The McGill-Queen's Iberian and Latin American Cultures Series is committed to publishing original scholarship that explores and re-evaluates Iberian and Latin American cultures, connections, and identities. Offering diverse perspectives on a range of regional and global histories from the early modern period to twenty-first-century contexts, the series cuts across disciplinary boundaries to consider how questions of authority, nation, revolution, gender, sexuality, science, epistemology, avant-gardism, aesthetics, travel, colonization, race relations, religious belief, and media technologies, among others, have shaped the rich and complex trajectories of modernity in the Iberian Peninsula and Latin America.

The McGill-Queen's Iberian and Latin American Cultures Series promotes rigorous scholarship and welcomes proposals for innovative and theoretically compelling monographs and edited collections.

1 Populism and Ethnicity
Peronism and the Jews of Argentina
*Raanan Rein*
Translated by Isis Sadek

2 What Would Cervantes Do?
Navigating Post-Truth with Spanish
Baroque Literature
*David Castillo and William Egginton*

3 The Pen, the Sword, and the Law
Dueling and Democracy in Uruguay
*David S. Parker*

4 From the Theater to the Plaza
Spectacle, Protest, and Urban Space
in Twenty-First-Century Madrid
*Matthew I. Feinberg*

5 Death in the Snow
Pedro de Alvarado and the Illusive
Conquest of Peru
*W. George Lovell*

6 Configurations of a Cultural Scene
Young Writers and Artists in Madrid,
1918–1930
*Andrew A. Anderson*

7 Beyond Intimacy
Radical Proximity and Justice
in Three Mexican Poets
*Christina Karageorgou-Bastea*

# Beyond Intimacy

*Radical Proximity and Justice
in Three Mexican Poets*

CHRISTINA KARAGEORGOU-BASTEA

McGill-Queen's University Press
Montreal & Kingston • London • Chicago

© McGill-Queen's University Press 2023

ISBN 978-0-2280-1643-4 (cloth)
ISBN 978-0-2280-1644-1 (ePDF)
ISBN 978-0-2280-1645-8 (ePUB)

Legal deposit first quarter 2023
Bibliothèque nationale du Québec

Printed in Canada on acid-free paper that is 100% ancient forest free
(100% post-consumer recycled), processed chlorine free

Permission for reproduction of W.H. Auden's "Law Like Love," from *Collected Poems*, was granted by Random House; and for the eBook version, by Curtis Brown LTD. Permission for reproduction of parts of Myriam Moscona's *Ansina* was granted by Vaso Roto; and for *Tela de sevoya* by Acantilado, Quaderns Crema SA. Permission to quote from Gloria Gervitz's *Migraciones* 2004, 2017, 2020 was granted by Abraham Maczka; and *Migraciones/Migrations* by the translator, Marc Schafer.

McGill-Queen's University Press acknowledges the financial support of Vanderbilt University towards production of this book.

We acknowledge the support of the Canada Council for the Arts.

Nous remercions le Conseil des arts du Canada de son soutien.

---

Library and Archives Canada Cataloguing in Publication

Title: Beyond intimacy: radical proximity and justice in three Mexican poets / Christina Karageorgou-Bastea.

Names: Karageorgou-Bastea, Christina, author.

Series: McGill-Queen's Iberian and Latin American cultures series; 7.

Description: Series statement: McGill-Queen's Iberian and Latin American cultures series; 7 | Includes bibliographical references and index.

Identifiers: Canadiana (print) 20220431906 | Canadiana (ebook) 20220431981 | ISBN 9780228016434 (cloth) | ISBN 9780228016458 (ePUB) | ISBN 9780228016441 (ePDF)

Subjects: LCSH: Gevirtz, Gloria, 1943-2022—Criticism and interpretation. | LCSH: Bohórquez, Abigael—Criticism and interpretation. | LCSH: Moscona, Myriam—Criticism and interpretation. | LCSH: Mexican poetry—20th century—History and criticism. | LCSH: Mexican poetry—21st century—History and criticism.

Classification: LCC PQ7171 .K37 2023 | DDC 861/.6409—dc23

---

This book was typeset by Marquis Interscript in 10.5/13 Sabon.

For Erica Segre

*Z"L*

# Contents

Acknowledgments  ix

Introduction  3

1  The Case for Abigael Bohórquez: Against Injury  29

2  *Enladinar*: Intimating with History  64

3  Breach of Intimacy  103

Conclusions: Radical Proximity  141

Notes  149

References  179

Index  195

# Acknowledgments

This book started at the end of an article I wrote years ago about one of my favourite films of all times. In *El secreto de sus ojos*, justice and intimacy are inaccessible to the spectator, they belong to the space behind the closed door of a judge's chambers. Throughout the process of writing, so many people have helped me clarify ideas, think and rethink them, and sustained my effort in different ways. Some are specifically related to the pages that follow, others are *amores* that have accompanied me through years of *migraciones*.

My colleague, mentor, and most of all friend, Cathy L. Jrade, read, commented on, and corrected every page of the manuscript, more than once. Her brilliance as a reader and a writer, her intellectual rigour, her generous camaraderie, her *complicidad*, her faith in the importance of poetry and poetry reading, and her encouragement, are present on every page. Needless to say, I am responsible for anything out of tune in this book.

Vanderbilt University has been my academic home for twenty years. I thank everyone at the Department of Spanish and Portuguese for creating around me an environment of intense and sincere collegiality throughout that time. I hold very close to my heart the generous friendship of my colleagues Andrés Zamora, Vicki Burrus, Ed Friedman. I thank Anna Castillo for her enthusiasm in organizing the summer writing groups in whose silent circle of benevolence I wrote in good company. The most intense conversations on poetry I have had in my academic life took place in the classroom I shared with graduate students. I cannot thank them enough for the dialogue and the challenge they represented as alert, avid, smart, young, funny, caring interlocutors. In the following pages, I have tried to answer some of the questions in front of which we found ourselves in radical proximity. Over the years, Perla Ábrego, Elena Deanda, Sarah Fluker, Miguel Herranz, Clara Mengolini, André Ramos Chacón, David Richter, Daniel Romero, Brayan Serratos, Fernando Varela, and Steve Wenz have offered me many occasions for learning more. I group together Denise Callejas, Karin Davidovich, and Alonso Varo, although I have concrete and very personal affection for each one, for the bond they created among themselves, an example of solidarity and support of which I was and am still a beneficiary. I am grateful to Elvira Aballí Morell for our long walks and conversations on just about everything in addition to literature and art. Finally, I thankfully refer to the insightful words that Charlie Geyer and I have shared in the classroom and outside it.

I cannot thank enough Martha Elena Munguía Zatarain for introducing me to Abigael Bohórquez's poetry back in 1994. As I started exploring the work of Myriam Moscona and Gloria Gervitz, I immersed myself in Jewish languages, culture, and history. I am thankful to the Lady Davis Trust for the fellowship that led me to the Hebrew University of Jerusalem, in the fall of 2018, where Ruth Fine and David Bunis welcomed me warmly. In Thessaloniki, Rena Molho, the historian and native speaker of Judezmo, offered me extraordinary insights into Greek Jewry and Sephardic life, in addition to being a shining exemplar of what it means to love one's métier and deeply enjoy it.

Ever since we met in 2002, José Medina has been my constant interlocutor and closest friend. This book is in debt to his scholarship and to the intellectual and affective horizons he has opened for me. The honest challenges with which José's thought has always presented me run through the following pages. Andy Bush is a generous reader and a dear friend. My attempts to explain to Andy the different steps of my research benefited from his insights, for which I will always be in debt. Carlos Thiebaut has accompanied me from afar in the process of writing; he has read and commented on parts of this book, and I have always gained clarity from his generous perspicacity. Maica Teba is a constant presence of support and guidance; she has helped me direct my thoughts and my emotions as they came to the surface while I was writing. I met Allyson González because of this book, and we share a multilayered experience of thought and affection. Nissim Lebovits's poetic view of words has untangled a great part of the manuscript through thoughtful suggestions and comments. Working

# Acknowledgments

with Nissim on the translation of Myriam Moscona's poems for this book was a great lesson in linguistic sensibility. I met Myriam Moscona in person at a conference in Jerusalem, in 2019. It took us about three seconds to recognize in each other a sisterly spirit; our friendship is one of the serendipitous moments this book brought about.

As I look back, two names insistently come to my mind: Esther Hernández Palacios and Nadine Ly, the two *maestras* who revealed to me the beauty of reading poetry. Esther taught the first graduate class I ever took on Mexican poetry, and I remember vividly her analyses of José Juan Tablada's *Li-Po y otros poemas*. Nadine revealed to my awed younger self how a reader grows with poetry, and she taught me to love instead of fearing the sometimes impenetrable verse of César Vallejo. They are with me as examples of personal and professional integrity to which I hope I will never stop aspiring.

This book is rooted in deep affects: back home, the people who have always enveloped, encouraged, and sustained the commitment to my professional life over so many years, always abroad; among them especially my sister, Maria Karageorgou, and my friends Emilia Bessis and Kleopatra Sklatsa. In so many other places, friends and colleagues have framed study in dialogues of emotion and trust; Ana María Amar Sánchez, Marisol Barbón, Simon Carnell, Julia Cohen, Nathalie Debrauwere-Miller, Cecilia Enjuto Rangel, Geneviève Fabry, Pedro García Caro, Alicia Lorenzo, Mercedes Lozano, Paul Miller, Alma Mejía, Santiago Morales, Kasia Moszczynska-Dürst, Christina Mougoyanni Hennessy, Irma Munguía, Michelle Murray, Fátima Nogueira, Paz Pintané, Rita Plancarte, Nidia Vincent.

My gratitude to the team that worked with me at McGill-Queen's University Press, Nicolás Fernández-Medina, Richard Ratzlaff, Matthew Kudelka, Filomena Falocco, Alyssa Favreau, Kathleen Fraser, Elli Stylianou. My gratitude to Vanesa Calpanchay and family for their diligent work on the index.

I wish this book were not dedicated *in memoriam* to Erica Segre. The brightest Mexicanist of our generation departed far too soon. I will always miss Erica's comments – *su sentido crítico insobornable* – laid out on the tender canvas of our friendship.

This book grew with my daughter Kyana in mind: for her being there, her patience and understandably lack thereof, her faith in me and her beautiful smile, in hope that the knowledge that comes from the quest into how words of deep beauty fight for change nurture always our agonistic intimacy, this very particular path to justice.

Τῆς Δικαιοσύνης ἥλιε νοητὲ καὶ μυρσίνη σὺ δοξαστική
(Intelligible sun of Justice and you, glorifying myrtle)

Odysseas Elytis, *The Axion Esti*

# Introduction

Justice pertains to a quality of the person, and, hence, of the community
itself. Since its primary role is to specify the conditions under which
personal harmony may be attained, it is, above all, a cognitive category.
For it seeks to disclose the factual circumstances which ground personal
harmony in this capacity, it aims at the widest possible understanding of
human being, both in its frailty and in its strength. Yet justice is a quite
special kind of cognitive category. Its concern is also with that rectification
of wrong which alone will allow for such harmony to be attained;
and it aims at restoring a kind of balance or equity within the person,
between persons, and for the community as a whole. Hence, a judgmental
component involving morality is necessarily interwoven with the
cognitive component. Finally, since no means may, in the largest sense,
effectively flow towards an end – in this case, *harmony* – unless it partake
of the quality of that end, justice also involves an aesthetic component.
In short, justice requires that the truth of the other be grasped as a
representation of the interplay of the powers of both, a representation
which is self-emending. In consequence, justice presupposes the idea
of *participatory* truth: namely, that kind of mutual entrusting which
is suffused by hope and, in the last analysis, identical with love.

Leonard C. Feldstein, "Toward Integrity and Wisdom:
Justice as Grounding Personal Harmony"

## RADICAL PROXIMITY AS JUSTICE

The central claim of this book is that three contemporary Mexican poets, Abigael Bohórquez (1936–1995), Myriam Moscona (1955–) and Gloria Gervitz (1943–2022) have created a lyric platform for justice through their poetic praxis. Between 1976 and 2020, faced with distinct horizons of violence proper to historical and personal contexts, these authors showed the ways in which the lyric discourse that is created in radical proximity between self and other(s) offers a model for justice.[1] Intimacy and fairness mirror each other as distant yet related qualities of togetherness. They both refer to a bond with another and to a quality of an individual's inner life. In this book I will talk mainly about the sphere of the relational. This perspective is dictated by the texts I analyze, whose aesthetic positioning is highly interpersonal and relies on sociability. *Poesida* (1996) by Bohórquez, *Anisna* (2015) by Moscona, and *Migraciones* (1976–2020) by Gervitz present poetic encounters between self and other in which dialogues, explicit or implicit, explore justice viewed as a social praxis, a theoretical problem, and a moral quality of one individual with regard to another.

Because these poets cast their literary works in the mould of responsible sociability, they are also capable of envisioning a world-other, in which one arrives past damage and distortion, through a being-together that is both agonistic and viable. In radical proximity, the binary of other and self turns into human habitat of affective, cognitive, and moral complexity. I contend that Bohórquez, Moscona, and Gervitz put their poetics to work toward the exploration of a space of converging singing voices. In the poems I read, self and other share limits in radical proximity. On this human horizon, individuality and sociability are conditions of encounters and crossings, freedom and limits. The three Mexican poets cultivate the relationship between other and self, as an elementary kind of sociability, and thus create embodied instances of discourse that come into existence endowed with moral qualities concerning our duty towards one another. In their works, poetry serves as a blueprint for justice.[2]

Because speaking instances share existential borders, definition of the lyric voices comes from orchestrated movements in which the frontiers between self and other constantly shift under the forces exerted in the poetic act. Voices combine auto- and allo-references, adopting intimacy as the main link to what lies outside the self.

# Introduction

Through the poetic locution this welcoming of another produces far-reaching vicinity. The resulting poetic affair is marked by flexible bounds of selfhood and alterity, which consequently are conducive to examination of the laws of interpersonal and social engagement, a search for and reparation of occasional or systemic injustices, consciousness of personal liability, and a probing of historical perspectives in moral thinking through literary and aesthetic premises.

By my interpretation, intimacy is the prism through which it is possible to see justice and poetry as the poles of a dialectic. The bifrontal orientation of intimacy – "most private, most shared" (Yousef 2013, 119) – resembles justice's dual nature as personal quality and interpersonal duty. The uniqueness of intimacy as a social setting of being with others, I argue, contrasts with institutional and social models built on the normativity of the law and on personal models of interaction that are by definition excluded from general theories of justice (Rawls 1999, 47). Intimacy, as the lyric modulation of a dialogical utterance and the reciprocal definition of sentient frontiers among people, offers the liminal ground on which to test and build social virtue. As it does so, it also places emphasis on the lyric genre's social and aesthetic energy. In the texts I analyze, a variety of modes of being close – desire, filiation, mourning – and qualities of experience – illness, diaspora, exile, rupture – show how poetic utterance *qua* the right word can shape and map out the rightful act. Connection on the edge, where self gives herself to another whom, *de facto* and not because of reciprocity, she receives, enables the transition from the individual to the structural. Because of this fundamental change from the personal to the structural, intimacy as radical proximity is lived always in the *polis*, within its institutions, the most fundamental of which is justice. Bohórquez, Moscona, and Gervitz present intersubjectivity as full-scale sociability endowed with a theory and a practice of fairness.

Almost forty years ago, at the beginning of a text that carries the emblematic title "Nomos and Narration" and serves as a foreword to *The Supreme Court of the United States 1982 Term Report,* Robert Cover brilliantly built the case for the foundational quality of storytelling in the codification of the legal system: "No set of legal institutions or prescriptions exists apart from the narratives that locate it and give it meaning. For every constitution there is an epic, for each decalogue a scripture. Once understood in the context of the narratives that give it meaning, law becomes not merely a system of rules to be observed, but a world in which we live" (1983, 4). The belief that justice and literature go together is a long-debated epistemological position. In the recent past, narrative and dramatic literary genres have been used to explain the ideological slant of concepts of justice. For instance, Maria Aristodemou in her feminist genealogy of the law and evaluation of androcentric legality contends that the marginalization of women is the core value of Western legal systems. Basing her claims on the analysis of texts as diverse as Homer's *Odyssey*, Aeschylus's *The Oresteian Trilogy*, Camus's *The Outsider*, Borges's "The House of Asterion," and García Márquez's *Chronicle of a Death Foretold*, she develops a concise gendered evaluation of Western cultures and jurisprudence: "The effacement of the mother, indeed her murder and the legal system's acquittal of that murder, is used to found not only the legal system, but civilization itself" (2000, 265). In the legal realm, storytelling has a conspicuous place: "Narrative is what we must tell juries or judges when we advocate for our clients. Narrative is also something we tell our clients about the law or tell our adversaries at the negotiation table. Narrative is what we do throughout the semester in our classroom. Narrative is the stories we construct for many of law's needs." So affirms Joseph Tomain, another jurist (2009, 786). From a philosophical point of view, Todd Mei points to the need for a narrative context for justice in order to recast Plato's banning of the poets from the *polis*: "In the philosophical attempts to apprehend the Good, it is the *poetical* that regrounds this understanding in life itself. This is because all things understood in human being are set within *a narrative context*, and it is this narrative context that provokes a reinterpretation of its changing situations according to the Good" (2007, 773, my emphasis).[3]

In contemporary political philosophy, *narrative activism*, a term coined by Michele Moody-Adams (2022, 188), appears as key to human rights movements. In her *Making Space for Justice*, the philosopher offers an extensive mapping not only of why and how getting hold, changing, and retelling narratives of disempowerment is crucial for social justice, but even more importantly of the fact that such involvement on the level of storytelling is necessary "for pursuing a just and genuinely shared political life" (2022, 220). Moody-Adams boldly asserts: "Narrative is the most important means that human beings have – whether through words, images, or some combination of words and images – of giving *meaning* to diverse perceptions obser-vations, and experiences" (2022 193–4, emphasis in the original). Perspectivism makes visible the intersectional oppositions within a

Introduction

pluralistic domain of social imagery. Moody-Adams considers such discursive strategy as structural to narrations and endows it with pre-eminence in the struggles for social and institutional justice, because of the different and opposing points of view it allows to emerge and come into agonistic clash (2022, 189–90).[4]

Martha Nussbaum's *Poetic Justice: The Literary Imagination and Public Life* (1995) is a book in which, despite the explicit reference to poetry in the title, only one chapter addresses this genre. Here the endorsement of literature as a player on the field of justice is constructed on the belief that judges and/or lawmakers *qua* readers benefit in their exercise of legal authority (1995, 2, 4, 5, 10, 53, *passim*), because literary imagination in the novel (and partly in plays) makes accessible the vicissitudes of lives to which these readers may not have empirical access. In the chapter devoted to Walt Whitman, Nussbaum examines the poet's attitude towards his civic duty at the crossroads of ethnography, literature, and nation-building. Exaltation of Whitman's agency for being all-encompassing, and therefore offering a concrete aesthetic context for the liberal democracy of the United States, is based on the fact that as a poet he was at the same time a man of action and a scholar (Nussbaum 1995, 79–83, 118–21). Nussbaum approaches this poet's justice mainly in a historical and thematic way.

Law relies on stories to set the foundation for its plausibility, to direct its normative powers. Without committing itself to standardizing rigidity, narration legitimizes the law. At the same time, the productivity of meaning and the proliferation of stories that champion a legal argument or its contestation undermine law's unique interpretation and therefore, somewhat, its vertical authority: narration sets the limits of law's intelligibility and application by exemplifying its permeability to uncertainty and rectification. As Cover notes, objection to the law is intrinsic to its power: "One must know the narrative to live as the problematic latecomer and usurper but bearer of destiny nonetheless, to have the fine-tuned sense of a horizon of will and of divine destiny at which the objective, universalized norm ceases to operate" (1983, 23). In its confrontation with the law, the individual plot – somebody's story – affects an entire community's moral positions. Feminist theory, that is, history told from women's standpoints, queer desire as a practice that goes against law's alleged applicability to all, and an ideal of justice that momentarily emerges from the ruptures that human action carves on the surface of legal reasoning, all bring about doubt and delegitimization of the law, in order to cast

8                     Beyond Intimacy

legality in new moulds. In my analyses of poetry, I will talk about these kinds of textual relations to the law. Nonetheless I am especially interested in the third type of interactions, which I claim Bohórquez, Moscona, and Gervitz aptly conduct as they lay the foundations for a poetic theory of justice.

The insights of Cover, Aristodemou, Tomain, Mei, Moody-Adams and Nussbaum illuminate the role of narration as a factor in lawmaking, yet they simultaneously point to a conspicuous exclusion – that is, theory, analysis, and interpretation of the relation between lyric poetry and the master virtue of justice. It seems that for these scholars, the literary universe crosses paths with justice to the extent that it also belongs to history and ideology, especially in contexts of restored legality and trauma. Voices that speak about class, gender, and racial asymmetries also find in narrative texts a wide field for arguing in favour of parity, which is one of the pillars of justice in the modern era.[5] Although there are no studies exclusively dedicated to the relation between poetry and justice, some scholars have explored the particular cases of poets who write on this topic. Worthy of attention are analyses of lyricism in the political context of the trauma suffered by Aboriginal children taken from their families in Australia. In addition to addressing historical injustice within the framework of race and ethnicity, Gail Jones in "Speaking Shadows: Justice and the Poetic," and Noel Rowe in "Just Poetry," focus on the way the rhetorical aspects of lyric poetry shape ideas and convey claims of justice.

Jones maintains that imagination can be the force towards rightful restitution: "Justice is not about repentance, so much as it is about recovering one's own and others' possibilities and potentialities – a kind of dream of plenitude for every life, one that requires imagining backwards (to regret historical mistakes) and forwards (to constitute a more just future)" (2008, 81). This view of justice as a movement in time – a legacy and a utopia – animates Myriam Moscona's imagination in *Ansina*, in which Judeo-Spanish, the language of Sephardic Jews, is the topic and the means of poetry. Moscona dwells on her own amnesia. Her endeavour is not to recover memory. Rather, in making an endangered language current, she crafts historical continuity. *Ansina* imprints an ample array of cultural meanings onto the present, motivating debates, struggles for power, and resistance to violence. To conspicuously place Judezmo in her own canon is a risky task because the poet draws from and addresses no current reading community. The voices of this verse collection live outside the functional moral frame of actual speakers. For all these reasons, ultimately, the poetic prowess is to write the gesture of social life on Judezmo's silence, and by means of such inscription to render visible struggles of justice latent in history that resonate in the present. Moscona's poetics of justice legitimates the law of the language beyond dutiful memory.

Another element that Jones considers in "Speaking Shadows" is cognitive opacity, a necessary phase in the quest for justice after historical events of atrocity and trauma. This state of language in which discernibility of reason is in danger goes hand in hand with justice's unattainability, opening the necessary space for mourning, an irreducible part of the process of repairing the world and building it anew (Jones 2008, 78). The epistemological wealth of such an element is that it triggers imagining through which it is possible to "envision *alternative ways of inhabiting experiential worlds* and to articulate the relevant *experiential counterpoints* through which things can look and feel quite different" (Medina 2013, 274, emphasis in the original). The intimacy between Judezmo and Spanish is tainted with linguistic opacity. Moscona invites reading from this point of view. Hence *Ansina* appears emitted and received from a limit of intelligibility and aesthetic appreciation. This liminal condition that both poet and reader occupy with regard to poetic language replicates the bewilderment with which we envision atrocity as cognitive subjects and obliges us to undertake ethical deliberation through *alternative ways of inhabiting* poetic experience on the verge of silence.

In her article, Noel Rowe argues that a poetics of justice puts forward a relational concept of fairness: "The I–you address provides a fundamental understanding of the relational self, and with that a relational understanding of justice" (2008, 47-8). The idea of justice as essentially relational echoes an Aristotelian principle. At the opening of the fifth book of *Nicomachean Ethics*, the philosopher posits that "[justice] involves relationship with someone else" (2014, 1130). The I/you condition of lyric enunciation formally approaches justice and poetic experience. While this sort of dyadic sociability is inherent to lyric poetry, the situation in which self and other share limits of subjectivity – namely, are in radical proximity – brings relationality to an extreme, where self and other exchange positions in containing and being contained by each other. Such is the case of social struggles and queer failure, Judezmo and Spanish, daughter and mother, in Bohórquez, Moscona, and Gervitz, respectively. In each paradigm, the intimate relation provides the context of the poetic act while also being an intrinsic part of it. In *Poesida*, *Ansina*, and *Migraciones*, subjectivity is a quality of active and liminal ambivalence, demanding discernment and legitimation, both of which are key to the three poetic collections.

Responsibility, a cornerstone problem in reflections on justice, is also a challenging issue in poetic production. One of the prominent moral and political philosophers of our era wrote that "the principle of liberty leads to the principle of responsibility" (Rawls 1999, 241).[6] The theoretical orientation of this concept of justice is far from the situational qualms of the relation between self and other in the poetry I study. However, Rawls puts forward a consideration that is essential in thinking about justice and poetry from the vantage point of intimacy. He affirms that his theory "is designed only for the special case of a nearly just society, one that is well-ordered for the most part but in which some serious violations of justice nevertheless do occur" (1999, 363). The sociability of radical proximity, I argue, entails this kind of relationship and thus is by default an endeavour both oriented towards and based on being fair. Intimacy carries the moral value we obey and the personal praxis that materializes when we stand morally close to another being in conditions of togetherness. In this situation, happily or not, we feel the responsibility for self and other as a part of who *we* are.[7] Intimacy is this well-ordered polity in which parity is possible but righteousness is always in the making, and thus eminently agonistic. The condition of closeness stemming from responsibility and not necessarily from contiguity in time and space, of togetherness systemically felt and carried out, gives lyric intimacy all its conceptual stamina and actuality. Bohórquez, Moscona, and Gervitz are concerned in their works with justice not only because at times they set the problem of inequality or wrongdoing at the centre of their inquiry, but also because, in the intimate lyric settings they create, the inner domains of self and other share spaces of being and praxis. Therefore, their lyric enunciations are ultimately essays on the creation and function of a fair polity that starts with a relational definition of being and goes all the way to the ethical values and the obligations that govern sociability at large.

Justice and poetry establish dialogue as two practices that take issue simultaneously with the acting of the virtuous self and the ethical weight of social and institutional human praxis in terms of obligation. In *Political Responsibility and Structural Injustice*, Iris Marion Young favours political liability as the ground on which to think and, most importantly, to act against injustices with which we are horizontally connected, and whereby we are institutionally related to others who are not immediately close. This is different from the liability we carry when we are personally involved in an act of injustice.[8] The purpose of this differentiation is to empower group activism against the conditions that propitiate unfavourable outcomes for fellow human beings, even when we do not create them as proper agents of inequality. What is important for my argument in Young's theorization of injustice as a structural phenomenon is that, despite the fact that she looks into massive social and historical processes, she never loses track of the connectedness between particular acts and their broad social ramifications. She posits that "we are connected by our own actions to the processes that cause injustice for others" (2003, 17). In terms of political duty, Young situates an agent within the frame of moral action, thus personalizing every deed within a much broader social process. Intimacy is a privileged space for dealing with political responsibility in these terms. This is because, in Young's scheme of things, even without personal liability, we still are responsible for others because they are *our space of being*, beyond ownership – affective, cognitive, conceptual, or material.[9]

Nancy Yousef locates intimacy at the crossroads of moral sentiment and idealism, as proximity that does not depend on sympathy, empathy, equality, reciprocity, or symmetry, but rather that includes "limitations, failures, and the disappointment of fellow feeling among our modes of being with one another" (2013, 119). This proximity complicates the opposition between affect and deference, empathy and epistemic connection, love and recognition, and enables a new, mainly spatial formation of intersubjectivity: "Between the affective fusion of sympathy and the remote regard of respect lies a realm of proximity – of mere coexistence with others, both familiar and strangers – that provides occasions for intimacy easily missed so long as equal recognition between persons remains the privileged epistemic and ethical archetype of relational experience (2013, 21). Diffused identity and spatiality are fundamental features of this type of intimacy, which does not transcend the relational meaning of the human encounter. Intimacy may translate in a personal realization that is barely communicated or sensed (2013, 81–98). In Yousef's conception, closeness shapes the self inwardly. Vis-à-vis such a mode of being close, I contend that radical proximity does commit to a process of cognition, namely, the epistemic change that results from the contact of the inner self with extimacy. I propose to view radical proximity as shaped by discourse, corporeality, cultural residues, affects, and impulses, but also concrete ingredients of memory and history. This compound of features acquires contours in the transactional relationality of those forming the intimate bond, in other words, when the outline of the inner self is affected by the frontiers of another. Unlike Yousef's definition of intimacy, which "as mere proximity is without content" (Yousef 2013, 3), radical proximity is born out of the materiality of contact, found not in physical proximity but in the involved entities' obligations toward the concrete circumstances of the encounter.

The difference between Yousef's vision of intimacy and the concept of radical proximity becomes evident in togetherness between one(s) who can carry moral responsibility and other(s) who cannot – nature, children, those who belong to the past or are yet to be our interlocutors, and so on. Here obligation is unilateral. However, the reverberations of being radically close integrate the two parties in the accountability of one moral agency: I inhabit a space of non-discrete separation with those others, as we mutually shape our limit of extimacy, in existence and duty, for one another. In radical proximity I am – or am not – just, not only because I am responsible for my acts, but also because being with another is my ethical deed. Responsibility for another appears here as a constitutional act that establishes justice as both a moral outcome and a condition of lived experience. In the poems that compose my subject of study, the lyric voice of the self exists in debt with others, and the quality of this bond – the duty to another – is the necessary and sufficient condition of its existence. The capacity of the self to articulate the right word is thus the self's obligation to make audible what lives in silence. Existence and duty look and mirror each other in an exchange of gazes, straddling the shared limit that radical proximity traces between word and act.

Scholars from different disciplines have offered perspectives on the meaning and cultural value of intimacy in our era. Many of them concur that intimacy is conceptually and politically contrary to identity, because (1) it is nomadic and anti-subjective (Arnould-Bloomfield and Pucci 2004, 6); (2) it adumbrates a sociability that consistently upsets and reorients classifications of self, self-representation, and other without being amoral, by introducing the ethical stance of the depersonalization of the self and the other (Volger 2000, 60–6, 76–8); (3) it mediates between the individual *per se* and the collective (Milne 2014,

204; Berlant 2000b, 3); and (4) it constitutes the animal residue of the human being, thus enabling inner alterity (Pardo 2004, 42, 47). The porosity of the self in the state of intimacy has also been traced linguistically. Pranee Kullavanijaya observes: "Power naturally puts a person in isolation ... Intimacy implies inclusion" (2000, 86). In Thai, a distinction is audible between the plurality of a "we" that multiplies by coopting others and a first-person plural that designates subjects invited to share one and the same space. Grammar allots to intimacy the interstitial location in which the individual disavows claims of authority while fighting for a horizontal congregation in parity. Without necessarily embracing symmetry, the difference Kullavanijaya observes in the personal pronouns that express relationality allows us to see that in intimacy the subject *qua* self becomes more tenuous, less nuclear, more diffused, less *self-ish*.

Argentine literary theorist Leonor Arfuch contends that intimacy heightens the dialogical nature of the word by nuancing the opposition between public and private. For Arfuch, intimacy is the privileged perspective from which to draw attention to the unequal distribution of visibility in our society. She argues that with greater exhibition of the private space – which she conceives as the site of the "universo afectivo y pulsional" – comes a larger "vigilancia del cuerpo social" (2004, n.p., "the universe of affections and drives," "surveillance of the social body"). In these terms, intimacy as a category of political connection is a form of resistance. Here, yet again, the intimate is a subtle fissure in a field of bold oppositions. Arfuch touches on the formation of subjectivities within intimacy, based on the theoretical contributions of Mikhail M. Bakhtin's dialogical imagination. The Russian philosopher spent a good deal of his intellectual life mapping out the moral nature of interpersonal verbal interactions (see his *Towards a Philosophy of the Act*, 1993). Furthermore, "logical and semantically referential relationships, in order to become dialogic, must be embodied, that is, they must enter another sphere of existence: they must become discourse, that is, an utterance, and receive an author, that is, a creator of the given utterance whose position it expresses" (Bakhtin 1984, 184). When we hear a dialogical utterance, we witness a person, a life at the threshold of a decision, thus an active consciousness (1984, 111). Word equals agency in literary dialogism because it is backed up by an instance in the process of becoming.

This is always too the condition of those implicated in intimacy; however, while intimacy entails shared boundaries, dialogism may exist even when the contours of the speakers – emotional, intellectual, cognitive, volitional, moral – are not affected by their being together. In intimacy, attentiveness allows for the ripple of a verbal act not to stop where the self ends, nor to conclude in the dialogue no matter how polyphonic this may be. Rather, in radical proximity, the voice hypostasizes space, continuously acquiring cultural gradations of cognitive and moral values; a decentred self, in constant movement, attentive to external rhythms, meets another as she finds herself surrounded by alterity. What is said and heard in radical proximity are embodied utterances, perceived as they cross the threshold of their agents' existence, creating echoes beyond the self and within the other.

Thus I argue that intimate words are tainted by the voices of others at the threshold of subjectivity, where there is no clear distinction of nuclear individual agency or reason, but rather interlocutors who exist in the frame of a stichomythia thick with mutual resonances. This environment is not identical to dialogic exchanges in the Bakhtinian sense. Intimacy presupposes dialogism, the exchange of embodied utterances, but not all incidences of dialogism fall under the category of the intimate. The achievement of such openness and receptivity takes the form of dialogic performances between self and other in modalities of time and articulation: the sequence of the linear present, the simultaneity of unison, the extemporaneity of memory or echo. The weight here is not put on agreement or conflict, but on the way the encounter within or with another is discursively inhabited by those who participate in it. To this point, intimacy with another is close to dialogism:

> In Dostoevsky, consciousness never gravitates toward itself but is always found in intense relationship with another consciousness. Every experience, every thought of a character is internally dialogic, adorned with polemic, filled with struggle, or is on the contrary open to inspiration from outside itself – but it is not in any case concentrated simply on its own object; it is accompanied by a continual sideways glance at another person. (Bakhtin 1984, 32)

The creation of the hero drives narration, and together with plot it generates a centre of gravity in a novel, which is after all the genre of the bourgeoisie's rise to power, in nineteenth-century, free-market Western societies. Bakhtin explicitly distinguishes between dialogues that serve the plot and dialogic exchanges that strive for the creation of a consciousness (1984, 252). He also contends that the development of a consciousness safeguards the hero from the reification of human beings and values in the capitalist era. He singles out a process of individuation that is the exclusive prerogative of the hero, whose independence from the point of view of the author and from any third-person objectifying perspective is the purpose of the artistic form in the novel, fully conceived and executed for the first time in Dostoevsky's polyphonic narrative (1984, 62, 252). Bakhtin's dialogism is a space where interconnectedness and autonomy happen and are indispensable for one and the same process: the revelation of the "inner man," the "man-in-man," "one's own self" (1984, 13, 62, 120, 252, 278). The ultimate purpose of the dialogic novel is to represent a consciousness in the process of its making: in Dostoevsky's universes, writes Bakhtin, "self-consciousness is the dominant of a person's image and ... the interaction of full and autonomous consciousnesses is the fundamental event" (1984, 73). By contrast, in the lyric poetry I analyze, autonomy is subjected to the creation of a shared universe founded on embodied words and actions that may be oriented inwards or outwards. The communal in the individual, the spiritual in the social, the affective in the historical, and the animal and inanimate in the human, share the space of intimacy and constitute the pathos of the lyric.

The backbone of a world lived in intimacy is precisely the presentiment of a fair common space, where parity is possible, a nearly just society, in words of John Rawls. Within intimacy no investment in oneself is possible because plenitude is the experience of otherness. François Julien boldly affirms: "On ne saurait être restreint, mesquin, médiocre, quand on accède à l'intime," because "ce que nous fait donc découvrir l'intime, en conséquence, mais discrètement, sans alerter, n'est rien de moins que ce qui, d'un coup, par la possibilité qu'il ouvre, met à mal la conception d'un Moi-sujet bloqué dans son solipsisme" (2013, 34–5).[10] The jurist paradigm of *audi alteram partem* finds here its ultimate consequence: a discourse that is never limited by the silence before and after; rather it expands as an antiphon, a ventriloquism, an ever more altered echo. The voices of *Poesida*, *Ansina*, and *Migraciones* do not refer to the self, but to the possibility of a compound agency. Intimacy reorients the problem of individual identity construed in terms of sovereignty, starting with the singing voice of Petrarch, the reflective discourse of Montaigne, the confessional utterances of Rousseau, and so on and so forth; it also allows for a daring form of sociability in which subjectivity comes as a result of forces different from those of social life, where proper distance and tolerance are safeguards against painful proximity.[11]

The three Mexican poets use lyric intimacy as a mode of convocation, beyond death, oblivion, and existential shutdown. Their poetry books respond to the law's mortal exclusions by creating a *polis* based in arduous discursive exchanges. The topic of difference, be it ethnic, sexual, or linguistic, is central to my analyses, although it does not rebound back to identity. Rather, radical proximity emphasizes the shared fringes of identities and alterities; it hints at the ever-changing embrace in which self and other exist. Queer dissidence and Jewish divergence are privileged perspectives on the agonistic slant of radical proximity as social positioning for justice and have often been used to clarify each other or to assign to one the social anathema of the other. Daniel Fischlin signals towards one function of the comparison: "Jew and Queer resonate as signifiers of a difference that refuses monolithic notions of identity categories. In the margins of identity lies an ineradicable difference, the otherness that frames, as do all margins, the orthodoxies of identity" (2003, 383). Drawing out the comparison in social terms, Jonathan Freedman considers that "both [Jews and queers] betoken a social otherness that has the property of constructing communities within communities, cities within cities, a people within a people whose group affiliations are deeply occulted yet who compose a powerful, destabilizing counter to ideological as well as social structures of the dominant culture" (2003, 340). Freedman's topography is one of the forms these two emblematic others of modernity take regarding Christianity and heteronormativity in the West. In fact, it is my contention that intimacy as radical proximity tends toward, aspires to, prepares, and strives for a form of embrace of equals through an effect of decentredness, ultimately revealing the position-self to be always already the outcome of agonistic engagement with otherness. Instead of the self, defined by a surveilled and vigilant frame/border, the lyric voices of *Poesida*, *Ansina*, and *Migraciones* offer the self as a receptacle whose malleability increases in proportion to the heterogeneity of the materials it encompasses, and that is contained and fruitfully tinctured, whatever be the cost of inclusion in threat and pain.

From a feminist point of view, this richly self-eroding receptacle that comes out of radical proximity with others is analogous to the *chōra* in Plato's *Timaeus*, as elaborated by Emanuella Bianchi, and its existence has specific legal consequences:

Introduction 17

> *Chōra* ... denotes the country as opposed to the city, the properly
> masculine public sphere of the polis. We may thus discern a
> commonality between the apparently unrelated *hupodochē* and
> *chōra*: each term lies beyond the polis, providing internal and
> external limits on, and conditions of possibility for, an ideally
> transparent realm of masculine discourse, commerce, sociality,
> and law ... [The] receptacle/*chōra* is knowable only through a
> dreamlike awareness or "bastard reasoning." It appears ... as
> a result of this reasoning beyond paternal law. (2001, 131)

The *chōra* expands beyond the frontier of the law. In its domain, justice
is achievable by crossing concrete individual and institutional limits.
*Chōra* is the mould and space of non-harmonious voices and movements, and it is also "the marking of errancy as feminine, and indeed
the marking of the feminine as errant, striking cacophonous,
arrhythmic notes" (Bianchi 2001, 135). In order to advance Bianchi's
argument, I explore how lyric intimacy goes beyond the binary setting
of *chōra* versus *polis* by complicating the relation of home and exile,
the binary normativity of gender, and the debacle of traditional expectations in terms of harmony.[12]

A radical turn in musical composition came at the beginning of the
twentieth century with the advent of atonality. Arnold Schoenberg
dethroned the consonance/dissonance scheme of tonal harmony,
changing also what counts as beautiful in music. In very much a mod-
ernist fashion, the composer appealed to a counterintuitive argument:
art is about comprehensibility ([1941] 1996, 234). Atonal music is no
different from tonal music in this – it also conveys an idea ([1941]
1996, 234). Tonal harmony drives the creator to "an almost somnam-
bulistic sense of security in creating" ([1941] 1996, 236), whereas,
because of its lack of hierarchy and harmonic destiny, twelve-tone
composition offers a new understanding of musical expression and
representation. For an art that has no referential load in terms of
semantics, to alter the expectations of coherence is to go against the
whole system of signification. Schoenberg asks the listeners to understand dissonances the same way that the ear accustomed to tonality
understands consonances:

> What distinguishes dissonances from consonances is not a
> greater or lesser degree of beauty, but a greater or lesser degree
> of *comprehensibility*. In my *Harmonielehre* I presented the theory

that dissonant tones appear later among the overtones, for which reason the ear is less *intimately* acquainted with them. This phenomenon does not justify such sharply contradictory terms as *concord* and *discord*. *Closer acquaintance with the more remote consonances* – the dissonances, that is – gradually eliminated the difficulty of comprehension. (Schoenberg [1941] 1996, 235, my emphasis)

The musician equates dissonances with remote consonances, thus giving a spatial dimension to sound perception and understanding. In this context, being close depends on accepting that distance in systemic relations is neither necessary nor natural, and thus that laws obey a teleology that can be systemically altered. Sustain the experience of time present, hold on to the space of each note, achieve proximity not beyond but on account of a non-hierarchical seriality, where no point of gravity dictates the distribution of sounds – these are all lessons on the emancipation of dissonance that shed light on social harmony. Schoenberg elaborates a non-teleological and thus non-utilitarian conception of music and of musical experience, one that affects, among other strongholds of Western aesthetics and thought, reasoning based on analogies and predictability. Correspondence between unfamiliar-dissonant notes blows up aesthetic comprehensibility and opens the way for ontological and moral changes. In the spatialization of music, the familiar begets the uncanny. Through this topographic egalitarianism each note's meaning is revealed in the note's reference to the one next to it.

Schoenberg's ideas are fundamental regarding intimacy as justice because they reorient the concept of harmony towards a non-hierarchical dimension. In these terms, the act of being in dialogue, affecting and transcending on one another, gives form to a principle of existence and a manifestation of volition, without the tyranny of a normative conclusion. The laws that govern such harmony are non-utilitarian, non-teleological. The first conclusion Schoenberg arrives at in his theorization of twelve-tone composition, namely that "the two-or-more-dimensional space in which musical ideas are presented is a unit," sustains an analogy to the dialogic nature of proximity: "Though the elements of these ideas appear separate and independent to the eye and the ear, they reveal their true meaning only through their cooperation" ([1941] 1996, 238). Harmony in atonal music relies on the meaningfulness of notes based on proximity; it is the cognitive product of an act, concrete yet unpredictable, whose sheer existence has no destiny other than the one potentiated by its becoming. While music conveys ideas, it does not tell a story *stricto sensu*, it develops no argument, it does not rely on a representational allegory. By abolishing the interplay of consonance/dissonance with regard to a tonal centre, Schoenberg's proposition establishes harmony as a *status quo* among entities in parity, by means of a principle that is also the measure of its applicability. Harmony becomes in this way the outcome of permeability, change, fluidity.

I read Schoenberg's new understanding of music theory as inhabiting the horizon shared by justice as harmony in philosophical thought. Starting with Plato, a well-organized society – namely, one in which each individual and group works according to their talents and natural aptitudes, ruled wisely by the philosophers – has been viewed as analogous to a tripartite being of mind, soul, and appetites, with the first of these in charge of the other two (Plato 2000, 434d–e; Johnston 2011, 86).[13] In positing this principle of social structure, Plato planted the seed for epistemic and moral mistrust of poetry with regard to justice by maintaining that art – the love of beauty (2000, 403c) – is at odds with justice as "virtue and wisdom" (2000, 350d). Art imitates appearances and thus is at third remove from the Form and *aletheia*. In the specific case of mimetic poetry, art may (and often does) place what is of low ethical value, weak and base, before the eyes of the public in attractive ways, "and it irrigates and tends to these things, when they should be left to wither, and it makes them our rulers, when they should be our subjects, because otherwise we won't live better and happier lives, but quite the opposite" (2000, 606b). Mimetic literary genres are clearly detrimental to justice and *aletheia*, the two principles that motivate the layout of Kallipolis. The philosopher places a moral value on affection, hence the rigour with which he separates the part of the *polis* accounted for and accountable by institutions from the intuitive part of relationality, which he confines to private spaces.[14]

Jill Frank posits that the multilayered delimitation between a just *polis* and the mimetic genres of literature is based on Platonic objections referring to all the domains of thought and act: "Mimetic poetry is condemned on psychological grounds for appealing to the irrational part of the soul, on epistemological grounds for belonging in the bottommost section of the divided line, on ontological grounds for being at the third remove from the truth, and on the ethical grounds for emancipating desire" (2018, 50–1). Condemnation of the moral aspect of literature takes on a particular value in the case of lyric poetry, for this genre is built on a premise unfathomable for the Platonic institutions of justice, moral philosophy included: desire as an imaginative force of union with another. Lyric poetry can rework separateness in terms of the sociability between self and what lies in extimacy, because of its categoric dependence on the I/you dyad. Viewed as elusive and unstable, the domain of togetherness becomes a space that is taboo for Platonic justice, and the genre of discourse that stems from it is viewed as an unruly vassal for the state and the mind.

Literary discourse stands opposite the receiver, often awakening a moral interest: "Readers can be moved by stories and map their own life narratives onto the stories that they read. And these same readers ... also want to talk about the stories with others, explore them, give them further complexity and richness through group discussion, locate themselves through the stories" (Waxler 2009, 679). A claim of moral legibility can thus be based on the necessity of doing justice to those who live by word only, because of the strange solidarity established between readers and characters, considering that the former align themselves with the latter's happiness or misery. This argument relies on the ethos of literary *personae*, the moral depth of the plot, and the possibility of empathy through which readers may be moved towards justice and against evil. Literature, as a representation of human lives, can thus be viewed as a measure of difference between moral systems and sociohistorical contexts: protagonists and events will by default be judged with regard to an array of moral standards. The literary text itself is the complete rehearsal of this process. In their own dynamics, the figures and acts of a fictional world are judged by their beauty, heroism, baseness, and ambivalence, and first and foremost they have to live up to words.

Fairness has always been a disputed term in the social arena. In *A Brief History of Justice*, David Johnston claims that from antiquity to the present day, despite the many different ways of conceiving justice – utilitarian, deontological, legal, social – a common feature has always accompanied this concept and its application in human society: reciprocity. For this theorist, balanced or unbalanced reciprocity lends justice the character of retribution.[15] The original *lex talionis* transforms as it incorporates the vector of desert and merit: "justice is realized when people receive the equivalent in value of what they have given (or when they give the equivalent in value of what they receive)" (Johnston 2011, 176). In his account of diverse theories of justice, Johnston does not consider poetic justice. However, this rhetorical device points to a deontological facet of literature and an aesthetic of legality. The term "poetic justice" was coined by Thomas Rymer close to the end of the seventeenth century. Angelika Zirker succinctly defines it as "the reward of virtue and the punishment of evil" (2015–16, 136), Thought of in these terms, poetic justice appears to be a more or less transparent system of ethical judgments based on exact and exacting correspondences among motivations, deeds, and outcomes. In literature, poetic justice works in lieu of usually inept institutional administrations of fairness, holding a standard of moral superiority because it appears as integral and proportionate to good or evil, clearly discernible, in the context of a life with moral purpose.

By the end of the nineteenth century, faced with late modernity's radical doubts regarding teleology and the unattainability even of fictional fairness, literature sought alternatives to justice: mercy, recognition, and sympathy entered to save face for a world and an art adrift (Zirker 2015–16, 140–3). Confronting the exultatory attitude of the Enlightenment, poetic justice gave way to elaborations on human virtue. Thus, knowledge stemming from literature intersected with virtue by moving away from the certainty of moral teleology and accepting a role other than judgment. From the nineteenth century on, narrative deliberations on the ethical aspects of human relations antagonized institutional justice by demonstrating its limits. Jeff Dolven's inquiry into the model of ethics implied by "poetic justice" sustains a counterintuitive proposition: "At the root of this durable idea of poetic justice is the fantasy that punishment is unnecessary: that the world is so constructed that all transgressions are revenged in the nature of things" (2001, 128). Two essentially contradictory thoughts are at the core of this idea. The first signals towards a systemic normativity of all acts: our lives belong to a system, supervised by a providential authority. The second is that in a world without any particular purpose, the only legitimate etiology is that of the act as a closed circuit of causes and effects that underlie the immediate finitude of human praxis. In Spanish, the proverb "en el pecado lleva la penitencia" (punishment is part of the sin, i.e., punishment inheres in crime) encapsulates the moral premise Dolven aptly deconstructs.

The scholar's attack against the ethics of poetic justice is construed on the basis of its retributive function, understood as reciprocity. Dolven's conclusion is unmistakably ironic: "The English practice of allegorical punishment ... especially as a state function, was on the wane by the time the phrase 'poetic justice' came into use, by the time it found its name. The eighteenth century began to enjoy the luxury of believing that such dangerous satisfactions had been expelled from the polis and exiled to the imagination" (2001, 140). Throughout the theocratic era, desire for justice materialized in the individual and social literary imagination and in public performance of punishment along the same lines. In this context of social morality, there was something to be gained by exposing flaws of human nature. On this basis, canonical literature and the law aligned with each other in that they participated in a world of clear didactic purpose, free will, and relentless accountability to a higher moral authority.

Through a complex argument that puts together historical evidence, philosophical principles, and the intuitions available to a recipient of beauty, Elaine Scarry presents a full account of how art and the moral structure of the law come together in the materiality of the aesthetic object. She contends that the bridge between justice and beauty is laid down by aliveness and distribution (1999, 90–2). This connection stems from the desire to infuse with life that which is uneven and suffering. For Scarry, beauty and justice are not analogous, but rather engender each other. In this sense, when one falters, the existence of the other becomes an awakening to the goodness and indispensability of the one that is stumbling. The critic does not distinguish between the various kinds of beauty in art and in other domains, such as the purely aesthetic, the ornamental, the natural, and the artificial. Moreover, with regard to how beauty and justice are related, her argument applies equally to the animate and inanimate worlds.

For Scarry, "the meanings of 'fair' in the sense of loveliness of countenance and 'fair' in the sense of distribution converge" (1999, 104) in order to build the conceptual common ground on which communication between the two realms of human activity – art and justice – can be fluid. In a world of painful inequalities, where the concept of beauty has been criticized for how its exclusion of non-canonical aesthetics exacerbates social unfairness, this literary scholar endorses the possibility that beauty and virtue may pertain to the same domain. She supports this mostly on account of the receiver's reaction to the work of art and its moral effect.[16] Alexander Nehamas offers a Nietzschean twist to these ideas, introducing the element of hope not as a moral feature but as a premise of uncertainty. Less optimistic and even more personal than Scarry, the Greek aesthetician points out that recognizing beauty does not make the individual who carries out such a cognitive act a more beautiful person, nor does it situate the one who identifies virtue on the side of justice. Nehamas locates the moral weight of beauty in the blurry territory of an expectation, ignited by the form and materialized in intense attraction, that is, in the need for proximity: "Beautiful things require attention and, if only for a limited time, an attachment both deep and intense; to abandon them, like being abandoned by them, is always a source of pain" (2007, 102). Nehamas claims that the desire for closeness to the beautiful object or person is unremitting and that it is based on the intuition of meaningfulness residing in the object (2007, 41). In the attempt to understand beauty, hope is set in motion. Through the gate opened by that which resides in the form of art or a person, the object of aesthetic appreciation promises a change for the happier for one's own self and world. Nehamas not only preserves but actually builds upon the good derived from the specific materiality of form, because he attaches to it an energy exerted on the observer, who in turn becomes the bearer of hope outside the aesthetic experience.

The question of form is at the centre of the definition of poetry vis-à-vis other literary and social genres of discourse, especially in modernity, when traditional versification has suffered substantial changes. One such change, the most radical in terms of the laws that govern separation between prose and verse, has to do with the integration of poetry and the poet within a lawful society. Immediately after the first publication of *Les fleurs du mal*, Charles Baudelaire found himself involved in a legal battle. His book was accused of immorality because of a misinterpretation. Elissa Marder studies this moment in Baudelaire's life and the onset of modern poetry from a point of view both historical and formal. She argues that modern poetry was founded on a reaction to legitimacy in terms of the law, as well as with regard to the legitimacy of interpretation. The clash between the poet and the legal system corresponded to the breakdown of the normativity in versification. To explain the emergence of the prose poem as rupture of poetic form in Baudelaire's *Le spleen de Paris*, Marder offers the following interpretation:

> Compared to the residual ideal of homosocial complicity that underwrites the verse poems, the voice that speaks in the prose poems maintains a very different relation to the law and the question of "justice" ... In transforming *malentendu* into a critical element of his theory of poetic production, Baudelaire turns away from all institutional forms of social justice and turns instead to something else – a form of violent poetic action that he calls "criminal jouissance." (2014, 73)

The target of Baudelaire's literary acting out is double: the law of poetry, and that of the *polis*. The idea is surely suggestive, notwithstanding that there had been attempts to break away from the mould of versified order before *Le spleen de Paris* – polymetric poetry being one such attempt – and that the prose poem had an important forerunner in Aloysius Bertrand's posthumous *Gaspard de la nuit* (1842). Nonetheless the point is well taken: Baudelaire contests the purpose of public welfare and the legal system that supports it. Despondent before the short-sightedness of his judges, whom he accuses of not understanding his *Les fleurs du mal*, Baudelaire turns his fury against art and destroys versification, namely the cornerstone of legitimate poetic creation. In the prose poem, he assaults and abuses code and tradition. The modern poet drives his art against its own conventions and declares that only outlawed words can sustain poetry's ethical and aesthetic commitment. He situates the lyric form before the law, in such a way that modern poetry arises from a major falling out of the poet-citizen with the legal system, symbolically and practically depicted in the poetic form.

Marder masterfully dissects Baudelaire's disappointment and defiance in the breaking-glass clatter of "The Bad Glazier," which overwhelms poetry's innermost core: "the work of creating *harmony*, melody, and *order* out of the base materials but as a rejection of base materialism [which] was once – once upon a time – associated with a very particular job description, *jadis*, the job of the poet" (Marder 2014, 75, my emphases). If we take the evaluation of this loud mishap one step further, the issue of form meets problems of social harmony and order: the fact that poetry cannot be heard and that the poet is not understood in a court of law means that lyric harmony has lost its place in social dialogue and that Plato is emblematically winning the battle against the poets.

On the one hand, distribution of labour, free market economy, luxury, urban development, and technology all turn the lyric poet into a delinquent. On the other, the city is clearly not the well-governed *polis*. Instead, the poet's misfortune exposes a dystopian world: the nightmarish outcome of the pursuit of order in architecture, mechanics, economy, in other words in the building of a fair society. In a gesture of defiance, which does not preclude self-loathing or destructiveness, the father of modern poetry dismantles the generic order by inviting the prosaic other into the house of lyric harmony. From this moment on, the qualities of poetry and justice will be subject to visceral assaults that will culminate in the avant-garde. Baudelaire's counterattack through the prose poem affects the external part of the overarching *structure* that threatens him, in one and the same act showing the intrinsic relation between the form of the law – the component of justice that is most visible and undisputed, yet for the same reasons also immediately vulnerable – and that of versification. He does so by rupturing the regulatory appearance of a commandment and thus expanding the poet's jurisdiction within and outside of the literary field, in the form of resistance and in the resistance to form.

The correlation between politics and poetic form, in Baudelaire's context, can be traced back to the Parisian struggles for bourgeois democracy. In *The Appeal of Poetry*, E.S. Burt points out that "the [1789] Revolution brought with it a heightened awareness of form, not only of the symbols and representations of the Revolution ... but also of the constitution, the forms of law, the order and administration of the state, and so on," and that the "poet withdraws strategically, so as to investigate the relation of public to private space." This introspective move, itself representative of a poignant relationship between lyric poetry and politics, becomes all the more intense when we consider, as Burt actually does, that the topic of the poetic critique is "a problem of justice" (1999, 4). Although Charles Baudelaire and Walt Whitman time and again have been considered modernizers of contemporary poetry due to their similar views of urban spaces (Berman 2011, 149–54) and time (Katsaros 2012, 99–109), the kinds of interactions between the *polis* and the poet they endorse are radically different: for Whitman in "The Poetry of the Future" (1881), renewal of lyric modes is the central proof of a nation's political modernity.[17] For the French, the labourer of verse stands opposite the legal system of bourgeois social rule. He wages war against society by exploding the limits that restrain him as a poet and as a citizen.[18]

In thinking the role of poetry in the quest for a fair society, one faces questions regarding both the moral value of poetry and its social efficacy. Does the beauty of the world fall short facing injustice? Is allegory (and literature is entirely allegorical in a sense) unable to actually capture the deed and its reverberances? Does one need to suspend memory in order to write poetry? Are beauty and poetry correlative to moral forgetfulness? Are being able to see beauty in anything, giving form to ideas, and formulating revelation trivial matters in the face of trauma, social death, and stigmatization? Is it that once we, as humans, have crossed the limit of wrongdoing, the only thing we can enjoy is by default words, never better placed than in a lyric poem? The poetry I interpret in the following pages patently shows that, in a world where human dignity is endangered, poetry enacts and incarnates a concept and an agency of justice.

The three poets awaken a sense of responsibility towards an other who is close, although not necessarily in time and space. By assuming a position of radical proximity, in other words, by letting the experience of another inform the lyric voice's being in the world, Bohórquez in *Poesida*, Moscona in *Ansina*, and Gervitz in *Migraciones* bring the injustice suffered and the fight against it to the front, thus reinstating the scene of harm from within the pain it causes. Instead of telling a story in which they remember the act of injustice, which many other types of discourse can and do achieve even more so than poetry, the poems and the voices of the three Mexican authors revive the moral horizon and the evil enacted on it, thereby allowing for a clash of moral positions. In this setting, they enable an array of voices to be heard in their singularity. The fact that lyric discourse functions as a hinge between the particular and the universal opens the way for such an endeavour to come to fruition with respect to justice imagined and depicted.

More than fulfilling a moral duty, which at times they also do, poetic actions and actors in *Poesida*, *Ansina*, and *Migraciones* internalize exteriority, embrace alterity, and enact what has happened to others within the intimate space of the self, one offered for the appeasement of the other's inalienable experience. In doing so, the poems function in terms of justice in a courtroom. According to the French jurist Antoine Garapon,

> Le procès est alors le théâtre d'une tension entre, d'une part, la qualification juridique préexistante aux faits qui réduit leur singularité, et, d'autre part, la toile de fond sur laquelle ils se découpent ... l'action du procès se déroule au présent. Son but dans ce sens est d'abolir le temps ... réduire à néant la régularisation que le temps semblait avoir procurée ... Il borne le récit, stoppe symboliquement le cours du mal ... La justice a deux fonctions principales : dire le droit et prononcer une peine. (1999, 116–18, 123)[19]

Here justice resonates with some of lyric poetry's constant features as a literary genre: time's arrest, universal subjectivity, actualization of time past in the present of articulation. On the basis of such

# Introduction

commonalities, and reversing Garapon's idea, if justice's commitment is to say what is fair and to sentence – *dire le droit et prononcer une peine* – Bohórquez, Moscona, and Gervitz assume through their poetry the commitment to materialize the grievance in the right word so as to give access to the responsibility and obligation of justice.[20] For this, it is paramount to set up a stage where the fate of another may be likewise the fate of the self, heard in orchestrated dialogue and lament. This scenery I call intimacy, the locus of a purposefully decentred self in its encounter with another.

Abigael Bohórquez's quest is social justice. His poetry resists injustice and strives for poetic experience. The relationality it struggles for is that of a social pariah. In *Poesida*, Bohórquez draws from the canon of Hispanic poetry and is intimate with AIDS victims. On the edge of health, beliefs, attitudes, and organized struggles, there lies a space where he tests social virtue: in being intimate, beyond desire, with the ill and destitute, on the verge of death and even posthumously. Poetry creates this space, shaken by conspicuous queerness and failure of vitality, rising from the precariousness of life. Bohórquez singles out the legal status of bodily intimacy in sex, epidemic, and death, as a right for those under threat by social stigmatization. The poet achieves his goal of articulating the right word in a careful equilibrium between the tradition of avant-garde poetics, found among others in Luis Cernuda, César Vallejo, Pablo Neruda, and the linguistic melting pot of the northern Mexican border.

Myriam Moscona strives for epistemic justice. *Ansina* is a poetry book written completely in Judezmo, also known as Judeo-Spanish, Ladino, Spanyolit, Haketia, and by other names, that comes after eight poetry books in Spanish and a novel in which the author intertwines the two languages. *Ansina* performs the emblematic gesture of speaking for the word itself as the sign of the absent other. By using Judezmo, the language the Sephardim took with them and preserved in diaspora after 1492, Moscona pushes against the boundaries of muteness from a place of linguistic posterity, already besieged by silence. On the one hand, Moscona replicates the position of as many speakers as she can imagine within the linguistic, ethnographic, scientific, and philosophical environment of her ancestors. On the other, she dwells on the language to the extent that she writes against the grain of its tradition, incorporating modernity, beyond the horizon of a community. The outer boundary of language – its expressive quality – presses against the inner space of words, expanding their generative possibilities. Only by testing the inner core of the linguistic system of Judezmo is Moscona able to do justice to the silence left behind by the death during the Shoah of the majority of the Sephardic Jews who lived in the Balkans. The poems depict what lies outside of the word and its negative, silence. Moscona is intimate with the uncanny through an exercise of duty against history and posterity.

Gloria Gervitz explores what a breach of intimacy can tell us about justice through the lens of a daughter/mother relationship. *Migraciones* has been rewritten multiple times over more than forty years. It follows the rhythm of feminist thought from identity politics to intersectionality and from the celebration of the female body and motherhood as one of its powers *par excellence*, to the necessity of breaking free from biological determinism. In the poem, mother and daughter sustain a symbiotic intimacy beyond kinship: they arduously debate their roles in the reproduction of their relationship. From the perspective of the daughter's poetic character, motherhood is an oppressive form of selfhood-building, based on imposed relationality: a mother is always a daughter, a daughter is potentially a mother. This two-way identification, a vicious circle of sorts, goes against the agonistic nature of radical proximity. The cry against motherhood becomes poignantly audible at a moment when the Supreme Court of the United States strikes down *Roe v. Wade*, curtailing the constitutional right to abortion. Under this light, the daughter's position in *Migraciones* is a stronghold of resistance against institutional violence towards woman's body. The bond of intimacy between mother and daughter in the poem rules over a dystopian love and dissolves the cycle of procreation. Queer sexuality – non-productive practices of desire and pleasure – and poetry – words that stem from radical proximity and that belong to others – are the two avenues through which the elegy for self and m/other will materialize, and by means of which justice will become the object of an ever-renovated desire on the horizon of women's constant migrations.

# I

# The Case for Abigael Bohórquez

## *Against Injury*

Hay muchas maneras de ser virtuoso. El amor es una de ellas.[1]

Pedro Castera, *Las minas y los mineros*

### INTRODUCTION

The formidability of Abigael Bohórquez's poetic language results from successive verbal explosions. Singled out, refracted, and examined verse by verse in painstaking detail, these blasts illuminate matters of life and death. Bohórquez's poetic power also comes from its questioning of the role of poetry itself in configuring civic values in democratic societies; his poems explore the ways in which people, institutions, countries, languages, and cultures come to connect and clash across borders, both physical (e.g., between Mexico and the United States) and figurative (e.g., rights and obligations, concepts and affects, material and spiritual disparities). Bohórquez's lyric voices sing out against social injustice also understood as depleted affect and intellectual impoverishment. Touching on class, race, and gender, the lyric struggles counter lumpenization of the outcasts – the orphan child, the destitute lover, the ignored poet, the drag queen, the citizen of the periphery, the indigenous – in hypercapitalist urban spaces. Close to the end of his life, Bohórquez looked illness in the eye and asked himself and the reader about the correlation of a poet's and a society's justice in the context of the AIDS epidemic.

In what follows, I focus on *Poesida*, the lyric collection that represents the high point in Bohórquez's engagement with the society of his time and opens his poetry to the future. The collection, written between 1990 and 1992, was published in 1996, a year after its author's death. Though the book was awarded the Premio Internacional CONASIDA in 1992, its daring content had made publication impossible during the author's lifetime. The title plays with the words poetry ("poesía"), AIDS ("SIDA"), and existence itself, as the past participle of the verb to be in feminine, "sida." *Poesida* refers to poetry both as that which exists (*poesía* plus *sida*) and as the daughter of the poet, using the classical Greek suffix "–is/ida," which marks a person as a father's female child.[2] The heading brings forth an important gender indeterminacy: *poesía* is a feminine noun, like the poet's daughter, yet the Spanish acronym for *SIDA* (AIDS) is masculine. From the very beginning, the collection points to plurivalent multiple meanings at the intersection of poetry, life, and gender. Bohórquez builds his poetic self in a layered, semi-chronological autobiographical account, at the same time that he offers a legacy already masterfully announced in the title.

Through colourful and dense encounters with lovers, fellow drunks, dead friends, his own mother, and many strangers, Bohórquez records the individual's desire for accountability, justice, and, of course, other bodies. The progressive irruption of different voices in the universe of *Poesida* transforms the lyric self's musings into dialogues. In terms of encounters with other bodies, seduction, intercourse, masturbation, fellatio, take place before the reader. The lyric stream of consciousness and the exchanges among poetic characters happen in the open; more importantly, they constitute a paradoxically intimate public sphere of relational practices: unsafe sex and lyric exchanges.

The collection's introductory poem presents the illusory border between life and death, a problem that will occupy the poet in literary, metaphysical, and social terms:

Poesida

Estáis muertos. Pero,
¿En verdad estáis muertos,
promiscuos homosexuales?
MUERTOS SIEMPRE DE VIDA:
Dice Vallejo,
EL CÉSAR. (2000b, 21)[3]

A three-way dialogue unfolds: the lyric self calls upon dead homosexuals and César Vallejo (Perú, 1892–1938). The Peruvian poet is invoked first as an aesthetic influence, when Bohórquez paraphrases his lines from *Trilce LXXV*, and then as a political authority through the pun based on Vallejo's first name. As "Caesar," invested with power of life and death, Vallejo offers the paradoxical statement "MUERTOS SIEMPRE DE VIDA" ("dead always of life"). Vallejo's poem raises the problem of existence versus the annihilation of human life.[4] Without ever pointing to a class or group of people, the Peruvian master uses apostrophic discourse to implicitly question any assessment of life that fails to recognize its ceaseless and inevitable attrition.[5] With poignant simplicity, he presents the drama of lives lived as cannon fodder, expendable because they feed history.

Bohórquez takes on Vallejo's lament of invisibility. In "Poesida" he weaves together archaisms, irony, colloquial language, puns, and literary tradition on the loom of eros vis-à-vis illness and *thanatos*. Echoes of the paradox of the living dead, famously explored in Santa Teresa's "Vivo sin vivir en mí," endow "Poesida" with undertones of mystical ascent and evoke the imagery of eternal life in spite of death, in a context in which unleashed sexuality takes the place of godly love. The poem's hieratic pitch is also evident in its verb forms. Like Vallejo's *Trilce LXXV*, "Poesida" employs the second person plural, an archaic form in contemporary Latin American Spanish. Summoned back from the afterlife, the "promiscuous homosexuals" enter the stage affirming their having lived, a statement built on the tense convergence of secular, religious, and literary voices of authority.

Inquiry into the reasons for ruined bodies, affects, and ideas take Bohórquez from the depths of his own life to the lives of others, and even to the underworld. Along the way he makes evident the gap between desire and death, on one hand, and biology and ideology, on the other. In dialogues rife with differential power positions, misrepresentations, and lack of recognition, Bohórquez's lyric voices emerge, giving intimacy a liminal definition.[6] I argue that because AIDS tests the limits of radical proximity as foundational to relational subjectivity, it also pushes forward a politically radical position: sensuality is a human right and thus a lawful pursuit by the individual in accord with the collective well-being. Endorsement and protection of this premise is legitimate and indeed mandatory. From the public stage of lyric poetry, in the absence of social structures capable of sheltering this basic principle of existence, Bohórquez launches a voluptuous human rights campaign.

In the eleven poetic compositions that comprise his book, Bohórquez explores different representations of sexuality, class, and gender through the public dimensions of feelings. He thereby pulls open the curtain that covers insignificant lives, revives the memory of sentient individuals within a time made of intimacy and words, and demonstrates the continuum between everyday violence and what has been judged as a "crisis." In doing so he reveals the predicament of characterizing as exceptional an exclusion and condemnation prepared systematically, while showing the need for justice. In *Poesida*, intimate interpersonal experiences probe a state of injustice. The collection exposes the helplessness of individuals and institutions facing human desire and pain. Bohórquez approaches this reality from the point of view of failure. Death by AIDS is not the endpoint of an illness; it is the outcome of social loathing. During the 1980s, queer sociability was brought to the fore only to sink into vengeful repudiation. The poet gives his characters a platform that they never had while living. He brings them back from the netherworld to sing their stories of disappointment, for their lives are over and their defeat is ensured long before actual death. Bohórquez will not try to dignify the deplorable circumstances of their trajectories. On the contrary, he will highlight the crudeness with which he and his comrades in sexual/social dissidence have lived and died.

The poet strives to integrate the infirm body into the body politic. He does so in the following way: the lyric self exposes his own life as one that demands to be recognized by others, then later on his own circumstances become the background against which the living-dead "promiscuous homosexuals" puncture silence and mourn with outrageous performances from the afterlife. The dialogue with the sufferers demands a great deal of courage on the reader's part, causing discomfort and anguish. To achieve a dialogue between the silenced and those who ought to listen, the outcasts and their accusers, the lyric voice straddles life and death, bridging oblivion and history.

In the spring and summer of 1989, *Daedalus*, the journal of the American Academy of Arts and Sciences, published two volumes under the title *Living with AIDS*. The collection included articles from the humanities, the social sciences, and the biomedical professions together with the voices of activists and people who at the time were living with AIDS. In his preface, the editor of the journal, Stephen Graubard, a historian and professor at Brown University, at the time, noted:

> We live with a disease that is incurable, that clearly has a
> long incubation period and is almost certainly already lodged
> in millions throughout the world who will one day show
> the symptoms of *their* condition. How are *we* to prepare
> for what awaits *them*? How are we to care for *them*? What
> can *we* do to minimize the risk of new infections? How, given
> all reasonable prognoses, can *we* prepare individuals and
> societies for the hazards that are impending? (1989, vii,
> emphasis added)

Clearly, Graubard believes that there exists a stark dichotomy between the affected "they, them, their" and the unaffected "we, us, ours." Among the polarizations he delineates, I believe the most painful is "How are *we* to prepare for what awaits *them*?" Bohórquez's poems fit right into this gap of the official rhetoric; they elucidate the fears that underlie such language, as well as its demand for protection of the healthy and control of the ill. The individuals who are only a ghostly speculation for Graubard become a firm presence in *Poesida*, a loud chorus exposing the porousness of safety and the impossibility of a they/we divide. As Bohórquez makes clear, nobody is spared: "they" and "we" live under the same regime, and what is deadly for the ailing "they" pertains equally to the ostensibly healthy "we." Bohórquez's mapping of death, desire, and justice in the era of sickness thus proposes a renegotiation of the border between the imaginable and the unimaginable.

At the same early moment of scientific attention to AIDS, contrary to Graubard's vertical separation and closer to Bohórquez's poetic endeavour, epidemiologist Nicholas Christakis wrote: "The pandemic ... suggests that we take an ecological view of health, a view that stresses the interrelatedness of the health of people throughout the world" (1989, 115). In this same light, I examine the epistemic and ideological context of works written in the United States around the end of the 1980s. I have deliberately read *Poesida* within this critical frame because I believe that Bohórquez's poetic attitude towards the AIDS pandemic captured and responded to many questions related to illness, citizenship, queer sociability, performance, and utopia throughout the first decade of the AIDS pandemic, for which I maintain that his poetic contribution was foundational and visionary.

34 Beyond Intimacy

## ABIGAEL BOHÓRQUEZ:
## THE MAN, THE POET, AND HIS READERS

Bohórquez was born in Caborca, a small town in Sonora, Mexico, on March 12, 1937, the only son of a working-class single mother, Sofía Bojórquez García.[7] He spent his childhood and adolescence in his hometown and in San Luis Río Colorado (Sonora). In 1955 he published his first poetry collection, *Ensayos poéticos*. Three years later he moved to Mexico City, where he studied theatre and scene direction (1955–58) at the Instituto Nacional de Bellas Artes. He returned to Sonora between 1959 and 1962, to teach at the Escuela de Arte Dramático at the University of Sonora. In 1960, *Poesía i Teatro* (Editorial Bartolomé Costa Amic), his first book, was published in Mexico City. The poems included in this volume under the title *Fe de bautismo* had already won first prize in the literary contest "El libro sonorense," in 1957. In 1962, with the support of Jaime Torres Bodet, a member of the poetic group Contemporáneos, Bohórquez returned to Mexico City, where he worked at the Instituto Nacional de Bellas Artes, first as a civil servant responsible for cultural promotion and management and then as director of the Departamento de Literatura del Organismo de Promoción Internacional de Cultura. He spent most of his adult life in public administration, at the Instituto Mexicano del Seguro Social, in Milpa Alta, Chalco, and later at the University of Sonora, always in positions related to cultural life.

He was the author of more than twelve poetry collections as well as numerous plays, oratorios, and monologues, which he staged on various occasions throughout his life. He was honoured in poetry contests in Oaxaca, Mazatlán, Guadalajara, Xalapa, Sahuayo, Hermosillo, Caborca, and Aguascalientes, to mention only a few of his recognitions within Mexico. In 1990, he returned to his native Sonora, where he lived in Hermosillo, taught literature at the University of Sonora, and participated intensely in the city's cultural life. By the time he died of a heart attack related to his alcoholism, in late November of 1995, he was highly respected in the cultural world along the Mexico-US border, where new generations of writers considered him their teacher, though he was never recognized by the Mexican literary establishment, which was dominated by Octavio Paz's poetic circle of *Vuelta*. The exceptions to this silence were the poets Carlos Pellicer and Efraín Huerta. In 1969, the latter wrote "Palabras por Abigael Bohórquez," a poem that

The Case for Abigael Bohórquez 35

shows deep knowledge and personal appreciation of this poet's work (in Bohórquez 2005, 27–8).

In the 1980s, slowly and reluctantly, critics started paying attention to Abigael Bohórquez as interest shifted to regional literatures. In 1989, the volume titled *Ya no estoy para rosas: la poesía en Sonora, 1960–1975* acknowledged Bohórquez's importance and provided a critical framework within which to read his lyric work. Five years later, that book's author, Martha Elena Munguía Zatarain, contributed an article on Bohórquez to *Latin American Writers on Gay and Lesbian Themes: A Bio-Critical Sourcebook* (1994, 70–2). In it she touched on the most important features of his poetry: attachment to literary tradition renovated by orality, dissidence, and the presence of strong social consciousness. In 1995, Fortino Corral published "El paraíso terrenal de Abigael Bohórquez," in which he read Bohórquez's poetry of social awareness as a defence of the dispossessed, a song of exile and uprooting, and a metaphysics of the flesh (Corral 1995, 235–41). In 2000 the poet and essayist Dionicio Morales wrote "Los resquebrajamientos del alma," a text that served as a preface to a new edition of *Poesida*, (in Bohórquez 2000b, 7–11). The same year, Morales was in charge of the introduction to an anthology of the poet's works between 1957 and 1995 (Morales in Bohórquez 2000a, 11–60). In the first article, Morales provides a succinct overview of the themes in *Poesida* as they relate to its author's previous artistic achievements. In the second, the critic offers a thorough study of the poet's work and life. Morales set the tone for other critics who worked on the same topic in the later years, especially after 2010, mainly in blogs and online literary gazettes and magazines.

Starting with the new millennium two articles offered a new perspective on Bohórquez's works. In 2004, Efrén Ortiz Domínguez analyzed homoerotic desire as social resistance. Applying the concept of the abject, he compared sexual difference in Bohórquez with marginalization rooted in racism and classism in another Mexican poet, Juan Bañuelos (1932–2017). In "Abigael Bohórquez o la voz sobre la frontera," I argue that in *Poesida*, Bohórquez surrendered the only privilege he ever had – his poetic word – to social outcasts. The use of choral structure throughout the book accompanies sexual, racial, and social dissonances, transforming lyric monologue into dialogism. This explosion within the lyric form gives Bohórquez's linguistic extravagance and stylistic innovations their deepest political meanings (Karageorgou-Bastea 2006).

By 2010, Bohórquez was gaining increasing popularity among young poets, critics, and bloggers. In *Abigael Bohórquez. La creación como catarsis*, Ismael Lares astutely pointed to the fundamental role of drama in Bohórquez's poetry (2012, 16). Between 9 November and 3 December 2015, Omar de la Cadena posted on the web an intellectual biography of the poet in eight instalments. This series closely followed Bohórquez as he moved from place to place, job to job, at different stages of his life. It thus provided a social context to his poetry by touching on his friendships with other authors, his relations with political and cultural authorities, and his trajectory as a man and as a writer. By basing his research on archival materials, de la Cadena filled a void in our knowledge of who Bohórquez was.[8] In "¿En verdad estáis muertos?," Bruno Ríos read *Poesida* as an autobiographical account that, through the nostalgia of desire, became a testimony to other lives (2014b). The current critical literature on Abigael Bohórquez is dispersed across websites, where different readers of his work offer their opinions, referring to their personal friendships and poetic apprenticeships at his side. Most of these sources emphasize the ostracism Bohórquez suffered at the hands of the Mexican literary establishment and contrast the richness of his poetic language with the scarcity of critical readings of his work.[9]

Throughout his lyric works, Bohórquez's poetic self oscillates between an erudite older poet and a social outcast immersed in the *bajos fondos* (the lower depths). He writes with a gargantuan appetite for words: his poetic vocabulary draws on the medieval and Golden Age lyric traditions, the provocative spoken language of the northwest Mexican frontier, Nahuatlisms, and the Yaqui and Seri indigenous languages of Sonora. Many of his neologisms are reminiscent of Vicente Huidobro's formal innovations in *Altazor*. However, unlike the Chilean's *creacionismo*, Bohórquez's linguistic revolution comes from the need to say everything, to live all lives, to stretch experience until it becomes comprehensible. Dissonant linguistic registers, amplified by satire and elegy, are key to the world of culture and sociability he crafts. From early on, Bohórquez used the dramatic monologue. Dialogue, implicit or explicit, became his poetic mode especially after *Acta de confirmación* ([1966] 2015) and *Canción de amor y muerte por Rubén Jaramillo y otros poemas civiles* ([1967] 2015). His mature works are heavy with civic engagement, specifically, with the poetically expressed faith that discourse can change society. Whoever sings

The AIDS pandemic in the West was first documented in 1981, when strange cases of pneumonia and cancer were diagnosed and treated in California and New York, in male patients generally in good health, whose common characteristic was the fact that they had sex with men. Up until 1996, when the highly active antiretroviral therapy (HAART) provided some hope for treatment, HIV and AIDS spread uncertainty, fear, loss, grief, and guilt across the urban gay communities in the West. Meanwhile, society at large treated at-risk groups – gay men, drug users, hemophiliacs, bisexuals, Haitian immigrants – with suspicion, moral condescension, homophobia, sexism, classism, xenophobia, and racism.[10] That same year, according to "A Timeline of HIV and AIDS," published by the US federal government on www.hiv.gov, "the number of new AIDS cases diagnosed in the U.S. declined for the first time since the beginning of the pandemic" ("A Timeline of HIV and AIDS," n.p., year 1996).

During the first decade of the pandemic, prejudices against homosexuals in most social and racial environments escalated to unprecedented levels. The separation between healthy and sick citizens became more extreme, and funding for HIV/AIDS research was obstructed. Not until HIV/AIDS began to reach the population that thought itself untouchable by the illness (Bersani 1987, 203) did conservative administrations in the United States (Reagan, 1981–89) and the United Kingdom (Thatcher, 1979–90) started addressing the health crisis in a more decisive manner.[11] At the same time, activism intensified throughout the 1980s in the face of tardy and deficient attention to patients. Members of the gay community were in many ways unified by rising homophobia, willful and obdurate negligence on the part of political officialdom, and newfound physical and social threats.[12]

While the media intensified mystifications of the pandemic, scholars in the humanities and social sciences needed some time to react. In *Policing Desire*, originally published in 1987, Simon Watney took issue with how media represented AIDS in the first few years of its spread in the UK. The book offered acute arguments against the paranoia of a public sphere shaped by misinformation, moralism, and homopanic. Watney related race, class, gender, and citizenship to social and epistemic authority through the lens of sickness and health, homosexual promiscuity and heterosexual marital restraints. The same year, Leo Bersani, departing from Watney's insights, wrote an influential essay titled "Is the Rectum a Grave?" in which he examined homophobia around the pandemic in relation to representations of masculinity and men's sexuality. He argued that the heterosexist culture of fear of gay men, in terms of which the health crisis was addressed, whether that culture was scientific, religious, or administrative, not only was not based on facts but also, more significantly, demonstrated "the comparative irrelevance of information in communication" (1987, 210). Bersani contended that the stereotypes on which homophobia was founded were in part buttressed by the "gay commitment to machismo," namely depictions of masculinity and gay male desire paradoxically common to heterosexist and gay imagination (1987, 208).

In 1988, Susan Sontag published *AIDS and Its Metaphors*, a coda to *Illness as Metaphor*. She offered two significant insights regarding the ways in which HIV infection had entered the symbolic realm through imagination and memory: "With the most up-to-date biomedical testing, it is possible to create a new class of lifetime pariahs, the future ill" (2001, 121–2). Sontag announced a dystopian future generated by scientific methods of classification. That nightmarish future coincided in Sontag's thought with the pre-modern past: "AIDS, in which people are understood as ill before they are ill; which produces a seemingly innumerable array of symptom-illnesses; for which there are only palliatives; and which brings to many a social death that precedes the physical one – AIDS reinstates something like a pre-modern experience of illness" (2001, 122). In Sontag's view, AIDS's timeline had significantly altered the flow of time and curtailed future hopes by recycling anxieties, much as epidemics like the Black Death had for Europeans in the 1300s.

Charles E. Rosenberg pointed to the striking contradictions that AIDS revealed regarding scientific and humanistic one-dimensional thought, positing that the pandemic was a postmodern and post-relativist phenomenon (1989, 13–14). Yet Rosenberg's most compelling idea – one that directly relates to *Poesida* and the way that Bohórquez structures the personal, social, affective, and cognitive experience of the disease – was what he conceived of the "epidemic incident as

The Case for Abigael Bohórquez

dramaturgic event" (1989, 3). Rosenberg argued that, just as often happens in a play, the pandemic nature of a severe health crisis had transitioned from an arbitrary set of mainly isolated initial observations to a painful recognition that the disease was a serial event for which nobody was prepared. A second element of theatricality through which we come to understand a pandemic, continues Rosenberg, is that, at least initially, it elicits social responses based on lay assumptions that, during the pandemic's spread, prove dubious or flat-out wrong. In this context, it becomes apparent that fear in the face of pathological contagion is an epiphenomenon to social anxieties. When the pandemic finally begins to reside, survivors search for a moral framework through which to understand what otherwise would, according to Rosenberg, be events of frightening randomness (1989, 3–9).

In Mexico, the first case of HIV infection was reported in 1983. According to the Mexican National Centre for Prevention and Control of HIV and AIDS (CENSIDA), from 1990 until November 2014, almost 190,000 people were living as patients or were seropositive, and 37 percent of the infected population in Mexico were unaware of their condition (2015, "La epidemia del VIH y Sida en México." *Hoja informativa – 01*). The same year that *Poesida* was finally published, an effective antiretroviral medication was announced in Vancouver at the 11th International AIDS Conference. That same year marked the first time that "AIDS [was] no longer leading cause of death for all Americans ages 25–44, although it remain[ed] the leading cause of death for African Americans in this age group" ("A Timeline of HIV and AIDS," n.p. year 1996).

## "ME PONGO A RECORDARME / A RECORDARTE / A MUERTE"[13]

*Poesida* opens with a prologue in which the author justifies the existence of his poems as a condemnation of homophobia, a document of lives thwarted by AIDS, and a plea for mercy for his own poems:

Del autor
Dentro de la otra violencia cotidiana cuya especularidad
sanguinaria se asume eficazmente sin escándalo hipócrita contra
los homosexuales aun ahora todavía, hizo su aparición el Sida ...
y los homosexuales atónitos y sometidos a la angustia de lo
desconocido, se vieron hostilizados a viento y marea,

zarandeados hacia las cámaras de gases de los más acreditados conjuros malignos y los tentáculos del abismal horror del *desempleo, separados de sus salarios, descaradamente exorcizados por la prensa y los pastores de la iglesia*, porque era castigo de Dios. Luego aparecieron muchos personajes en la trama de la muerte: los mismos ciudadanos y las concubinas de los ciudadanos, y los secretarios y los choferes de los ciudadanos y los chimpancés domesticados de las mujeres de los ciudadanos y los rintintines acelerados de las alcobas de las mujeres de los ciudadanos y el perico y el gato comelón. Y los Conasidas y los condoneros se pusieron de moda, el problema fue poco a poco sazonándose y la especulación fantaseadora cedió a la preocupación preventiva que desde la importancia científica o la condoficción por el temor a una venganza cósmica, perdura este día ... Cuánta gente pública y privada desapareció muerta de arcangelismo, de ninfomanía, del susto, porque el Sida era la muerte que no se atrevía a decir su nombre; cuánta gente pública y privada se fue poniendo flaquita, sin pelos y se murió de dulce muerte primaveral; de fiebre de heno, porque se le fue la tripa, de Sida nunca, lo que diría el Comendador. Traigo este *documento* cruel pero solidario para pedir comprensión infinita para los ciudadanos del mundo que han muerto víctimas de este cáncer finisecular y bondad para estos poemas del paraíso perdido que algún día que mi imaginación no alcanza a predecir reenconrtaremos: "Poesida," poesía testimonial de quien pudo escribirla con todas las palabras de que es capaz un hombre, en Hermosillo, Sonora, a los veinte días de marzo de mil novecientos noventa y uno. (Bohórquez 2000b, 13–4, emphasis added)[14]

Here the author offers a social landscape ruled by bigotry, fear, and death. As an activist, he denounces the attitude of secular, religious, scientific, political, and media elites; as a poet, he issues a daring invitation: to look into death and beyond. Readers will witness the poet's struggle to detach *eros* and *thanatos* from HIV/AIDS, unearth the skeletons stigmatized by the epidemic, and deliver their memory to the symbolic universe within which societies negotiate the meaning of catastrophes for their history and their future.

The symbolic value of epidemics has a long literary tradition. From the plagues in the Old Testament, to the devastated city of Thebes in Sophocles's *Oedipus Rex*, Petrarch's *Canzonieri* inspired by Laura's death from the Black Death in mid-fourteenth-century Florence, the backdrop of *I promessi sposi* by Manzoni, Daniel Defoe's *A Journal of the Plague Year*, Mary Shelley's *The Last Man*, Jack London's *The Scarlet Plague*, and, more recently, of course, the allegorical masterpiece by Albert Camus, *La peste*, Gabriel García Márquez's *El amor en los tiempos de cólera*, and José Saramago's *Ensaio sobre a cegueira*, writers have found in these catastrophes a fertile aesthetic and ideological ground for representations of social malaise and the ways human beings react to it. Epidemics are conducive to reflection on pre-modern conceptions of divine punishment, modern depictions of scientific failures, apocalyptic fictions of war, authoritarian regimes, and colonialism. Historians and social scientists, too, have paid attention to these public health phenomena. Some of them have come to explain key social changes based on how societies react to epidemics. Suzanne and James Hatty argue, for instance, that the masculinization of Western culture started in the late Middle Ages and early Renaissance as a result of how epidemic crises were related to the female body (1999, 25). Furthering Foucault's lessons, Lauren Berlant argues: "We learned most recently from AIDS, after all, that the epidemic concept is not a neutral description; it's inevitably part of an argument about classification, causality, responsibility, degeneracy, and the imaginable and pragmatic logics of cure" (2007, 763).

Bohórquez's public and critical reaction represents a clear consciousness of what public health crises entail. Besides showing in his prologue the permeability of symbolic domains – "especulación fantaseadora," "la condoficción" – and material ones – "los Conasidas," "la preocupación preventiva," "la importancia científica" (2000b, 13) – the poet announces an elementary and thus fundamental contradiction in the social reaction to AIDS: by signalling sexuality as the root of what is unhealthy, epistemic and decision-making centres potentially place every member of the society – even those who are not sexually active and indeed not yet born – in the outrageous position of being unlawful victims. Seen through the prism of homophobia and public hygiene, a disease that destroys an individual's immune system – whether that of an intravenous drug addict, a newborn, a blood transfusion patient, a prostitute, a gay man, or a Haitian immigrant – threatens to undercut the integrity of the body social. HIV/AIDS victims have one thing in common: their encounters with others afford a deliberate level of proximity that is unbearable for society to witness. They share semen, blood, needles, and DNA. Thus they show the permeability of the contours of selfhood and, by historical extension, of gender, social class, race, and nation. In the context of AIDS, death not only ends life but also reduces individuals to corpses, for it attempts to erase and thus to redefine the contours of intimate contact with alterity, both physically and symbolically, as well as across time, in memory, in the present and in the utopian future.

Bohórquez announces in the prologue to *Poesida* the grief for that which Agamben will claim years later in the context of biopolitics:

> If there is a line in every modern state marking the point at which the decision on life becomes a decision on death, and biopolitics can turn into thanatopolitics, this line no longer appears today as a stable border dividing two clearly distinct zones. This line is now in motion and gradually moving into areas other than that of political life, areas in which the sovereign is entering into an ever more intimate symbiosis not only with the jurist but also with the doctor, the scientist, the expert, and the priest. (1998, 72)

Firm in his decision to explore and remap sovereign individuality, and in this sense to provide the kind of justice that literature is capable of administering, the lyric self in Bohórquez's poems endorses failure and radical proximity as performances that escape institutional surveillance and criminalization.

Jack Halberstam has made the case for failure as a particular feature of queers, which he locates on the ground of affects as political strategies. Those who fail, he argues, "remind us that there is something powerful in being wrong, in losing, in failing, and that all our failures combined might just be enough, if we practice them well, to bring down the winner" (2011, 120). In Halberstam's thought the act of losing thus acquires a purpose. Unlike the characters analyzed by Halberstam, mainly from children's mainstream movies, Bohórquez's poems do not oppose the winner. They yearn for a queer *locus* more in the sense argued by José Esteban Muñoz in *Cruising Utopia*. Taking issue with autobiographical writing on public sex, drag shows and artists, poems, plays, and ballet, the Latino scholar has argued that queer utopia is not a future aspiration. Rather, its potential for projection onto the future is based on queerness already here, performed at the heart of heteronormativity. The power of queer performances hinges on their non-commodification. Insubordination against the norms of hypercapitalist economy and its surrogate heteronormativity, as well as the ability to short-circuit the system from its producing centre, allow acts of queer performance to live a life of memory. Whether it is Giorno's prose, an activist's article, Bishop's poems, or Aviance's shows, "queer world-making" (Muñoz 2009, 37 and *passim*) comes "into play through the performance of queer utopian memory, that is a utopia that understands its time as reaching beyond some nostalgic past that perhaps never was or some future whose arrival is continuously belated – a utopia in the present" (Muñoz 2009, 37).

Bohórquez's poetry sustains many theoretical articulations with the perspectives exposed up to here, yet unlike Halberstam and Muñoz, the poet does not champion sovereign agency as the opposite of injustice. On the contrary, he is invested in confronting the reader with actions that stem from spontaneity, lack of organization or purpose. Those who have failed in *Poesida* – the lyric self included – are already dead either physically or figuratively. Therefore, restitution within the polity and the benefits that come from inclusion in the national aggregate are of no use to "estos ciudadanos del mundo" (Bohórquez 2000b, 14); their failure is already consummated before we start reading.[15] For Bohórquez, what is at stake here are the violent changes imprinted on the body politic through the effective social positioning of those who refuse to build or simply cannot build a life within normativity – namely those who even in death present a menace to society. The ideal place for these individuals is the netherworld, and the lyric voice joins them there. He thus testifies to the social history of a group by inhabiting dead bodies in emancipatory necrophilia. In *Poesida*, expansive sexuality and lack of transcendence replace eternal values. Fortino Corral has already pointed out some of these features of Bohórquez's Eden. When it comes to spiritual directionality, Corral finds that

> no se trata ... de un descenso a los infiernos sino, en todo caso, de un desesperado asalto al paraíso. Un paraíso que debe continuar justamente en el momento en que se prueba la fruta prohibida ... Este paraíso supone una moral peculiar basada en una espiritualidad estrictamente corporal, que se traduce en cierto aire de ociosidad banal e intrascendente, una emotividad fragmentada con rápidas y azarosas crestas, penetración sin compenetración, aliento agitado pero breve, vitalidad sin fertilidad. (1995, 239-40, emphasis added)[16]

Bohórquez believes in an unconditional paradise and convokes the lyric strategies to reach it.

The overall sense of the collection is simultaneously posthumous and utopian. It begins in the underworld, where the lyric voice encounters the "dead promiscuous homosexuals" and the most important twentieth-century Latin American poet, César Vallejo, yet it also surpasses death. It extends to a future in which society will have healed from AIDS and love will again be in the hands of the youth. In "Desazón" ("Unease"), the lyric self assesses his life as a series of experiences viewed from "esta playa vieja / ya en sí moridero y desamores" (2000b, 27, "this old beach / in itself a loveless graveyard"). "Carta" ("Epistole"), a letter addressing a skull, is a nuanced epitaph in which the lyric speaker, although consciously in touch with life, sees himself as an "osamenta de amor" (2000b, 33, "skeleton of love"). "Tergiversito" is a reflection on life as a form of death (2000b, 37). "Slogan" ends with the declaration "y he muerto" (2000b, 43, "and I have died"). When AIDS is announced on the TV, the lyric self is immersed in death again: "y otra vez estar muerto" (2000b, 56, "and once again dead"). In "Duelo," Bohórquez laments the lives of those who are dead since they were born and with whom he actively identifies "aquellos / que, desde que nacieron, / son confinados, etiquetados, muertos" (2000b, 68, "those / who, since they were born, / are confined, labeled, dead"). The series of poem-vignettes titled "Retratos," in which Bohórquez tells the story of AIDS victims, all start with the verb to be in the past: "era/n". The tenth of these vignettes depicts the lyric self: "Éste era yo, perplejo: zurcía, bordaba, jugaba con muñecas, / cantaba amargo, descreído de Dios" (2000b, 82, "This one was I, perplexed: / I used to mend, embroider, play with dolls, / sing bitter, doubtful about God").

In "Cantares," the tone changes. Bohórquez compares the voice that sings to an apparition – "un fantasma se alza entre las ruinas / pájaro de mala muerte yo" (2000b, 53, "a ghost rises among the ruins / bird of deadly omen I" – echoing the historical menace of Marx's *Communist Manifesto*. Almost at the end of *Poesida,* the lyric speaker appeals to the future despite being already in the underworld. He speculates:

[Cuando] el AIDS sea un slogan de los ochentas
habré de ver qué digo
de donde esté:
Lázaro resucita cada día. (2000b, 86)[17]

The hope of resurrection confronts dystopian social contracts that rule even beyond death. Bohórquez's inquiry aligns with Achille Mbembe's questions: what is the place "given to life, death, and the human body (in particular the wounded or slain body)? How are they inscribed in the order of power?" (2003, 12). Against this power of exile and sanction, the Mexican writer places a force that seeks to reinstate the dead among the living through a *post-mortem* process of naturalization (Bohórquez 2000b, 14). Throughout the book and insistently in "Retratos," Bohórquez's lyric self descends to the underworld and dies together with others. In this journey, like a contemporary broken Odysseus, a decrepit Orpheus or Dante, guided by the figures of *doña Sofía*, or those of the lost lover, the fellow poet, his doppelgänger "Abigael," the lyric persona accounts for lost lives. Lyricism reveals and brings into the open what is unknown, unfamiliar, yet intensely imagined, namely the intimate life and death of the "damas caballeros de la fosa común" (Bohórquez 2000b, 84, "ladies gentlemen of the common grave"). Endowing his elegy with answerability, the poet establishes conversations on the ethics of death. In the context of such a memorial ceremony, the orphaned corpses of thanatopolitics will be bodies rescued by love, friendship, and desire.

The poem "Slogan" announces the appearance of AIDS in the life of a group identified by the pronouns "we, us, ours." The singing voice narrates in lyric terms the spread of the pandemic: "Y, fue que, un día, el BUEN vecino / estrenó la película, como un trigal en llamas: / AIDS IS COMING / AIDS IS HERE" (2000b, 41, English and small caps in the original).[18] The first incidents of HIV/AIDS are seen as a movie originating across the border from Mexico. Contrary to the post-colonial imagery of an ailment with animal roots, stemming from Africa, in *Poesida* it is the superpower that spreads a conflagration in Mexico, just as it exports to this country cultural objects. The influence of the United States resonates also in the idiolect of Mexico's northwestern frontier, alternating with English translated word for word from Spanish. The poem has a chorus: *"because to die for AIDS is different / from what anyone supposed"* (Bohórquez 2000b, 41, English and emphasis in the original). Here, AIDS is not presented as something you die of; rather, it is a temple for its martyrs, it is the other face of an overwhelming sexual appetite, itself so close to death:

Sobrevino el terror,
*the happy birthday of dear* DEATH TRACY;
uno
entonces,
enamorado todavía de las cosas oscuras
tornó a mirar a su izquierda, a su derecha,
detrás, al frente,
queriendo ver espejos donde tocar un rostro fértil;
pero llegó algo que vino enemistado,
desapartando y no es igual la vida:
*because to die for* AIDS *is different*
*from what anyone supposed*;
y devino el horror impenitente
de que éramos muriendo o vamos a morir
o estamos muertos
y obstinamos: dead-drunk
rock,
dead-end
rock,
deadfall
rock,
deadly gone world
rock,
o yeah,
*because to die for* AIDS *is different*
y ai'nos vamos, carnal
haciéndonos poquitos,
esfúmate, pass bye
no chingues, puta muerte,
*because to die for* AIDS *is different*
*like to spit on olden olden God,*
rock
rock
rock'n rolling,
a pesar de aquel día. (Bohórquez 2000b, 41–2)[19]

A bilingual dialogue signals the diversity of possible interlocutors and audiences. The poetic form straddles English and Spanish, representing in and of itself the interconnectedness of cultures, an integral topography for the spread of the pandemic.

The Case for Abigael Bohórquez 47

Earlier in the book, Bohórquez uses the phrase "la raza baldía" to refer to those who disparage the people threatened by AIDS (2000b, 27, "barren race"). In "Slogan," he extends a call for support to a community already dismantled by this undefined "something" that converts solidarity into estrangement ("pero llegó *algo* que vino enemistado, / desapartando y no es igual la vida," emphasis added). The insistence that AIDS is an indeterminate "something" recalls Reinaldo Arenas's *Antes que anochezca*. In the introduction, titled paradoxically "El fin" ("The End"), the Cuban dissident confesses not to know what AIDS is, adding that the perfection of the virus suggests the possibility of its origin in a human laboratory, and denouncing the governments of the world for taking pleasure in an epidemic that has targeted marginalized groups. In Arenas's perception, the outcasts who fall prey to this illness do not aspire to anything except to live and thus are natural opponents of doctrinaire autocracy (1992, 10–11). At the end of the book, in "Carta" ("Letter"), Fidel Castro is directly referred to as the sole person responsible for the author's exile and the destiny attached to it: hardships and AIDS (1992, 347). The political burden Arenas attaches to his decision to commit suicide adds one more piece to the backdrop against which Bohórquez writes his book.[20] The Cuban writer juxtaposes the treacherous equanimity of global politics against the different groups threatened by AIDS, attributing to those viewed as pariahs only a meagre aspiration: "no more than to live" (Arenas 1992, 11). Although the Mexican shares with the Cuban the feeling that the outcasts have suffered the major blow in this crisis, the former gives the relation between illness and political life an agonistic turn that links the pauperization of life and the shrinking of human rights with late capitalism.

For Bohórquez, AIDS is a condition directly related to the marginalized and to death with no time specificity: "de que éramos muriendo o vamos a morir / o estamos muertos." The protagonists of "Slogan" nonetheless get a second chance at humanity by defiantly persisting. Existential obstinacy is depicted through repetition and songlike rhythm. Semantic overlaps (o estamos muriendo ... *o yeah*) infuse the poem with reminiscences of an era of resistance through rock music. Following in the footsteps of the Woodstock crowd, Bohórquez places the world of *Poesida* in a much broader historical context. This insertion identifies gay men with the pathos of being in love ("uno / entonces / enamorado todavía de las cosas obscuras"). Despite grief and fear, love for dark things and all that comes with it will provide the framework of history and future for the odd community of the "dead always in life."

48 Beyond Intimacy

"Slogan" is a poetic descent to Hades, by means of which the lyric voice assumes its queer poetic origin in Walt Whitman and Federico García Lorca. The Mexican poet treads uninhibitedly upon his poetic ancestors' footprints and boldly reorients the direction they signal: "¿me celebro a mí mismo y me canto a / mí mismo?" (2000b, 41, "I celebrate myself and sing / myself?"), asks the lyric self, replicating within question marks, and thus twisting, Whitman's assertiveness of the self in the opening of *Leaves of Grass*. The interrogatory here is disquieting: all optimism proper to Whitman's creation is lost, and all exuberance, but not to the detriment of the quest for a poet's justice. Instead of singing the lyric self in his sumptuous encounter with the world, or as the poet of the nation, the land, and the times, Bohórquez's voice originates in a time of wild sexual activity and follows the fatal destiny embodied in the same kind of men that Lorca condemns in "Oda a Walt Whitman" ("Ode to Walt Whitman"):

> Pero sí contra vosotros, maricas de las ciudades,
> de carne tumefacta y pensamiento inmundo.
> Madres de lodo. Arpías. Enemigos sin sueño
> del Amor que reparte coronas de alegría.
>
> Contra vosotros siempre, que dais a los muchachos
> gotas de sucia muerte con amargo veneno.
> Contra vosotros siempre,
> *Fairies* de Norteamérica,
> *Pájaros* de la Habana,
> *Jotos* de Méjico,
> *Sarasas* de Cádiz,
> *Apios* de Sevilla,
> *Cancos* de Madrid,
> *Floras* de Alicante,
> *Adelaidas* de Portugal. (García Lorca 1988, 160 and 162)[21]

"Slogan" replies to this list with another in which queer desire assumes agonistically its agency in a relentless festival of pathos:

> Porque hubo días hasta la desvergüenza,
> donde fuimos      *tan lúbricos*
>                  *tan móviles*
>                  *tan fértiles*

> *tan plácidos*
> *tan sórdidos.* (Bohórquez 2000b, 42)[22]

Whitman and Lorca function as poetic and sexual landmarks. However, they also offer concrete intertexts that serve as major critical points for both *Poesida*'s voices and the book's artistic inception of a queer world that exposes gay culture's inner homophobia.

At the end of *Poesida* the poet's voice offers the energy and privilege of the word for others to articulate their own afterlife. While Whitman celebrates everything the lyric self touches, his universal and at the same time historical self, Bohórquez's mission is quite different: "Vengo a estarme de luto por aquellos / que han muerto a desabasto" (2000b, 67, "I come to mourn all those / dead of dearth"), he affirms in "Duelo." The protagonists of queer sexuality and sociability abhorred in Lorca's poem perform in Bohórquez's drag shows. Their lascivious avidity, effeminate looks, and antiheroic acting are precisely what makes them worthy of praise and elegy. Bohórquez thus appears deeply critical of his two literary predecessors: unlike Whitman, he detaches himself from monologic lyric omnipotence, while against Lorca's inner homophobia, he subscribes to the relentless queer tone of his fellow outcasts.

The lyric voice turns often to others: friends, acquaintances, the mother, a stranger, a lover, a fellow poet. Despite their differences, these entities share the same world of love and death. In "Carta," the loving companion takes the shape of an anonymous second person, the receiver of the letter (Bohórquez 2000b, 33). In "Slogan," it is the lover (2000b, 43). In one of the "Retratos," it is the mother, who also appears, together with the lover, in "Cantares" (2000b, 54–5). In many of the "Retratos," it is a whole group of drag performers, male prostitutes, and decadent old queens decimated by AIDS. Unlike Arenas, who viewed this same group as passively resistant to governments, the pariahs in Bohórquez's world come from a lineage of social rebels. "Cantares," the book's longest and richest lyric text, weaves together desire, poetry, and politics. There are many literary and cultural resonances in the poem, such as Antonio Machado in the title, various Mexican *boleros* in the body of the poem, Pablo Neruda's "Puedo escribir los versos más tristes esta noche" ("I can write the saddest verse tonight"), which is turned into the rough "Puedo aullar esta noche," and the disenchanted "ya aullé / y no consigo nada" (Bohórquez 2000b, 53, "I can howl tonight," "I already howled and achieved nothing").

Among this continuous quoting, one reference stands out – a veiled, daring inversion of Neruda's epic cry "Sube a nacer conmigo, hermano" (1997, 140, "Rise to birth with me, my brother"), from *Canto general*'s "Alturas de Macchu Picchu" ("The Heights of Macchu Picchu"). In this part of the poem, the Chilean's epic voice appeals to the dead ploughman, the weaver, the shepherd, the horse-breaker, the mason, the water carrier, the goldsmith, the potter. He conjures them up from oppression and death to revolution. In "Cantares," Bohórquez addresses "doña Sofía," the unmarried mother, whose social transgression the lyric self assumes with the same ambiguous feeling of shame and pride with which the mother accepts and loves her gay poet son (Bohórquez 2000b, 56). When AIDS breaks into the scene, the lyric voice dies a figurative death, from which another presence saves him. The poem becomes a display of gratitude towards this other, whose affective ambiguity prepares the ground for a queer reading:

> en el televisor:
> el sida, el sida, el sida, el sida
> y otra vez estar muerto;
> sacudo la cabeza
> y ahora es que respiro emocionado
> emocionado de que *tú me levantes*
> *desde el polvo*
> quelamor el
> ¿amor?
> algún día algún día algún día
> de aquestos
> por la calle. (Bohórquez 2000b, 56–7, emphasis added)[23]

The bastard son, the ostracized gay boy, the ignored poet, the queer man and those on stage with him – all are fraternally compared here to the Latin American working class whom Neruda's verses address in "Alturas de Macchu Picchu":

> Sube a nacer conmigo, hermano.
> Dame la mano desde la profunda
> zona de tu dolor diseminado.
>
> No volverás del fondo de las rocas.
> No volverás del tiempo subterráneo.

No volverá tu voz endurecida.
No volverán tus ojos taladrados.

Mírame desde el fondo de la tierra,
labrador, tejedor, pastor callado. (Neruda 1997, 140)[24]

In a masterful turn filled with genuine emotion not at all weakened
by the witty sexual innuendos, Bohórquez takes from class struggle
and the most authoritative literary tradition the impulse to come out,
sing, protest, fight, and enact sexuality in public. The forthright tone
warrants a queer translation:

on the TV
AIDS, AIDS, AIDS, AIDS
and there I am dead again;
I shake my cock's head
and now I breathe hard
overwhelmed by the hard-on you gave me
by a good fuck
thisfuck this
¿love?
one day one day one day
of those days
in public.

Bohórquez couples the dead-serious, socially conscious working-class
macho-men with the marginal queers, cast out by poverty, race, prejudice, sickness, while pairing himself with the manly bard Pablo
Neruda. Significantly, though, and unlike the Chilean rhapsode, in
Bohórquez's poem the voice is not that of the hero. The dead will rise
and help the poet come back through poetry and sensuality. By means
of this twist, in *Poesida,* the lyric self locates the ripe fruit of private
lives/deaths, lustful and morbid, within Latin American social and
literary history. The poetic endeavour of recasting Neruda's 1950
poetic saga in drag unveils the tension within the linguistic domain
that serves as material of representation for both social and sexual
disparities and violence.

Poetry, desire, and life seal the fate of *Poesida*'s protagonists. In
"Tergiversito," we read: "Nuestras vidas / eran ríos / que fueron dar
a encamar que / ¿fue el vivir?" (Bohórquez 2000b, 37, "Our lives /

were rivers / that took people straight to bed which / ¿was this living?").
Bohórquez radically reorients Jorge Manrique's moving *Coplas a la muerte de su padre* (*Verses on the Death of His Father*) from filial love to the urgent need for sex. The possibility of distorting Manrique's foundational poetry is already announced in the title, an endearing twist on the verb *tergiversar* (to distort). The verb comes from *tergum*, Latin for "back," and *vertere/versum*, a turn of the plough, or a line of writing. "Tergiversito" can be translated as a noun: "the little twisted line" or "the little man turned around"; but also as a verb: "I twist the little poetic line," a creative yet ironic synonym for poetry; or "I turn somebody facing down," which may well evoke anal sex.

Through puns, Bohórquez presents in "Tergiversito" different lives and their literary, natural, and sexual avatars. The poem ends with an open question regarding the reality and value of "living," seen from the distance of death, an already befallen end. Bohórquez invites his readers to answer and thereby he converts musings to dialogue. Silence at the end of the poem does not mean the end of the conversation. The previous enjambments are proof that the verse does not end at the end of the line. Rather, it throws itself to silence, eliciting continuity and answers. By the same token, the abandoned life does not end in death; rather, by provoking questions, it reopens injustice and abandonment. Bohórquez is aware of his own condition: decrepit, poor, aging. Yet in the face of AIDS he feels indebted to others, and thus he sets off to understand how sensuality becomes the key to personal freedom in public space, sex, and readership. By underscoring the commonality between queer sex and life itself in the final line of "Tergiversito," the poet invites his readers to grasp the limits of sociability, the concepts and institutions on which this quality of social living relies, and its relationship to queer radical proximity.

AIDS seen through the eyes of someone who has sung the pleasures and pains of the flesh arrives as one of a series of ignominies: poverty, public humiliation, ostracism, misery, alcoholism. Before *Poesida*, Bohórquez had practised his rebellion against normativity through poetry and sexuality. He had protested against and denounced the social status quo. He had also indulged his reader in poetic acts of unabashed sex. In a way, the poet exerted sovereign agency as such. However, AIDS has exposed the fractures of what agency and sovereignty mean. "Desazón" ("Unease") is a seven-stanza poem that tells a life story. The first four stanzas start with a temporal clause: "Cuando ya hube roído pan familiar," "Cuando ya hube sentido," "Cuando ya hube saboreado," "Cuando hube salido" (Bohórquez 2000b, 25–6, "Once I already had gnawed on my family's bread," "Once I had already felt," "Once I had already tasted," "Once I had come out"). The verbal tense, past anterior – an archaism – gives the past a sense of closure, both autobiographical and linguistic; it functions as a mausoleum of time. Everything the poetic voice has lived belongs to another story. Each stanza accounts for a phase of the lyric voice's life and his faith in God.[25] This appeal comes more as a bitter coda than as a claim of unconditional loyalty or metaphysical belief. A miserable childhood spent in hunger watching those who had everything; an early youth of social awareness and braveness; the awakening and practice of homosexuality; an adulthood of brothels, pawnshops, lustful confessional boxes, poetry, triumphs (2000b, 26), are over and done with.

With the advent of AIDS – "Y de repente, el Sida" (2000b, 26, "And suddenly, AIDS") – life comes to a full stop. Bohórquez will use this stasis to exploit the odd and multiple meanings of the word "sida":

¿Por qué este mal de muerte en esta playa vieja
ya de sí moridero y desamores,
en esta costra antigua
a diario levantada y revivida,
en esta pobre hombruna
de suyo empobrecida y extenuada
por la raza baldía? Sida.
¡Qué palabra tan honda
que encoge el corazón
y nos lo aprieta! (2000b, 26)[26]

AIDS and the lyric self's being – a synecdoche for queer lives – are identical twins for the poetic voice's grammar of life. Tenuous yet meaningful is the link between AIDS and sexuality, insinuated by the word "hombruna." Typically used to characterize a manly woman, this adjective is hardly ever said about a man. Here the word is used not as a qualifier but as a noun. It designates a masculinity oddly defined by a feminine adjective, and by extension a group that stands vis-à-vis the "raza baldía," depleted of resources and strength, a condition that resonates in "hombruna," a quasi-paronomasia of "hambruna," famine. The elegy marks its own end in this squeeze of the heart in which life, too, has already happened, has been "sida."

The poem ends with an undertone of indifference:

Afuera, al sol,
juguetean los niños,
agrio viento,
con un barco menudo
en mar revuelto. (2000b, 27)[27]

The artist depicts the indifference of the world towards disgrace; he uses nature's lack of empathy as a mirror in which plenty of insensitive bystanders, from the light-hearted children playing in the sun to the most committed readers, seem amused by or totally oblivious to the dangers menacing unregistered lives. Bohórquez calls sharp attention to the subject by having two different agents in its place: the children and the bitter wind. The syntactic indeterminacy bifurcates the interpretation: either the little boat is endangered while in the hands and play of children, or it is at nature's mercy on the open sea. The poet stages the confrontation between play and history, children and nature, individuation and diffusion, proximity and remoteness, and adopts both perspectives of the binaries. Sometimes he is part of the peril threatening the "little boat," even while from afar he is a spectator. This ambivalence causes the effects of AIDS to be connected whether to a society of inadequate caregivers or to natural laws blindly observed. Helpless and fearful, the sufferers from this point on, symbolically embodied in the little boat, become the focus of Bohórquez's poetic composition.

"Mural" brings the reader face-to-face with the ailing and the moribund. As the poetic self reminds his reader, queer men *die* for passion outside mainstream forms of socialization. Their deaths are integrated into the mood and rhythm of the city, of mass culture, and of personal isolation:

Siempre los vi morir de la otra muerte urbana.
Nunca de trance natural.
Talvez se acaban de beso a beso
...
bajo las regaderas de los baños,
o el cachondor de los cines a tientas,
forniqueciendo
en las cuevas umbrías,
o en los bares hediondos
...

The Case for Abigael Bohórquez

mirándose al espejo, viejísimos,
esqueletos de aquella primavera
que, de repente, se quedó sin hojas,
sin la delicta carnis hasta ayer verdesIDA,
arrugaditos, desventurados,
mientras un loco aullido de terror:
¿por qué?
les sale finalmente por la boca
extenuada.
Nunca he visto morir a uno, qué mejor,
pero siguen. (Bohórquez 2000b, 61–2)[28]

"Mural" crosses the watershed marked by AIDS. Fear accompanies queer lives in urban settings at every moment. There they share death, sordidness, and affective deprivation. Positioned in late modernity, the seekers of passion in the public space grow older and lonelier, and they never die of natural causes. Bohórquez suggests that death lurks in the blind need for other bodies. The protagonists of this poem are bound to embrace decadence and to fade away in their passionate ordeals. Thus, although AIDS is undoubtedly a destructive addendum to the frantic quest for sexual intimacy, it is not actually a turning point with regard to the loveless ranks of men getting older and decrepit. Even so, there is something treacherous about the illness and the lives it has been taking. Bohórquez highlights the change produced in the body erotic by AIDS with a neologism: "verdesIDA." Just as with the title *Poesida, ser* (to be) and the illness *Sida* (AIDS) come together in the paradoxical rebirth of primaveral nature: "verdecida." Here, Bohórquez crafts an illumination: death and renewal are always present through sexuality. For a fleeting moment, queer vibrancy, characterized by hypersexualization and urban environments, populated by practitioners of public sex, and disruptive of the organization of time and space that José Esteban Muñoz identifies with heteronormativity (2009, 154), equals its lethal condition to the liveliest of seasons.

Faced with death and society's hostility, the poet stands in mourning. In the next poem, he declares the reason for his poetry:

Vengo a estarme de luto
porque puedo.
Porque si no lo digo
yo

56       Beyond Intimacy

> poeta de mi hora y de mi tiempo,
> se me vendría abajo el alma, de vergüenza,
> por haberme callado. (Bohórquez 2000b, 68)[29]

This definition of the poet's métier as the act of – civil – duty to disobey and his declaration of a personal moral stance converge in the title, "Duelo," which means both opposition and mourning. Compassion and vehemence cross in this poem. Its protagonists are illuminated by two kinds of light: that of the poet's eyes, and that of their social detractors. The reader is thus confronted with a mobile perspective that obliges her to take sides. The place this third party might occupy is either one of closeness, interpreted as provocative sameness, or one of prejudice, which produces disambiguation between the subject and object of the discourse. Bohórquez takes the risk of setting out both attitudes because, in order to be able to occupy the former and therefore find and offer comfort, it is imperative that he present the record of insults and injuries: "caravana de las carcajadas," "paredón de la befa pública," "muro del asco" (2000b, 68, "parade of guffaws," "firing line of public scorn," "wall of shame"). The stage is set, and the spectacle is about to begin.

"Retratos" ("Portraits") is a series of eleven compositions portraying a group of queer men already dead. These working-class citizens pose in front of our eyes, identified mostly by their artistic names, mainly female, and by their day jobs, habits, dexterities, dreams, wives and kids, vibrant nights. What they all have in common is an ordinary life, disrupted at one point. In the case of Lesbia Roberto, "fue cuando vivió para no contarlo" (Bohórquez 2000b, 73, "it was when he lived not to tell the tale"); for Pájara Gustavo, it was just "una mañana" (2000b, 74, "one morning") when he was found dead; Daniel L'amour "ahora ocupa un lote bajo tierra" (2000b, 75, "now he owns a plot underground"). To the platoon of queer proletarians the turning point comes in the form of an order: "Se les dijo bien claro: Pelotón, marcha atrás" (2000b, 76, "they were told loud and clear: Platoon, back out"). In the series of vignettes, Braulio Ayeres represents a change of direction: he arrives at the crossroads where everyone dies a sad death when he suddenly integrates with nature "de la noche a la mañana" (2000b, 77, "from one day to the next"). After this poem, all characters descend to the underworld, the poet included. Death is a synonym for a cast of human figures that lived inadvertently and by the same token slipped into non-existence.

The Case for Abigael Bohórquez    57

Although not yet physically dead, the lyric self joins the group, for, like the others, he follows the rhythm of inconsequential actions: "Éste era yo, perplejo: / zurcía, bordaba, jugaba con muñecas, / cantaba, amargo, descreído de Dios" (Bohórquez 2000b, 82, "This one was I, perplexed: / I mended, embroidered, played with dolls, / sang, bitter, incredulous of God"). Through this affiliation, ordinary life implicitly equalizes art and death. Claims of agency and sovereignty are discredited by "Retratos." Bohórquez presses to the point of exhaustion the matter of being, evaluated in terms of its distractedness and dissemination. Everybody dies in dispossession, and nobody protests. The poet bypasses activism. He plants his headquarters on the turf of a heartbroken yet sober griever. Through the rhythmic anaphora of the first line in several "Retratos" – "Éste era" (Bohórquez 2000b, 73, 74, 75, 77, 81, 82, "This man was"), "Ésta era" (2000b, 76, "This woman was"), "Éstos eran" (2000b, 78, 79, "These men were") – the lyric self shows death to be not only a tiresome *ritornello*, but also a force that erases differences. The result is a present of shadows that lasts while the poem continues.

Lauren Berlant's seminal article on the concept of slow death addresses the critical problems posed by the kind of existence singled out in *Poesida*: the life and death of those who strive not to be lost in a seriality of events with no outstanding qualities.

> An event is a genre calibrated according to the intensities and kinds of impact. Environment denotes a dialectical scene where the interaction reified as structure and agency is manifest in predictable repetitions; an environment is made via spatial practices and can absorb how time ordinarily passes, how forgettable most events are, and, overall, how people's ordinary perseverations fluctuate in patterns of undramatic attachment and identification. In an ordinary environment, most of what we call events are not of the scale of memorable impact but rather are episodes, that is, occasions that make experiences while not changing much of anything. (Berlant 2007, 759–60)

The lost lives of the men in "Retratos" need to be revived not only against society's will but also against their own repetitiveness. Bohórquez speaks of characters who go through life and death in a continuum of affect and time. These individuals are emblematic of an endemic condition rather than representative of an epidemic crisis.

Bohórquez's poetic memory struggles to activate a process of individuation in the absence of a salient purpose of resistance or contestation on behalf of individualized victims. In such a context, an "activity exercised within spaces of ordinariness ... does not always or even usually follow the literalizing logic of visible effectuality, bourgeois dramatics, and lifelong accumulation or fashioning" (Berlant 2007, 758). *Poesida* tears away the poetic veil of prototypical life with the unambiguous rhythm of colloquial language, and with allusions to the popular tradition of *boleros, rancheras,* and nursery rhymes, as well as with the alternating verses of *arte mayor* and *arte menor*. The poems make audible the ordinary voices of lives at risk and guaranteed deaths.

Crisis implies among other things the possibility of consciousness as the outcome of a historical moment, of activism, and, in many cases, of artistic production. In *Poesida*'s context, the failing bodies overwhelm any such possibility. Consciousness proves inadequate in the face of AIDS' deadly effect among the outcasts. The poet himself must go beyond death if he is to say something meaningful regarding the accumulated loss. Posthumously, he turns back, not like Orpheus, but rather as Eurudice, to look at the spectacle:

Oh travestis casi perfectos de los carnavalitos,
oh vedettes culimpinados de los gimnasios,
oh locorronas de las sacristías,
oh pobrecitos de aldea
apedreados por el vecindario
cercados por los perros,
ahorcados y quemados en la noche sin tregua. (Bohórquez
    2000b, 84)[30]

The accumulated insults result in a lynching. Interpellation by and reappropriation of the injurious name, as Judith Butler theorizes in *Excitable Speech*, are here at work, *avant la lettre*. What interests me in the mirroring between art and rhetoric is what Butler announces as a fearful permeability between linguistic injury and physical survival: "If language can sustain the body, it can also threaten its existence" (Butler 1997, 5). In *Poesida,* the body has already been threatened and annihilated. To the extent that AIDS attacks their immune systems, the characters endow words with sacrificial power, in this way becoming socially immune to linguistic violence. That which was an insult before will now make the body recognizable beyond death. Injurious terms are used for a process of identification that underscores desire. The bodies are killed once again, beyond physical death. The life and death of queers is still onerous. However, the ritual of aggression turns into a ritual of closing, and what has started as an offensive definition ends up as an identification.

A look at transvestites, gym-queens, homosexual priests, and closeted bisexual men accentuates the discomfort borne by individuals and by the poet as their spectator. The successive apostrophes create a suspense that ends in bitter awareness: the social anathema that comes with homosexuality. What starts as a lament turns towards contemplative sublimation by means of which linguistic wounds become landmarks of being, places to dwell on and from which to articulate poetry as a claim:

> entremedio,
> lucisombra,
> cachagranizo,
> leandro;
> por eso sé que
> ahora sé
> qué canto. (Bohórquez 2000b, 84)[31]

Poetic soundness does not necessarily lead to a moment saturated with the potential of consciousness and transformation. Rather, ordinary quietism carries out loss as a process of drifting away, just as the almost nonsensical alliteration of the final verses does with poetry's purpose. Deep acceptance does away with the effervescent rhetoric of social institutions, public health authorities as well as that of activism. Bohórquez's characters denounce the logic of crisis-handling as a strategy for managing people; they enter death endowed with the lives they have lived, not by the hand of the hope of vindication.

The protagonists of *Poesida* take the lyric voice to a new place, that of the sufferers who distance themselves from the dramatic need for heroism and whose poignant integrity is a major claim for justice. The creation of a lyric chorus in the context of a historical tragedy responds to the demand for action with solemn abandonment. Among the members of the cast, the standard-bearer is depicted in a remarkable poem:

60   Beyond Intimacy

Éste fue Braulio Ayeres
que de la noche a la mañana,
contrajo, de raíz,
magnolias de consunción,
que consiguió ver despojos
de haber dado fragancia,
impávidos rescoldos de haber pasado por el fuego
y de no haberse hecho santo,
constancia de no haber sido
como pudo ser
su personaje inolvidable,
pavesas de haberse dado holgadamente
a la desventuranza,
indicios de que una vez probó,
delicuescentemente,
la miel sobrada del amor,
pruebas irrefutables de mala suerte
y mala muerte
en la tenebra del hospital. (Bohórquez 2000b, 77)[32]

Braulio is singled out from among the queer men of *Poesida*. First, his life does not extend into past times, through the imperfect tense "era," which is used to present the rest of the characters in "Retratos." His existence is extinguished at the moment he shows up on stage, it is simply past: "fue." His case seems redundant: he got infected and died. Nonetheless, *contraer* is a rich and ambiguous verb: it means to shrink, to get infected, to serve as a value that extends from particular to universal standards, to summarize a meaning, to get married, to assemble tightly together two things (*Diccionario de la Real Academia Española*. s.v. *contraer*). In each of these different meanings there is a more or less obvious sense of distilling, squeezing, mixing – a transformation in the main material of an object or of a subject. "Magnolias," the object of this verb in the poem, does not harmonize with any of these meanings.

The poem "contracts" its own significance progressively through syntactic parallelisms. A series of ambivalent acts produce ephemeral gratification or surprise regarding Braulio. He is staged as the protagonist of frivolous transformations as well as of purposeless actions. He shrinks magnolias from the root up, he sees the remnants of the process whereby delightful scents are created, he dies in his ashes without becoming a saint, he holds the record of who he could have but did not manage to become. To summarize Braulio's acts in the past – Braulio in his "ayeres" – he dwells on different past temporalities, composed always of an action at odds with its production. Death comes as one more of the character's unfortunate or thoughtless efforts. Braulio's encounter with love is delightful, irrefutable, doomed. The only regret regarding his life is that he could not become "his own unforgettable character," and that is what the poem achieves by telling his story. Braulio stands before the reader, dead several times before he becomes a number in a hospital. His lived experience is incommensurate with the magnitude of the AIDS epidemic. However, such crisis vanishes before the concatenation of actions proper to a miraculous life of expansion, despite its short-lived or even frivolous outcomes. For Braulio, as for the reader, death is divested of its power to define the dead.

## A POET'S STAKE

In 1995, Martha Nussbaum argued that narrative prose, especially that of the realist novel, can be of great use to judges, policy- and lawmakers, for it triggers the imagination and makes fathomable the circumstances of literary characters who are far from the readers' world. Through this effect of recognition, emotions shift and more empathetic judgments and policies addressing everyone's quality of life are possible (1995, 1–12). To sustain her claim, Nussbaum advocated for a moral rendering of the imagination and rational emotions. She also made the case for raising the novel above other literary genres because "the novel is a living form and in fact still the central morally serious yet popularly engaging fictional form of our culture ... The novel is concrete to an extent generally unparalleled in other genres ... Novels (at least realist novels of the sort I shall consider) present persistent forms of human need and desire realized in specific social situations" (1995, 6–7). With regard to poetry, Nussbaum took as her champion the democratizing spirit of the poet, expressed in Walt Whitman's *Song of Myself*:

The poet is the instrument through which the "long dumb voices" of the excluded come forth from their veils and into the light. To attend to the way things are with the excluded and the despised as well as the powerful, to insist on participating oneself, through sympathy, in the degradation of the degraded,

62 Beyond Intimacy

to accept only what others can have on the same terms, to
give voice to the pain of the excluded, the intimidation
of the harassed – this is a norm of democratic judgment.
(Nussbaum 1995, 119)

The role of the two literary genres and their authors – novelists and
poets – in affecting social justice is clearly very different. Nonetheless,
Nussbaum did not seem to acknowledge the division and thus she did
not follow up regarding the implications in terms of how imagination,
empathy, and social change may be produced by the two different
kinds of writing and reading experience. The novelist creates characters who move one's imagination and foster one's empathy. By contrast,
Abigael Bohórquez's *Poesida* shows a poet-judge, lawmaker, politician,
in a society that needs the poet's voice as protest. The poet sets the
stage for justice, she does not just mobilize fancy and emotions to
affect the reader's judgment. Bohórquez's poetry violently enacts
offences; it does not provide restitution, which is just an illusory wish
outside the institution of justice. Poetry strives for systemic justice: it
testifies and demands a fair trial for those already judged, it pronounces
an appeal, and thus points to the pitfalls of justice.

There is clearly a common thread linking Whitman's lyric self as an
all-encompassing democratizing advocate and Bohórquez's all-lost
mourner: artistic responsibility. Whitman, at the age of thirty-seven
and in good health, set the poetic foundation of a powerful nation,
whose extension and potential, optimism and enthusiasm, found fertile
ground in a democratic regime. He connected population, history, and
nature in an emblematic self who would defend those in need.
Bohórquez puts forward a poetic voice empowered by those others
already judged and condemned by the society of his time, following
a historical pattern of hatred and radical ostracism. The poet looks at
the future, and his aspiration is both utopian and posthumous:

Cuando el alba aletee otra vez
y vuela al mundo la claridad,
y quizá yo no exista,
y los jóvenes asuman nuevamente
la fuerza comosea del amor
en el sexo cualquier,
y el AIDS sea un slogan de los ochentas,
habré que ver qué digo

de donde esté
Lázaro resucita cada día
entre los minerales del estiércol
y *la paloma de la masacre*
volverá a hacer pichones
bajo el cielo. (Bohórquez 2000b, 86, emphasis in the original)[33]

For those dead in the carnage of AIDS in a hostile, continuous present, the poet augurs rebirth in generations of utopian sexual desire and freedom. He himself aspires to poetry, to the fecund word, "la paloma de la masacre," a robust dove hovering over hecatombs. The extinguished lyric self incarnates in others, proliferates within them from beyond the limit of death, with a question mark regarding what he will have to say in this utopian future. Bohórquez does not, even after death, speak of personal mission or redemption. He rescues hope in the emblematic freedom of desire, within a society that still does not know how to amend its endemic unfairness. A poet's justice stands for the agonistic *process* that links the bloodbath to the future.

# 2

# *Enladinar*

## *Intimating with History*

Komo es posivle de kultivar el espirito de este puevlo? Avladle de·la fízika, de·la atraksyón, de·la óptika, de·la akústika; avladle de·la kimya, del ekuivalente, de·la koezyón i de·la afinidad, del imponderavle i del impenetravle; dezidle todo esto i el no puedrá entender, porke esto no egziste en su idyoma.[1]

David Fresco, "Un puevlo mudo"

### TOWARDS *ANSINA*

In the pre-modern era, Judezmo distinguished the Jewish population of Andalusia from the Christians and Muslims. After 1492, it became the diasporic language of these Iberian Jews as their exilic community established itself mainly around the Mediterranean and confronted early modernity.[2] By the beginning of the twentieth century, the last in which Judezmo was employed in Jewish communities as a native tongue, some of its speakers had internalized its epistemic subordination: the language had long been identified with the domestic domain and working-class Jews and thus was associated with ignorance and inferiority in relation to other Western languages, including Castilian Spanish.

The orality of Judezmo is a commonly accepted fact. Be it in medieval Toledo, Ottoman Izmir, twentieth-century Mexico City, or present-day Israel, Judezmo's natural linguistic environment seems to be largely oral. Yet to assume a homogenous use of the language during modernity – namely from the end of eighteenth century on – is to flatten a multifaceted landscape and to simplify deep and intense sociolinguistic relations. For one thing, the notion of an almost exclusively oral code renders unproblematic the division between orality and script with all its cultural and philosophical implications. Furthermore, an unvaryingly oral view of Judezmo replaces the complex history of that language with a nostalgic fiction of uniformity, smoothing out historical pleats of rich significance and erasing differences among groups of Judezmo speakers over time. Such complex panorama of debates, I argue, gives *Ansina*, Myriam Moscona's 2015 collection of poetry, its full meaning. I maintain that the book takes part in a long-standing struggle against epistemic injustice. The topic of epistemic injustice and resistance has been theorized by José Medina, in *The Epistemology of Resistance*. Here the philosopher sustains that social injustice is intrinsically related to issues of personal and interpersonal knowledge, social imagination and perception, as well as the challenge of disseminating some kinds of knowledge, more privileged and epistemically more authoritative, while silencing others. Medina proposes epistemic resistance as an attitude referring "to a mode of relationality that is crucial for democratic sociability – in fact, the heart and soul, the epistemic centrepiece, of a democratic culture" (2013, 4). The lyric voices of *Ansina* connect with one another and the world by putting forward this kind of relational sociability based on knowledge, imagination, and historical recollection carried out by a language in silence, radically proximate to death.

In comparison to other modern poets in Judezmo, I contend that *Ansina* brings the voices that have populated a history of centuries into radical proximity with the present and the future, thus bridging the gulf between the ambit of life and the afterlife of a language. Moscona's poems mark a constant movement from the social sphere to intimate relationships and back again, touching upon politics, science, literary tradition, love, linguistics, ideology, and more. *Ansina* sets the foundations for a contemporary lyric encyclopedia of sorts, one that through updating and furthering old paradigms enacts the memorial and cultural archive of epistemic struggles within the Sephardic diaspora.[3]

In "Eskrivir de amor o sensya" ("Writing on Love or Science") one of the poems in the section titled "De sensya" ("On Science"), the lyric speaker offers this declaration:

Me permeto dezir a todos vozotros, profezores ke pasan todo
el diya eruktando danrivabasho, ke no konozen la lingua
muestra... Meldan kuentos, sienten frazes, ma estan al rovés...
Dafuera adientro van a dar un veredikto?

Muncho se puede
dezir en esta lingua
espandirme en eya
naser ainda puedo
i eskrivir de amor o sensya

no se topa la lingua
solo para servir
kantikas o para enlazar
ermanos

la lingua sirve
para el rakonto
de estreyas
para studiar
insektos
para apanyar
ladrones
i kriyar ijos
i pajaros
en la techumbre
de las kazas
(para limpiarse
los dientes
la lingua
se guarda mui
detrás)

no solo se topa
en la universitá
la lingua es mas ke
un revivido
es la konsentraziyon

desto
i de akeyo

no es la suma es
la resta
de la suma
el divisor y el dividendo

es la tardada
en ke los ojos
se ensierran
en sí
i por adientro
a la klaridad se echan (Moscona 2015, 54–5)[4]

The poet examines her language's ties to a broad world in which speaking and writing are not only instruments for private communications but also bridges between the familiar and the unknown, be it in mathematics, delinquency, or death, the uncanny *par excellence*. From the beginning, Judezmo is a disputed territory between the speakers and the academic ambit, the prose that opens the text and the verse that follows. Furthermore, it is orality that establishes a dialogue with the written universe of scientific research, the aesthetic use of language that converses with epistemology. Poetry is a reaction against a verdict on Judezmo's viability; Moscona's text represents orchestrated, polyphonic, palpable evidence of aliveness.

In juxtaposing scientific research to childrearing, and metaphysics to dental hygiene, the poetic self attaches the language to the body. The language of "Eskrivir de amor o sensya" represents and expands creatively the world's defiant complexity, despite its being written in a post-vernacular language and a dying systematization of the real.[5] By means of these tasks that the mind and the body perform, Moscona offers her readers a hint of the edifice they are about to enter. *Ansina* cannot be read as the aesthetic elaboration of a currently spoken language. Rather, it is a depiction of what exists in radical proximity with what has ceased to be.

The locus of linguistic competence is already shaken by the diglossia of the book: Spanish frames the poems in Judezmo through a series of paratexts: "Exordio," (Exordium), "Aclaraciones ortográficas" (Spelling Clarifications), "Glosario" (Glossary), and "Agradecimientos" (Acknowledgments). Given the language in which this frame is laid out, and more emphatically given the glossary at the end of the book, *Ansina*'s reader is thought of mainly as a Spanish and only secondarily a Judezmo speaker. If linguistic competence and native command are the guarantors of understanding what lies *dibaxu* ("beneath" in Judezmo) poetry, *Ansina* unveils the epistemic region over which this poetry soars: language's simultaneous foreignness and familiarity.[6] In addition to this poetic manoeuvre, because of its connection to the sphere of the house, *Ansina* is a *mother's* tongue, the vehicle of popular

68 Beyond Intimacy

aesthetics and traditional literature. However, the book signals also a *tour de force* regarding death, the utmost uncanny, opened up as a world of inner clarity ("i por adientro / a la klaridad se echan"). In this way, Judezmo is twice foreign: because of its differences from Spanish and its post-vernacular perspective. The main language of the book constitutes thus a *de facto* paradox.

David Bunis makes a convincing case for Judezmo as the language of Iberian Jews. He asserts that it was a variation of the language spoken by Christians on the Iberian Peninsula prior to the expulsion in 1492 and that it was generally written in the Hebrew alphabet: "There is an extensive written documentation of traditional Jewish Ibero-Romance from the Middle Ages into the present. Pre-expulsion writings include personal correspondence, rabbinical ordinances, and communal records" (2017, 3; on this topic, see also Bunis, Chetrit, and Sahim 2003, 105). This language, rich in elements of Hebrew and Aramaic, especially in matters related to religious life, had incorporated lexicological items of regional vernaculars and was "distinct from varieties of Ibero-Romance used by non-Jews in Iberia" (Bunis 2011b, 24). While in Spain, Jewish groups identified both internally and vis-à-vis others on the basis of religion.[7] However, the existence of Judezmo as a vernacular offered a linguistic dimension, anchoring the Jewish Iberian communities in secular tropes of being, together with everyday material culture and practices.

A large part of Judezmo's divergence from the Castilian Spanish was a result of education. A strain of the language was developed for the literal translation of Jewish sacred texts. This variant, called Ladino, followed Hebrew syntax and was geared towards a faithful rendering of the Torah into a language that young boys with no knowledge of the holy tongue could understand and make theirs. The accuracy and adherence to orthodoxy of such translation tool was supported by specific techniques, and as printed materials started becoming widely available, also by glossaries. The first printed texts in Ladino date from the sixteenth century. According to Bunis, "the oldest surviving examples [of Ladino] are a translation of the Psalms (Constantinople, c. 1540), the trilingual Hebrew/Ladino/ Judeo-Greek Pentateuch published in Constantinople in 1547, a portion of the Latter Prophets and Writings published in Thessaloniki between 1569 and 1572, and a 1580 manuscript translation of the Early Prophets; the Latin-letter Marrano Ladino Bible was published in Ferrara, 1553" (1992, 401).[8] The influence of this learning and memorizing tool has had profound consequences, as the publications prior to expulsion support, although its importance extends beyond religious and educational reasons (Bunis 1992, 401; 1996b, 337–57). Because of its proximity to the Jewish Iberian vernacular and its distance from Hebrew, Ladino became a way to expand the sphere of education, for example, in the case of Jewish women's access to religious texts:

> According to Nahmanides (b. Gerona, 1194–1270) ... the Book of Esther was publicly recited in Romance on Purim in some communities of Castile, Catalonia, and Aragon, ostensibly for the benefit of women. Objections to the practice were voiced by R. Nisim of Gerona (d. Barcelona 1380) and R. Isaac Bar Sheshet (d. 1480), who were concerned about inaccuracies in the translation and feared that the vernacular version might supplant the Hebrew text. But Spanish-born rabbi David ben Zimra of Egypt (1479–1573) approved the recitation of the translation ... and it eventually became a widely accepted practice among the Ottoman Sephardim. (Bunis 1996a, 340)

An inner tension between Hebrew and Ladino is evident here. The holy tongue represents written orthodoxy, historically produced by educated men and synchronically available to them. Ladino, the language of translation, places in radical proximity orality and script, variation and monumentality, the house and the synagogue. Ladino bespeaks the gaps among gender, class, and age groups within Sephardic communities. Furthermore, as a means of translation between Hebrew and Judezmo, it evokes both religion and life in multiethnic environments, before and after the expulsion from Spain, and thus it becomes lively proof of a historical antagonism between the visionary return to the Promised Land and the reality that daily life in diaspora entails. It is the oral nature of Ladino that seals the intimate link between the holy and the quotidian, that brings closer the uneducated and the cultivated, the lower classes and the elites, while making visible the spiritual needs of women and children in a man's world.[9]

This religious practice had profound effects on the way identification with a past was asserted. According to Bunis,

> in training their pupils to translate the Bible spontaneously (a type of translation referred to in Sephardi Hebrew texts

as *milibam* "from the heart," and in Judezmo texts as *de kavesa* "from the head") the elementary-school teachers were perpetuating a tradition of oral Bible translation and interpretation which harks back to Targumic (or Jewish Aramaic) oral translations and interpretations of the *meturgemanim* mentioned in the Mishnah. Among the Sephardim, the technique came to be known as *(en)ladinar*. (1996a, 339–40, my emphasis)

Moving swiftly between various linguistic registers and agents, the passage guides us towards a concept of translation related to memory: an act of understanding intellectually and affectively, of inferring and imagining, anchored in the particular needs of time and space even while surpassing temporal and spatial exclusivity. The title of the essay – "Translating from the Head and from the Heart. The Essentially *Oral* Nature of the *Ladino* Bible-Translation Tradition" (emphasis in the original) – subtly summons the opposition between cognition and affection as the deep structure that corresponds to other binaries such as writing and speaking, voice and silence, boys and girls, spiritual experience and secular life, the synagogue and the surrounding non-Jewish community. The intended pun highlights memory's double origin in the heart and in the mind, a connection of long and fruitful epistemic life in the form of the art of memory.[10]

In *Ansina*, Moscona brings up to date the symbolic power of *enladinar*, as a twist in the development of the art of memory. The crossing from the hieratic to the ordinary performed in this linguistic code makes current the creative power of translation as a form of remembrance and imagination. The Mexican poet recalls a range of original texts and writers: the God of the Torah, the prophets of the Hebrew Bible, San Juan de la Cruz, León Hebreo, José Martí, Paul Celan, Edmond Jabès, Marcel Cohen, Juan Gelman, among others; and she does so by heart and through the mind. Moscona remembers the language *in* the language: she fuses Judezmo and Ladino to the landscapes of another language and finds a home for them in another culture. She fights for the dignity of those forsaken by justice then and now, the pariahs of late modernity – women, working-class adults and children. The poet's choice of language is a symbolic return to a double origin. On one hand, the languages of *Ansina* build a cognitive and emotional connection between the cities of departure and the places of arrival; poetry draws on the evocative power of ruins, in a stroll through the memorial geography of Sephardic communities. On the other, intimate exchanges in Judezmo constitute searches for a new home in the Mexican literary canon.[11]

I contend that by articulating Judezmo *from the heart and the mind*, Moscona follows in a path already established in the history of Judezmo, and because of that she is able to seek justice for those involved in ancestral tensions. Specifically, her nuanced practice of *enladinar* – the intimately weaving together of traditional *loci* and secular modernity – rearticulates voices and debates from pre-exilic times; recalls and solves ideological tribulations among Sephardim; revisits cultural animosities between the Jews of the Levant and the *intelligentsia* of East European Jewry. Finally, *Ansina* reopens the cases of struggles between the rich and educated, on one hand, and the poor, on the other; between women, as theological outcasts, and men, as the heirs of god's wisdom and will; as well as between different generations of speakers.

## JUDEZMO'S POLYPHONY

In the centuries that followed the expulsion of the Jews from the Iberian Peninsula, Judezmo evolved constantly as the speakers' diglossia of Castilian vernacular and Hebrew for religious observance was amplified by contact with the multitude of languages spoken in the North of Africa, France, Italy, and the Ottoman Empire. Once in diaspora, "Judezmo served as a kind of Sephardic international language" (Bunis 2011b, 31). For the most part, Jewish communities flourished in urban settings. The Ottoman Empire under Sultan Abdülmecid's rule underwent an administrative reorganization, known as the Tanzimat (1839–76). One of these new provisions was the reorganization of the regime for religious minorities that had previously lived in relative legal and administrative autonomy, and the extension of equal citizenship to all subjects of the Sultan, whatever their religious affiliation. The education that was supposed to open the way to these changes was offered to all children, and the language of that education was Ottoman Turkish. Westernization was under way, but not without tensions for the minorities and the position they held in the empire.[12] At the same time, the Jewish Enlightenment (*Haskalah*), an intellectual movement of mainly German and East European Jewry, reached the Ottoman Sephardim, with the aim of inserting Jews into modernity through education. Modern times brought a discrete separation of religious and secular life, so that part of the Jewish population distanced itself from traditional ways, such as those related to dress codes, education for women, travel, and socialist ideas that affected workplaces. These changes did not touch all social groups in the same way or at the same time.

After the late eighteenth century, upper-class Jews of the Ottoman Empire came into closer contact with the West. An important early influence here was a small group of Jews with Italian and Portuguese roots who had immigrated to the Ottoman Empire after its expansion in the West in the fifteenth and sixteenth centuries. The *francos*, as they were called, maintained a tight bond with their places of origin, as well as with their customs, which were significantly different from those of Oriental Jews. Contacts with Western Europe became more extensive in the eighteenth and nineteenth centuries as a result of commercial exchanges, leisure travel, and secular education, especially after the Alliance Israélite Universelle (AIU) was founded in Paris, in 1860. The AIU began establishing schools in the Ottoman Empire in the 1860s, propelling a nuanced process of secularizing young Jewish girls and boys:

> The rabbis continued to teach Hebrew and religious subjects even in the modern schools under the auspices of the Alliance, whereas the core of the curriculum was decidedly European (in particular French) in orientation.
>
> The conflicts between traditionalists and reformers should not be seen as a conflict between religious and secular elites, though. Different alliances were forged and broken ...
> In the end, it is probably best to understand the controversies of the late nineteenth century not only in terms of an ideological-cultural clash between modernizers and traditionalists, but also as a political power struggle in which members of the old notable families, the new *franco*-elites – usually under the protection of foreign consuls – and different factions within the rabbinate fought over influence and conflicting economic interests. (Lehmann 2017, 108)

With the administrative reforms of the Ottoman Empire in the nineteenth century came pressure for full integration, which meant adapting linguistically to Turkish, the language of the Muslim majority. At the same time, the modernization and the cultural openness that the times demanded brought about the quest for proficiency in the languages of Western Europe, and in other languages common to the multiethnic cultural environment that Ottoman Jews shared with Greeks and Armenians.[13]

The anthology of biblical commentary *Me'am Lo'ez* (1730) marked an early effort at inclusiveness as well as the beginning of a transformation of the public sphere. It offered educational opportunities in religion to various groups, including women, who had occupied the margins of education and were confined to the private domain (Lehmann 2017, 105–6).[14] In the late eighteenth century, a literature of non-rabbinic content, in Judezmo, began to develop in the Jewish communities of the Balkans and the Ottoman Empire. Later, influenced by the German-Jewish Enlightenment, Sephardi intellectuals began publishing books on history, astronomy, and geography (Bunis, Chetrit, and Sahim 2003, 109). Around the mid-nineteenth century, a periodical press also appeared. Judezmo writers grappled with the lack of terminology for expressing the fast-evolving changes around them. In addition to this extralinguistic difficulty, authors complained about a lack of grammatical rules and written norms. It seemed that the language lacked a modern (i.e., authorial) literary tradition compared to those of Western Europe. Among Judezmo native speakers and intellectuals there were those who defended and those who disparaged their mother tongue:

> From the second half of the nineteenth century, enlightened Sephardim expressed increasing scorn for Judezmo and advocated its replacement by other languages. In 1868, inspired by German-language monographs on the glories of Medieval Spain Jewry by Haskalah historians, the editor of the Viennese Judezmo periodical *El nasyonal* proposed that Judezmo speakers abandon their traditional language and adopt Castilian, to be written not in the Jewish alphabet but in Latin letters. (Bunis, Chetrit, and Sahim 2003, 111)

This disdain was hardly exclusive to Judezmo. Around the same time in the nineteenth-century Balkans, the presence of diverse languages and regional dialects became an issue for other national communities, who had to reimagine themselves as part of the historical process of nation-states building, for which linguistic homogeneity was pivotal.

At the turn of twentieth century, David Fresco (Istanbul 1853–1936), a prolific journalist, periodical editor, and literary translator, published in *El Tyempo* (1872–1930), a Judezmo newspaper written in Hebrew letters (which he directed after 1893), an article titled "Un puevlo mudo." The editor passionately condemned Judezmo as the reason why the Ottoman Jews had been excluded from cultural advancement within the empire, compared to other minorities. David Bunis collected and transliterated into the Latin alphabet several of the pieces in which the attitude towards Judezmo of this most conspicuous public figure is evident. In 1901, Fresco declared that the Jews of Turkey were a people that "no tyene lingua!" (Fresco [1901b] in Bunis 2019, 175, "does not have language," my translation). Fresco attributed the lack of intellectual development of the Sephardim to their language: "porke es la lingua que kria o desvelopa onde el ombre la fakultad entelektual" (Fresco [1901b] in Bunis 2019, 176, "in human beings, it is language that grows and develops intellectual ability"). Unlike other minoritarian ethnic and religious groups, he argued, Ottoman Jews had no access to art or science, because modern philosophers and literati had not been translated into Judezmo. This was because other people had languages, while Sephardim had merely a "žerigonza," jargon, the sign of an "hazinadura" (Fresco [1901b] in Bunis 2019, 176, "illness").[15] In 1924, in "The Language of the Israelites of Turkey," Fresco evaluated Judezmo in terms of its distance from Castilian Spanish and diminished the former's status (Fresco [1901a] in Bunis 2019, 176–9).

According to the journalist, among the various benefits unavailable to Levantine Jews due to the linguistic deficiency of their *žerigonza*, literature and justice stood out: "Kon este idyoma el no puede tener *ni ležisladores, ni literadores*, ni savyos, ni poetas ... Lo oprimen, lo eksplotan i el no puede levantar su bos, demandar *ğustisya* i proteksyón" (Fresco [1901b] in Bunis 2019, 175, "With this language it [the Sephardic community] cannot have either legislators, or authors, or sages or poets ... It is being exploited and cannot raise its voice to ask for justice and protection," my emphasis). This people, continued the author, lacked even knowledge of its rights: "No save reklamar sus derečos ... el no tyene ni lugares de orasyón, *ni tribunales, ni teatros*, ni konsyertos" (Fresco [1901b] in Bunis 2019, 175, "It does not know how to claim its rights ... it does not have places of worship, or courtrooms, or theatres, or concerts," my emphasis). Fresco's animosity against Judezmo is in fact quite unjustified: Ottoman Jews did enjoy freedom of worship and considerable autonomy with respect to legal issues that could be resolved in rabbinic tribunals. Nonetheless, the relationship he traces between justice and literature is noteworthy, for it strengthens the connection between the two on the grounds of the language.

Current speakers and writers may or may not be fully aware of the controversy into which the uninterrupted use of Judezmo led their ancestors at the end of the nineteenth century.[16] David Bunis takes a close look at contemporary discussions about the viability of Judezmo on the virtual forum Ladinokomunita. The scholar points out elements in common between today's deliberations on behalf of the Sephardim worldwide and the dialogue among Ottoman Jews, a war of sorts, regarding the state of their linguistic affairs (2016, 325). From a poetic point of view, Moscona echoes, refracts and potentiates cultural dialogues, in many of which Judezmo is both the vector and the reason of debate. Passionate defenders and detractors have left an imprint that the language carries as a sign of exuberant polyphony, and it is precisely in the vein of this tradition that *Ansina* can be read in order for the effervescence of its claims to be heard and, hopefully, keenly answered. Besides being the code of the house, the mother, and the vessel for oral translation of sacred texts, Judezmo, or Judeo-español or Ladino or Dji/Djudió or "el español muestro" or Španyolit or Haketía, is a language of cultural disputes and ideological controversies. *Ansina* reignites an array of voices and places them in contemporary settings, seeking justice for a language beyond silence.

### ANSINA

Myriam Moscona is a first-generation Mexican. Her maternal and paternal families came from Bulgaria to the Mesoamerican country after the Second World War. Bulgarian Jews were protected by the country's government and the broader Christian society against deportations and thus survived the Holocaust: "los búlgaros veían a los judíos búlgaros como búlgaros y no como judíos," writes Moscona in *Tela de sevoya*, her first Sephardic literary work (2016, 33, "Bulgarians considered Bulgarian Jews as Bulgarian and not as Jews"). Unlike the Ashkenazim of Eastern Europe, whose immigration was sponsored by international Jewish organizations – the Jewish Colonization Association, the Hebrew Immigration Aid Society, and the Joint (American Jewish Joint Distribution Committee) – and who were directed towards the United States and Latin America, Sephardim followed earlier patterns of immigration based on community, kinship, and social bonds, and thus they were oriented towards destinies previously explored by individuals or families of their own ethnic group, town, or language: "The Sephardim were scattered throughout the continent and divided into small nuclei that identified with their communities of origin. The history of each individual community was shaped by the confrontation between its cultural and social heritage and the conditions in the respective country" (Bejarano 2012, 4). Different countries and even cities of origin marked Jewish immigrants as more or less religiously observant, poorer or richer, more or less educated.

Twentieth-century Jewish immigration to Mexico from the Balkans and the Near East has been studied in relation to literature since the 1990s, when Rosa Nissán (Mexico 1953–) published the autobiographical novel *Novia que te vea* (1992).[17] This particular corner of Mexican literature and its criticism seem quite homogenous: they revolve around autobiography, memory and its coexistence with present issues of belonging, as well as the ethnic, religious, and civil forces the diasporic context exerts on characters' lives. Other related themes are search for identity, gender bias, and the intense secularization of Jewish communities. All these topics point to a common area: language. Judezmo is viewed as a vehicle of unique vivacity that has heightened the element of heteroglossia in Mexican canonical literature (Halevi-Wise 2012, 188; Lockhart 1997, 167). The importance of these literary works hinges on the oral vivacity of a language in which centuries of everyday life resonate and on its similarities to the predominant language of Mexican society.[18] The characteristic of this language probably mentioned most often is its acoustic prevalent feature. Judezmo is a "tender" sounding other to the different Spanish idiolects, and in some cases a more "feminine" alternative.[19]

Between 1978 and 1994, a series of poetry collections marked a revival of Judezmo literature. Clarisse Nicoïdski (France, 1938–1996), whose family came from Sarajevo, wrote *Lus ojus Las manus La boca* (1978, *Eyes Hands Mouth*) and *Caminus di palavras* (1980, *Paths of Words*); Israeli author Margalit Matitiahu (Israel, 1935–), from a Salonican family, presented, in bilingual editions of Judezmo/Hebrew, *Kurtijo kemado* (1988, *Scorched Courtyard*), and *Alegrika* (1992); and Juan Gelman, an Argentine of Ashkenazi origin, published *dibaxu* (1994), in a bilingual edition of Judezmo/Spanish.

Intimating with History

A text that has been equally influential in the attention given to Judezmo is *Letra a Antonio Saura* (2006, *Letter to Antonio Saura*), by Marcel Cohen (1937–), a French-born author of Turkish-Sephardic origin. In all these works, the tone is nostalgic and language serves as an emotional anchorage in the personal and shared past of the authors. The prevalent topic is loss related to new diasporas, the Holocaust, and family history. For the two women poets, the mother's death triggered a need to reminisce in the language of childhood. Matitiahu defends her choice of Judezmo on the horizon of Israel's policies of linguistic homogenization (Balbuena 2016, 62–3), while Nicoïdski confesses that Judezmo is for her "la otra lingua que era 'de la familia', del 'secreto', del susto y – quisas – de la vergüenza. Había hecho de nosotros 'los escondidos'. Además, comparandola al francés me parecia sin noblesa, sin gramatica y sin … literatura" (2014, 12).[20] When her mother dies, the French writer realizes that in losing her, "se iba definitivamente un poco de esta lingua de [su] infancia," (2014, 13, "a part of this language of [her] childhood disappeared"). Thus the reason for this writing is "para que quede la empresa de su voz" (2014, 13, "in order to keep the imprint of her voice"). Monique Balbuena reads Margalit Matitiahu's poems in *Kurtijo kemado* and *Alegrika* as straddling a nostalgic attitude towards the annihilated past of Salonican Jewry and contemporary poetics, "in this double binding of past and future" (Balbuena 2016, 89).

In 2008 and 2011, Denise León (Argentina, 1974–) published *Poemas de Estambul* (*Poems from Istanbul*) and *El saco de Douglas* (*The Pouch of Douglas*), respectively. In these two poetry books, the Sephardic diaspora plays a principal role, and the poems in Judezmo are accompanied by translations into Castilian Spanish. The 2011 book comprises three sets of prose poems in the voices of women: "Luisa (1914)," "Klara (1939)," and "Alegre (1971)." Luisa, a young girl from Izmir, laments the departure of the father, who escapes persecution during a time of war, migrates, and dies. At the same time, Luisa observes the mother as mourner. In the family history, there is a horizontal separation: in the upper part of the page the poems are in Castilian Spanish, while in the lower, in parentheses and italics, they are provided in Judezmo. The orientation of the poems towards a quest for self-discovery, albeit embedded in biographical recollection, separates León from other contemporary Judezmo authors and paves the way for Moscona's multilayered lyricism.

78 Beyond Intimacy

The historical tragedies surrounding the production of contemporary poetry in Judezmo, be it the Holocaust or, in Gelman's case, Videla's dictatorship and the *Guerra sucia* (Dirty War) in Argentina, converge with personal losses. Such elegiac condition weighs on those critical approaches that find in the poems a profound nostalgia, great authenticity, and a gendered slant, nested especially in the choice of language. Notwithstanding the accuracy of such readings, I contend that Moscona's poetry retains the agonistic quality of Judezmo *qua* vehicle and materialization of social confrontations and synergies. In *Ansina*, Moscona creates lyric voices that maintain an exophonic position towards language. Judezmo and Mexican Spanish are proximate enough that they refract each other. Judezmo's possibility of participating poetically in a current world is measured and asserted vis-à-vis a living language, with which it is in dialogue, through insistent heteroglossia. Justice as parity is the guiding principle of the close company that Judezmo keeps with Spanish-speaking readers in *Ansina*.

Moscona revisits and renews linguistic practices that have stayed alive for centuries: she translates today's physical and spiritual world into a version of the language that she recovers by heart and makes current by head; she adapts her words to scientific knowledge; she uses language to recover history, to draw readers into unfamiliar linguistic domains and aesthetic problems, and to mark ideological territories. Speculatively creating not only a world in Judezmo but most importantly the other as an ambivalent reader on the verge of silence, Moscona inhabits at the same time her own exophony – writing poetry in a language other than a poet's native tongue.

So far, literary criticism has mapped out the author's belonging to Jewish and specifically Sephardic traditions in Mexican and Latin American contexts. Scholars such as Alessia Cassani (2019), Florinda Goldberg (2013), Darrell Lockhart (2018), and Jacobo Sefamí (2002) have analyzed how Moscona's production ties into these broader horizons of identity inquiry. Sefamí places the poet within the production of Sephardim and Mizrahim, under Deleuze and Guattari's category of minor literature (Deleuze and Guattari 1986, 16, 18; Sefamí 2002, 148n11). Darrell Lockhart underscores the biographical or autobiographical slant of the author's literary works related to Judezmo in order to place Moscona in a group together with Rosa Nissán, Vicky Nizri, Jacobo Sefamí, and Angelina Muñiz-Huberman. Lockhart nevertheless recognizes that Moscona's prose is of quite a different nature:

While *Tela de sevoya* has much in common with its Sephardic counterparts in Mexico, what sets it apart is the rather innovative way in which Moscona incorporates Sephardism not as a trope or an ethnic flare with which to flavor the text and provide a glimpse into an otherwise hermetic world, but as the central axis of the narrative. She thus makes Sephardism the nucleus of her text in a way that is not overly stylized and hyperliterary, and yet invites the reader into an authentic and rather *intimate* representation of a world that in the vast majority of cases would be foreign to him or her, while maintaining its universal appeal. (Lockhart 2018, 113, my emphasis)

Regarding *Ansina*, he notes:

*Ansina* is divided into five thematic groupings of poems that not only delve into the evocation of a Sephardic past or a bygone age and homeland to be lamented in poetic verse. Her poems also employ Djudeo-Espanyol as a language of science, of literary creation, of wisdom, and of humour. In other words, she showcases Djudeo-Espanyol as a language of everyday use, even if in reality it is not entirely the case. (Lockhart 2018, 118)[21]

The novel, *Tela de sevoya* (2012), and the poetry collection exhibit (a) refraction and (b) thematic variety. The two characteristics are intrinsically related, for they depict an open-ended world that lacks uniformity. With this brand of vitality, Moscona draws from the past while also preparing the next step in the dialogue that Judezmo and Sephardim sustain in their new linguistic and cultural homes. Alessia Cassani finds Moscona fundamentally different from contemporary poets such as Matilda Gini Barnatán, Viviana Rajel Barnatán, and Juan Gelman, who also write in Judezmo: "Myriam Moscona … expresa el apego a su cultura a través de referencias a la Cabalá, a la tradición judía en sentido más amplio, a los maestros de la espiritualidad rabínica o a los poetas judíos contemporáneos, y *no en un repliegue nostálgico*, en el recuerdo de sus antepasados o en el recurso a un estilo o a temáticas ligadas a la poesía medieval. Al contrario, su estilo es prosaico, desenfadado, coloquial" (Cassani 2019, 75–6, my emphasis).[22] As Cassani points out, Moscona's references to Judaism have a sophistication that is secular and cultural rather than religious and metaphysical.

Furthering this observation, I see in *Ansina* not only the colloquial and casual but also the learned and esoteric.

The choice of language demands that the reader be located outside the space of *Ansina*. Moscona addresses in her paratexts the implications of this positioning. In "Exordio" (Exordium), she attributes her choice of not translating the poems to the impossibility of rendering into Spanish the affect and effect of certain expressions typical of Judezmo, pointing at the same time to a problem of all translations. The examples showcasing her claim are telling: "Dio Patron del mundo" and "Dio Santo i alavado" (Moscona 2015, 11, "God Master of the Universe," "Holy and Blessed God"). In a book of poems in which religious thinking takes a broader cultural perspective, the mooring of untranslatability in two expressions of sacred content directs the attention to identity: on one hand, the variant of "Dio" emphasizes the existence of a Jewish language, one that distinguishes the speaker from those around her who use another kind of Spanish; on the other, "Dio Santo i Alavado," evokes the traditional practice of *enladinar*.[23] Here the complex universe of Judaism plays a cultural role that is as identity-critical as the religious differentiation that the same expressions would have marked in pre-1492 Iberia. The echoes of Jewish liturgy contain a profound linguistic and sentimental value that infiltrates the layers of translation from Hebrew to Ladino, from the sacred to the secular and the poetic. Each of these metatheses of meaning creates diverse conditions of outside-situatedness for the readers.

Other tensions surround the book, such as the one between the prosaic "Exordio" and the poetic "Eskrivir de amor y sensya." In the former, Moscona affirms Judezmo's holy and also secular aptitudes; in the latter, the lyric voice protests against the idea that this language may only be suited for oral poetry and the realm of the family. An exquisitely layered, voracious appetite for intake and outpouring is encountered in "Eskrivir de amor i sensya," in which Moscona launches a conversation with history thematized in terms of what professors who "barf all day long" do. An abrupt emotional reaction shines and sounds just like a firecracker, in the gerund "eruktando," through which *Ansina* takes issue with the classification of Judezmo as a severely endangered language in the UNESCO *Atlas of the World's Languages in Danger*. Moscona converses with writers such as Marcel Cohen, Clarisse Nicoïdski, Margalit Matitiahu, and Juan Gelman, countering a retrospective view of Judezmo with the effervescence and vitality of a contemporary book that advances current debates and hopes.

Moscona offers two reasons for her decision not to translate the texts of the book into Spanish: first she claims that "la connotación lúdica del asombro coloquial perdería su huella." Then she bases her choice on the fact that Judeo-Spanish is "el habla que [le] permite entrar en otra dimensión del tiempo, en una más íntima, familiar y primitiva" (2015, 11, "the trace of playful connotation, which amazes in colloquial discourse, would be lost," "the oral expression that allows [her] to enter another dimension of time, a more intimate, familiar, and primitive one"). "Asombro" is the key word in the first reasoning: the elaborate orality of the book asks the reader to place words in an active, dialogical context charged with expectations of awe. The second justification has to do with a personal need to re-enact the familiar within the parameters of the foreign. Moscona does not go back in time; rather she actualizes time in space.

*Ansina* touches on a wide range of topics: family and identity ("De empolvaduras," 2015, 17–31, "Of Dusty Spaces"), the history of Sephardic diaspora before the Holocaust ("De morideros," 2015, 33–42, "Of Death Places"), the universe and its laws of physics ("De sensya," 2015, 49–57, "Of Science"), spirituality, one of whose forms is religious faith ("De kreaziones I undimientos," 2015, 43–9, "Of Creations and Sinkings"), literature ("De eskrivideros," 2015, 59–71, "Of Writers"). A variety of voices step forth from the depths of history into the multifaceted universe that comes alive in *Ansina*. This created world depends mainly on transformations from one lyric speaker, time, or aesthetic value to another. *Sui generis* permutations and metamorphoses invite the reader to connect dots that go beyond linearity and causal logic: Isaac Abravanel and his exodus enter a painful dialogue with Paul Celan (Moscona 2015, 37–9);[24] a dissonant universe resonates with love (2015, 52–3); nature becomes culture (2015, 24–5); family history expands to cover different times and spaces (2015, 27).

What gives this book of poetry cohesion is the way in which contemporary Judezmo builds uncanny causality between contemporaneity and history. Moscona extends sequences of past acts that lead to extravagant ends in actuality ("Un iliko," 2015, 30, "A Little Thread"; "Lo ke fue," 2015, 31, "What There Was"). Judezmo's permeability to the present is most striking in the fourth section, "De sensya." Here, Moscona's strategy translates the insights of an educated eye into words that oscillate between the fluidity of the colloquial and the precision of the epistemic in order to unmask

82                                  Beyond Intimacy

paradoxes of reason. The poet emphasizes the existence of governing
laws of the universe, only to highlight ironically the aporia of living,
wanting, dying. Unlike other contemporary poets writing in Judezmo,
she often turns to the cultural forces of laughter. The poems claim a
multilayered belonging to the Sephardic, Mexican, and Latin American
literary canons, and this interconnectedness constitutes *Ansina*'s
actuality, solidly relying on the refusal to offer a translation into
Spanish. This strategy, as Cynthia Gabbay astutely observes, "reevalúa
el parentesco especular entre ambas lenguas, al mismo tiempo que …
da el debido espacio para reimpulsar al djudezmo en la literatura
latinoamericana" (2022, 89).[25] By requesting a place within the Latin
American canon for a book written in Judezmo, Moscona anchors
her aesthetic endeavour in the present.

"Embrolyo en Fortaleza" ("Confusion in Fortaleza"), from the first
section of *Ansina*, gives the coordinates of the political sphere within
which the book discerns communicative and loving "embrolyos,"
complications that are personal and communal, intimate and political.
The poem is a dialogue between two voices. Ecology and intimacy
blend here to deliver a *puerpo* (body) of political and historical uses
of the *lingua* (language):

Embrolyo en Fortaleza
    ande se toparán las flores
    ke etchan por los lavios
    bafos de miel?

estás pensando mal?

        agora avlo
        del kampo
        i de un guerto
        de buena
        estampa
        no avlo del puerpo
        tuyo

        estas sintyendo
        kualo
        kero dezir?

penso de subito
en las flores
de brasil
enfrente de la afrika
rota

avlo de tu puerpo
ma de un puerpo politiko
organisado
en payises
ke kultivan
tayos para alevantar
la lingua

este eskritiko avlar keria
de todo eyo
     ama solo avla de ti. (Moscona 2015, 24–5)[26]

The honey-perfumed mouths and naughty thoughts of the first stanza
weave a canvas of proximity that will be further populated with
exchanges regarding the body, geography, history, political thought,
and colonialism, only to end in a *tour de force* with reflections on
love and poetry. The voice starts by singing a *beatus ille* in honour
of Fortaleza, in northern Brazil. Soon this praise gives way to a
historical and linguistic dystopia. Brazil, the great Lusophone country,
whose richness from colonial to postcolonial times has been built on
slavery, racial and religious violence, and social inequalities, is
reflected momentarily on the African continent, which has been
cruelly exploited and subjected to Western rapacity for centuries. The
poem tacitly points to a host of concerns, such as the past trade in
slaves, ecological destruction, and present-day racial discrimination.
The "tayos" that different nations "kultivan" in order to "alevantar /
la lingua" bring to mind peoples of ethnic miscegenation as well as
cultural clashes between the most agricultural, least technologically
advanced economies of our time and the First World giants of political
and financial power. "Talla" ("altura moral o intellectual," *Diccionario
de la Real Academia Española*, s.v. talla), the "moral or intellectual
height" found in voices of protest and denunciation, resonates in the
word "tayo." The poem brings to the fore dispossession, injustice, and

utilization; it criticizes financial expansion that impoverishes some countries in favour of others, and it denounces discrimination between lives and bodies whose freedom and dignity are worth defending and others considered disposable. In the end, as in much of modern poetry, the voice turns inward: it refers with tenderness to her poem as "eskritiko" and confesses her willingness to speak, thus locating her existence between writing and orality. The poem is outlined as a two-faced enunciation with a certain initial purpose, and with a *de facto* distinct point of arrival. Throughout, however, it is hinted that all reflection is somehow a discussion with another person, a dialogue, an ethical act in Bakhtinian terms.

Another possible reading places the problem of politicization prior to telling the story of a Judeo-Spanish speaker who addresses her language. The first verses ask about the fate of those who can speak this sweet language of "honey perfumes."[27] Bad thinking can also mean a bad omen, a sign of a sinister fate. The voice answers this by putting a certain distance and shifting the discussion to the terrain of representation and reference. It seems to say to its interlocutor: "I am not talking about you [my language], I am talking about the world." In a brief moment of intense concentration, the poem depicts the territory on which social life unfolds and a living language materializes in institutions. It is not by chance that Moscona relates the survival of her stateless language to "the payises," for linguistic unification is a cornerstone of the nation-state, a measure that places minority languages on the periphery of the national body.[28] The poetic self voices an accusation towards the political desires for homogenization and expresses a longing that her language be accommodated in organic social formations.

In both readings, what stands out is the amalgam of anti-colonial indictment and intimacy. What lies far and beyond the voice's reach, namely geography, history, the structure of modern states, results as intimate as the interlocutor whose body the lyric speaker brings to her mouth through the poem ("avlo de tu puerpo," "[el eskritiko] solo avla de ti"). Moscona's lyric voice makes the foreign personal and thereby attaches to the individual a responsibility for that which seems at first outside her moral incumbency or affective obligation. In the poem, the relations between Brazil and Africa, but also the history of nation-state formations, lie as close to the speaker's heart as the space, moment, language, and passion she shares with a lover. The personal and linguistic commitments of love appear commensurate with

# Intimating with History

cognition of political science, agriculture, and the history of slavery. Intimacy is thereby construed not only as a matter of affection, sympathy, and symmetrical knowledge of another, but also as based on social and epistemic fairness. Furthermore, Judezmo proves to be a language capable of rendering audible the word of poets, lovers, and political activists.

*Ansina* takes up the task of speaking about the law, in the prose poem "La letra beth: el muro ב" (Moscona 2015, 45, "The Letter Bet: The Wall ב"), which in addition to Kabbalistic resonances contains a reflection on people's observance and questioning of the law. In the poem, knowledge of the universe is contingent on a limit conceived and depicted in the form of the letter "bet," a synecdoche for scripture, with all its sacred connotations, and for language in general. Science, religion, and poetry abide by the law of the letter ב, which in the poem represents the visual threshold between permissiveness and prohibition, and thus the letter of the law:

> Todo esta avierto i puede ser de studio posivle. Atras del muro
> de la beth, nada ai ke un bivo pueda provar, i por ese silenzio
> los poetas eskriven i por ese silenzio los profetas traduzen
> las suias profezias i por ese silenzio los geometras de los
> sielos multiplikan, i por ese silenzio se fazen kadenas de orar.
> (Moscona 2015, 45)[29]

Using the format of the prose poem, a patent rupture of the poetic law of versification, Moscona proposes a contemporary mysticism, responding to the silence of God, protected by the wall of law.

The poem harbours religious and secular resonances. Just as in a primer for young Judezmo readers, a reminiscence of the eighteenth-century tradition of *Otsar aHayim*, for instance, Moscona's text radiates allusions to the secular heritage of modern Judezmo. At the same time, through the religious universe evoked by the letter ב, it refers to the yearly cycle of the Torah reading, based on the sequence of fifty-four *parashot*. Both threads get more complicated as the poem departs from the alphabet in a swift flight towards poetry, science, and the Kabbalah. Using the letter bet visually as a flipped house, and semantically, for "ב" in Hebrew is the etymon of the word חיב, beith, house – Moscona creates concentric circles of knowledge, through which she brings the wide world, in the form of literature, astronomy, and eternity, into close proximity and complicity with the speaking

86 Beyond Intimacy

instance. The poem plays with spatial commensurability between human beings and a vast chronotope. The former are represented by the body: "organos serrados por la piel," (2015, 45, "organs closed inside of the skin"). The latter is a cosmic extension open to knowledge and understanding: "Todo esta avierto i puede ser de studio posivle," (2015, 45, "everything is open and possible to study").

Moscona chooses a strange verb to refer to the uncertainty of life's sense: "Atras del muro de la beth, nada ai ke un bivo pueda provar." In Judezmo, *prova* means "proof, trial, attempt" (Kohen and Kohen-Gordon s.v. *prova*). *Provar* also evokes mouth and taste. A synecdoche for both the language-word and the tongue-food, the letter ב brings eternity to a material, palatable context: "Endelantre de la letra beth, todo está avierto para ke puedas saziarte del saver" (Moscona 2015, 45, "before the letter bet everything is open so you can quench your hunger and thirst of knowledge"). The verb *saziarte* alludes to a process of eating and drinking, while *saver* also relates to the noun *sabor* and the verb *saber*: knowledge that enters through the intimacy of tasting, eating, imbibing. Cognition and comprehension are foods grounded in history and culture but also in the love that goes into their preparation, and, of course, into the mystical union of body and spirit.

The poem is written in two counterposed frequencies: mysticism and human will. This confrontation occurs by means of a series of synonyms within the semantic field of taste and cognition, to the point that all paradoxes are subject to dialogues between quietude, stemming from the sacred, and effervescence, emerging from the taste of the ordinary. A hieratic tone resounds in the solemnity of "la prima letra del primo versikulo, del primo kapitulo, de la prima *perashá*" (Moscona 2015, 45, "the first letter of the first verse, of the first chapter, of the first parashah"), intensified by repetition twice early in the poem, and once at its closing. Different stylistic devices bring about a texture of disparities, laying out a verbal bridge between what can and cannot be internalized through poetic representation. Silence as the other of the word encompasses utterance, in the same way that the prose in the poem merges with lyricism through rhymes ("provar / orar / pedalear," "to prove / to pray / to pedal"), asyndeta ("estreias, arvoles, insektos," "stars, trees, insects"), anaphors ("i por ese silenzio," "and because of this silence," repeated four times), and the *estribillo*-refrain ("la prima letra del primo versikulo, del primo kapitulo, de la prima *perashá*"). Finally, the *eternidad* ("eternity," emphasis in the original) of the last line offers a choice of discernment:

Intimating with History

eternity can be seen as posterity beyond the threshold of death, but also as the quality of the endless process of being called history.

*Ansina* is built on a form of spatial and temporal transpermeability of elements and discursive instances. There is contiguity between opposites and often among unrelated acts or ideas; contiguity in the form of derivative logic that at times reveals similarities and at other times ties together fleeting thoughts; a sustained propagation even in short-circuits. This same challenged nearness also governs sociability in *Ansina*. "Un bomboniko" (Moscona 2015, 22–3, "Little Candy") and "La Kordela de Moebius" (2015, 51, "Moebius Strip") are two poems that derive an understanding of love from history and science respectively. "De trokamientos" (2015, 20–1, "On Exchanges") is another strange example of centripetal and centrifugal techniques of reasoning, where a pattern of mutations between states of disability leads to insights on death and love.

"Loka por el deskonozido" (Moscona 2015, 27, "Crazy about a Stranger") gives this same thematic thread a playful and daring twist. The poem appeared for the first time in *Tela de sevoya*, under the rubric "Kantikas" (Moscona [2012] 2016, 78, "Poems"). *Tela de sevoya* has an experimental structure. Five narrative series under different titles – "Distancia de foco," "Pisapapeles," "Molino de viento," "Del diario de viaje," "La cuarta pared" ("Focal Length," "Paperweight," "Windmill," "From the Travel Diary," "The Fourth Wall"), and one poetic, "Kantikas," ("Poems") – alternate to tell stories somehow interconnected, although of non-narrative/linear continuity. In the novel, snippets of Sephardi times past are interwoven with a world of dreams and the travels of a narrator in search of her family's roots in the Balkans.

Placed between an excerpt of the series "Molino de viento" and one of "Del diario de viaje," originally untitled, the poetic text of *Ansina*'s "Loka por el deskonozido" connects dreamlike voyages to the geographical travels of the protagonist.[30] In the chapter from "Molino de viento," the narrator arrives at a train station with no name and tries to communicate in different languages with the only person there, an old woman, to no avail. She finds her own name on a sign, takes the sign and leaves the station with a sense that she has been saved from a lonely and purposeless arrival at the unknown location (Moscona [2012] 2016, 76–7). After this episode, there appears the poem (Moscona [2012] 2016, 78), which in *Tela de sevoya* gives way to a section of "Del diario de viaje," where Moscona's narrator and her travelling companion arrive to Plovdiv, the Bulgarian city where the former's father was born. There they are supposed to find shelter in the house of Rabbi Samuel and his wife. This occasion allows the reader to know that the narrator finds observant Jews backward, especially because of the conditions of life of women in Orthodox Judaism. The narrator and her friend are secular, independent women, and, as such, foreigners within the traditional world of what a rabbi's household ought to be. In an inner apologetic monologue, she wonders whether she needs to disclose her secularism:

> Quizá deba explicarles que no somos religiosas, que somos impuras, que mezclamos lácteos con carnes, que los sábados nos vamos de fiesta, que adoramos a nuestros amigos 'gentiles', que además veneramos a la Virgen morena de Tepeyac, que estaríamos dispuestas a marchar en una manifestación del orgullo 'goy', pero que somos judías y amamos nuestra condición. (Moscona [2012] 2016, 80)[31]

As she rehearses seeing herself from the point of view and expectations of a religious man, the narrator offers in this passage all the reasons for raising doubts about her Jewishness: non-*kashrut* eating practices, activities during the Shabbat, a predilection for the *mestizo* Virgen of Guadalupe, and affective welcoming of infidels. In this passage, she outlines herself as a Jew diverging from traditional definitions and embracing alternative identities through solidary synergies ("estaríamos dispuestas a marchar en una manifestación del orgullo 'goy'").[32] Rabbi Samuel turns out to be a character sharply opposite to what the narrator had anticipated. This rebuttal of expectations, personified in the old man whose laughter explodes from time to time in Moscona's novel, culminates in an explanation of his rabbinic identity:

> Nos confiesa que él no es en realidad un rabino formado ...
> – *En mi chikez me ambezí a meldar evreo kon mi padre. Dospues de la gerra nadien kedó aki ke supiera fazer los resos i orasiones, ansina fue ke dije 'aki esto yo'. Fui del partido komunisto ama agora pasí a ser el raví de Filibé.*
> Y el estruendo de otra carcajada hace que la superficie del café turco se mueva con las ondas de su risa. (Moscona 2016, 82)[33]

The passage brings together half a century of history alluding to the expansion of Zionism and the revival of the Hebrew language that the old man learned as a child from his father; the Holocaust and the subsequent Jewish immigration to Palestine/Israel; the ascension of communism in Bulgaria; and the withering of Sephardic presence in the Balkans. Rabbi Samuel embodies deafening incongruities, which he works out through his laughter: earthy, impactful, bright. This sound from inside the body expands in waves through his cup of Turkish coffee – which functions as a soundboard in the "kantika" "Loka por el deskonozido" – thus opening the pages of the novel to discourses of doctrinal opposition. Such is the quality of the rabbi's inner life: a difference potentiating what is non-absorbable by identity.

Extimacy illuminates the innermost space of identity, and envelops the possibility of intimacy, namely the welcoming of otherness within. In the novel, this element creates an environment of empathy; in "Loka por el deskonozido," this same feature culminates in a relation of fairness between two strangers. *Ansina*'s poem tells the story of a casual encounter between the woman who serves as the lyric voice, and a man. She greets him and offers some speculations regarding the role the man might have had in key moments of her life. The voice enters the world of the man speaking from within his cup of Turkish coffee, in a poem in which mischief accompanies the solemnity of history and the impulse of desire:

Loka por el deskonozido

injunto de mi
un senyor beve kafe turkí
kravata verde i ojo hazino
imajino ke sabe kualo estó pensando

en la machina del tiempo
avrá sido     mi padre?
              mi partero?
              mi entierrador?
Los pajaros pretos suben al folyaje
– notchada buena – le digo –
so yo ken avla adientro
de su tasika de kafe

kero ke me tope afuera
en los kaminos de letche i miel
ainda konesensia no le tengo
ma kero bezarlo

lo savia de antes:
no so mujer de muncho fiadero. (Moscona 2015, 27)[34]

The nexus woven between the two characters resembles the encounter between the reader and the text, namely, an approach to what it means to be near a stranger. The poem sets the context based on random details, revealed in swift strokes that point to the colour of the man's tie, his Turkish coffee, his sick eye. Proximity deepens as a bond takes shape in the poem. The connections of presence and action, self and the other, event and meaning, emerge from the form in the lines "ojo hazino / imajino." Enjambment, interruption, and continuity through alliteration and paronomasia allow a two-way transference of qualities between the eye and the imagination, the woman and the man, what we read, even if we do so with sick eyes, and what we imagine when we enter in communion with the words. The particularly porous nature of self and other is the outcome of cognition, senses, imagination, and concept. The protagonists are connected by weakened sight but also by a powerful imagination ("save kualo estó pensando," "so yo ken avla adientro / de su tasika de kafe"), an asymmetry that favours the immaterial over the material despite the representational slant of the poem and the undercurrent of desire. While the lyric self does all the talking, and thus guides the course of the encounter, her thoughts enter the man's world as they stay close, in silence. In the changing valences of the father who is at the same time a "partero," an "entierrador," and the object of a forbidden desire for his daughter, family relationships are reworked beyond law and taboo, while gendered division of labour in the private sphere transforms fatherhood into midwifery, and the handling of the afterlife becomes a matter taken care of at home and at birth.

Several elements of the poem speak to a cultural environment in which conversing in Judezmo is still possible: "kafe turkí," "notchada buena," "so yo ken avla adientro / de su tasika de kafe." The lyric self is located somewhere in the Balkans, Turkey, or Israel, among Judezmo speakers in diaspora, believers in using coffee grounds to tell the fortune. The plausibility of this world stems from the self's desire to be part of another person's sphere. Falling in love with a "deskono-zido" propels the poem towards a world where the furtive encounter between strangers brings fortune and serendipity: "kero ke me tope afuera / en los kaminos de letche i miel." The word "afuera" locates the poem outside the ambit of traditional Sephardic communities, outside the family and the familiar. What makes viable this transition from self-compactness to diasporic scattering is the irony with which the lyric voice unites past, present, and future in the two final lines: "lo savia de antes / no so mujer de muncho fiadero." Far from enunciating a reprimand, the reflexivity of these final lines infuses the text with a playful defiance. The nostalgic affection for the world from which Judezmo and the poem arise – the solemn world of birth and death, written in a patriarchal key – is revisited on the basis of a woman's desire. This will to power, similar to Rabbi Samuel's laughter, sends the woman and her words into a daring inner diaspora. The poem evokes this dispersion through hope for the future journey in "kaminos de letche i miel," the traditional Sephardic wish for a traveller.

The twin texts "Kantika" y "Loka por el deskonozido" revolve around trajectories and travels, strangers who come together, personal identity confronted by belonging, language, solitude, and community. The crucial difference between them hinges on how these topics are resolved in narrative sequence and lyric concentration, respectively. In prose, being in unexpected places or finding oneself accompanied by strangers illuminates the narrator's search within; these contacts with others amount to a reflective look that starts as outward but then turns inward. In poetry, proximity with others is not converted through exchanges into personal consciousness. Moscona shows that a poetic other stands his or her imagined ground; word does not outsmart silence, and silence does not extenuate words. The poetic encounter of strangers is sustained, perhaps fleetingly, in a tense embrace, rendering audible radical proximity as unbearable togetherness. Poetic experience, in "Loka por el deskonozido," is the realization achieved in ignorance and even in madness; it is not the recognition of self and other, which is a process of assessing differences, but the *de facto* and painstaking creation of a social space and time, with the necessary structures and institutions that enable this shared chronotope to be sustained, albeit just for the brief duration of the lines.

This sociability finds different expressions within individual poems of *Ansina* and in the relations among different texts, as happens, for instance, with "Lo korolado" (Moscona 2015, 37–8, "Tainted"), a text followed by another poem with the telling title "Otruna version" (2015, 39, "A Different Version"). In these two poems, Spanish and Judezmo mirror each other. This reflection makes clairvoyance possible within blindness. Here, the poetic character of Isaac Abravanel takes the place of Paul Celan in his death and poetry, while the tragedy of the expulsion is lived through the atrocities of the Shoah. Moscona groups together items that do not harmonize, without ever suppressing their lack of conciliation, as a way to heighten dissonance and at the same time to put in relief the necessity of radical proximity for the emergence of meaning. "La risposta," a poem written in Spanish and Judezmo, resonates in rich fractal imagery of striking dissonances:

La risposta
   *¿Sabías que*
   *encontré en mi cuaderno*
   *una especie de dibujo fractal?*

   *La respuesta y la pregunta eran gemelas*
   *y hacían todo un sentido...*

   *(Como esa película japonesa*
   *que me hizo llorar*
   *con el kimono de mi madre puesto*

   *Era el kimono*
   *que usó en Madame Butterfly)*

   *Antes de cualquier cosa*
   *lo ciño a mi cuerpo*
   *aunque el cuerpo de mi madre*
   *fuera la niña*

ay de muzos los dos
ke vinimos de una
larga hazinadura
kon dulzura en el avlar
      – dos bokas
      – dos hazinos
       muerden con la klave de...

kon la yave
de ké?
de kualo etcho se trata?
de esparsir kon estas bokas?
ke kompletesh kon tu vida kurasion?

avrakadavra
mas mejor tuerto ke muerto

ay de muzos los dos
ke vinimos
di una lunga hazinadura

topimos rasones para matar u morir?
miralo bien
naldo el etcho
en un fraktal de eletchos
ermozeado en el kimono de la madre
lo supitesh de antes, janum

la repuesta prenyada
torna a demandar
(Moscona 2015, 28–9, emphasis in the original)[35]

The poem's story is elusive, yet very clearly there resonates an elegy for the mother, an opera singer. Two more characters populate the poem. Their intimacy hinges on both being sick and speaking with particular sweetness. Differentiation between mother and daughter is tested on the scale of proximity and separateness, marked by the limit of the kimono. The garment refracts the space of bodily existence as well as the time that sets apart the two women. If in the lines *"aunque el cuerpo de mi madre / fuera la niña"* we were to read "fuera" as outside, the nuclear locus of the maternal body would appear to contain the little girl and also to expel her into the open. This ejection is also the reason for an uncertain existence, if "fuera" is read as the subjunctive of the imperfect of the verb *ser*. In this reading, the kimono is a synecdoche for the dead mother. With respect to a trajectory from extimacy to intimacy, namely, to the innermost kernel of memory and present, the kimono evokes the space where the body of the mother was once contained. Refracted under the light of two chronotopes, that of the mother and that of the daughter, the body changes roles to the extent that the two instances exchange places with regard to each other.

Several binaries in the poem address discourse: the question and answer that feed into each other; the two mouths, of which one is musical, and the other a key that strives to access meaning; the two terms of the inner rhyme and paronomasia between "etcho" and "eletcho." The poem expands in concentric circles, sustaining paradoxical spatial and timely connections. The idea of a "dibujo fractal" creates a matrix from which multiple images emanate.[36] The harmony of proportion and sameness is shattered nonetheless by the tone of mourning regarding the purpose of speaking up against which the mouths set themselves. The poem as *risposta* is also the root of questions. The lines refract just like existence within the fabric that covers the dual body of the mother-singer and the daughter-lyric speaker. The self belongs to the ample landscape of otherness, and vice versa.

Another perspective on the poetic sociability of radical proximity and its importance as a blueprint for relations of justice is found in "Dos madres tengo yo." Here the ambit of encounter is the family. The lyric self arrives in a city where the languages of her two mothers flow and meet like two rivers. The title echoes the celebrated poem "Dos patrias tengo yo" ("I've Got Two Fatherlands"), by José Martí (Cuba, 1853–1895), in which the *modernista* poet laments the colonial night of his fatherland and offers to sacrifice himself for its freedom. In "Dos madres tengo yo," Moscona takes issue with several of the pillars of our contemporary societies: monolingualism, patriotism, and the proverbial singularity of the mother, playing out José Martí's solemn elegy in the key of an alternative homosocial family of two mothers, where equality and playfulness substitute for the confrontation of father and son, and the sacrifice of the latter in the colonial hands of the former:

> me topo kon una sivdad
> me rekordo'
> ke ayi moravan
> mis dos madres
> i mojo los piezes
> en los riyos
> ke de unas i otrunas aguas
> arrivan al lugar

*cuéntame la historia otra vez*

i a mis dos madres
siento avlar

en distintas
kantikas
avlan las dos (Moscona 2015, 41, emphasis in the original)[37]

In the word "piezes" (feet) resonates the rhetorical term "pie," "cada una de las partes, de dos o más sílabas, de que se compone y con que se mide un verso" (*Diccionario de la Real Academia Española* s.v. *pie*, "each one of the parts, of two or more syllables, of which a poetic line is composed and in which it is measured"). The image of legs submerging in a river evokes a poet's dipping her pen in ink. The *kantikas* (rhymes, little songs) come from afar, singing diaspora, filiation, and gender. Flowing and affable, from the fluvial bodies of the two mothers, one young and dark-haired, and the other old with white hair, a song springs, one that resists historical suffering and turns anamnesis into present, vibrant, intimate laughter.

Following Deleuze and Guattari's designation of Frantz Kafka's literary creation as "minor literature," Jacobo Sefamí attributes and applies this concept to the literary production of Levantine Jews in the Americas (2002, 148). The deep politicization of minority literatures, due to their roots in collective values (Deleuze and Guattari 1986, 17–18), the deterritorialization and reterritorialization of the "mouth" as the site of feeling, sensation, and reason (1986, 20-2), and the examination of the language's limits of expressivity (1986, 23) are characteristics found in minor literatures that also sustain *Ansina*'s aesthetic endeavour, as in "Dos madres tengo yo." As Monique Balbuena maintains, the contestatory slant that Deleuze and Guattari point to regarding minor literatures as specific to their location within a major language and tradition is restrictive, for Jewish literatures have always lived in multilingual environments (Balbuena 2016, 18). Balbuena's conceptual and critical approach in *Homeless Tongues* is geared towards unsettling Deleuze and Guattari's position in favour of "[doing] justice to the multiplicity of Jewish writing" (2016, 18). I maintain that Moscona's case does not fit into either one of the two views. Rather, in "Dos madres tengo yo," the poet takes issue with the inner multiplicity of Judezmo as a way of transcending linguistic boundaries, spatial limitations, temporal restrictions: Moscona's straddling languages, canons, and chronotopes echo Judezmo's historic versatility. In this sense, the language as an anthropological entity is both the tenor and the vehicle of the poetic adventure. To be a witness to Moscona's poetic utterance is to become conscious of the crossroads – the city of two rivers – where the daughter stands; it is to be shaped as a listener and a reader, as a participant, an observer, and a student of language and its history; it is to affirm linguistic continuity and difference, exotopy and exophony, as historical and literary forms of radical proximity.

Almost at the end of the book, Moscona goes back centuries in search of the root of injustice:

> Demandas
>
> ansina me *dijo* juan ke *te dijera*
> "ven y arrova il rovo que rovatesh"
> ansí me *dijo* el juan ke *demandara*
> ansí voló la pajarada entera
>
> en la chikez
> en tiempo de demandas
> *de la voz*
> abrevaba
>
> ken ke se ajarve de kaveyos ke no yore?
> . a la ida del Dio ya estoy entrando
> kada uno i kada kual empiés estamos
> avre, *englute, boka mia*
> ke no kero *avlar* solo al *tour* del paladar
> (Moscona 2015, 70, my emphasis except from
> the word *tour*)[38]

In what "john" asks the lyric voice to do resonates the line "y no tomas el robo que robaste?" from "Cántico espiritual" ("Spiritual Canticle"), by San Juan de la Cruz (Spain, 1542–1591):

> ¿Por qué, pues has llagado
> aqueste coraçón, no le sanaste?
> Y, pues me le has robado,
> ¿por qué assi le dejaste
> Y no tomas el robo que robaste? (Juan de la Cruz 1989, 137–8)[39]

# Intimating with History

In the context of Moscona's poem, the Carmelite monk of *converso* ancestors is an acquaintance and interlocutor of the lyric voice within a Judezmo linguistic community. In fact, this familiarity between the modern poet and the saint takes precedence over the poetic palimpsest of San Juan's lines because of the colloquial tone that Judezmo imprints on both poems. The translation of the mystical love is refracted in the oral flare of "Demandas," provoking a chain of resonances that goes from the relaxed initial *correveidile* (run-go-and-tell-them) to an elaborate reflection on metaphysics and aesthetics.

Moscona's version of a spiritual song manifests the choice of informal communication in different ways: proper names in lowercase, use of nuanced punctuation marks, dialogues among voices that are often overheard, recycling of one saying in another mouth. The authority of speaking comes from rewriting the place of enunciation. For a moment, Judezmo pushes San Juan and his poem, itself an intertext of King Solomon's Song of Songs, outside their historical milieu, back in time, before conversion, but also forward, to *Ansina*'s contemporaneity. By acting out how San Juan's verse would have sounded before the expulsion of 1492, the Mexican poet re-enacts the history that led to the infamous edict against Iberian Jews and Muslims. In bringing his song to the present, "Demandas" locates San Juan and his interlocutor in a time of dialogue between the Jewish vernacular, its hieratic other – Ladino, its cultural and racial other, through Castilian Spanish of the Golden Age, and Moscona's post-vernacular Judezmo. The text goes beyond literary intertextuality, dialectological inquiry, and historical restoration. At stake in acting out the claim – request, lawsuit, question, palimpsest – is an ethical imperative whereby imagination brings into radical proximity Hebrew, Ladino, Judezmo, aural Castilian and contemporary Mexican Spanish, on one hand, and mysticism, secular poetry, religion, and history, on the other.

Imagining a world besides the one we live in, a constant literary exercise, is an act of justice, for it involves bypassing identity in favour of exercising ancillary epistemic virtues such as curiosity and self-estrangement (Medina 2013, 16–18, 42–3). In "Demandas," the imagined lyric world is filled with inner dissonances. The lyric voice actualizes the passion found in San Juan de la Cruz's lines and sets the stage for an elegy. She complicates the Golden Age poetic echo by locating the origin of *arrova* (to marvel) in the verb *robar* (to steal). At this point, an inclusive humanity has taken the place of the community ("kada uno i kada kual empiés estamos"). Ultimately, Moscona proposes an autophagic practice in "Demandas": she privileges eating and silence. The lyric self opposes two eras and two uses of the mouth: drinking as a child from the voice to ease her thirst for answers (en la chikez / en tiempo de demandas / de la voz / abrevaba"), and stuffing her mouth to silence in the present. The entry to a godless life ("a la ida del Dio ya estoy entrando") coincides with a decision to lead a speechless existence, the reasonable result of a lonely life ("avre, englute, boka mia / ke no kero avlar solo al *tour* del paladar"). While the mouth quenches hunger, it also avoids non-palatable speaking. Deleuze and Guattari saw eating in Kafka's works as the reterritorialization of a deterritorialized speaking mouth through taste (1986, 20). The alienation of the mouth, for the Czech author, came about because of the language that he had to reinvent to polemically express the social displacement German meant for his community. In "Demandas," Moscona eats her words, unable to reterritorialize the mouth in isolation. Finally, what was love for San Juan de la Cruz becomes self-mourning, diaspora, and muteness in the contemporary text. The gulf between present and past closes, cause and effect exchange places ("ken ke se ajarve de kaveyos ke no yore?"), the sign of lament and despair can also be read as the cause of the pain for which the sufferer weeps.

The exotopy of discursive instances in "Demandas" turns the focus of the poem onto language itself. "Outside-situatedness" (Bakhtin 1999, 67), or exotopy (from Greek ἔξω, outside, and τόπος, place), is a fundamental moment of aesthetic creation and contemplation. It constitutes a break away from an empathetic connection with the characters and the voices of a literary work, and thus overcomes identification; in this way, it hypostasizes the characters and voices within the text (Bakhtin 1999, 66–7). According to the Russian theorist, this attitude of purposeful distancing and differentiation is fuelled by love: "Only love is capable of being aesthetically productive, only in correlation with the loved is fullness of the manifold possible" (Bakhtin 1999, 64). *Ansina* drives the reader – and, I suspect, the writer as well – to an outside-situatedness empowered by the confluence of linguistic familiarity and foreignness. In the ambit of "Demandas," the reader is obliged to tabulate their linguistic competence within Spanish. The poem holds me accountable for what I know, or what I do not, regarding the language and its history. Spanish turns momentarily into a foreign territory, and *Ansina* situates me as a reader in diaspora at home, by replaying the process of learning the language and thus revealing in it the authoritative structure which commands my respect. The task [learning a foreign language] is difficult and the goal is distant and perhaps never entirely attainable. *My work is a progressive revelation of something which exists independently of me.* Attention is rewarded by a knowledge of reality. Love of [a foreign language] leads me *away from myself towards something alien of me, something which my consciousness cannot take over, swallow up, deny or make real.* (Murdoch 1996, 89, my emphasis)[40]

*Ansina*'s languages enhance what Iris Murdoch proposes as feelings of love stemming from the cognitive effort of learning a foreign language, because they make patent that the independent reality of a language belongs to both the foreign and the mother tongue. *Ansina* begs to be read through intuition rather than knowledge. Moreover, Judezmo is not just another Spanish dialect or idiolect: it is the language of the marginalized, persecuted, exiled other, and it has historically been this other's distinctive mark. Echoing constantly its others – Biblical Hebrew, Ladino, and Castilian Spanish – Judezmo imposes itself as *koine*, thus it overcomes diaspora and exile, it bridges times and geographies. Judezmo illuminates not only the history of the Spanish language but also the reader's road to linguistic competence. Except that the reader/speaker travels backwards: from proficiency to the awakening of linguistic consciousness.

*Ansina* ends with a "Glossario" (Glossary). The lexicographic paratext that Moscona provides here is not foreign to the cultural history of Judezmo. For centuries, printed glossaries have been used for the religious education of the young, but also by adult, educated Sephardim: "Among descendants of the Jews exiled from Spain in 1492, extensive glossaries of the obscure words of the Bible and Talmud began to appear in writing in the sixteenth century" (Bunis 2011a, 343). Their composition, according to the linguist, signals a literalist principle, in other words, it obeys the obligation to follow the letter and the spirit of the holy texts. At the same time, as the Judezmo scholar argues, because glossaries used to have an educational purpose, they were composed for utilitarian and pragmatic reasons (2011a, 343, 346). Moscona seems to follow some of these principles. She translates Hebrew words such as *meshorer* (poet) and *mazal* (luck). With the religious term *perashá* (*parashah*), the poet-lexicographer offers an explanation for the technicalities of the yearly

100 Beyond Intimacy

reading of the Torah. For the term *shejiná* (*shekhinah*), she chooses the Kabbalistic translation of the Hebrew word: "el principio femenino de Dios" (the feminine divine principle) over the mainstream religious translation referring to the presence of divinity, who surrounds everything. She translates some Judezmo words that come from vernacular languages spoken in the Ottoman Empire and points out their linguistic origin – for example, *janum* and *pashá* from Turkish, and *meldar* (to read) from the Greek verb μελετάω, which means to study. Moscona clarifies colloquial words and expressions, for instance, *chuchurela* (diarrhea), and *kavesa de lenyo: de poco entendimiento* (log head: not very smart). Finally, she elucidates the significance of archaic Spanish lexemes, or words that do not follow contemporary grammatical rules.

The principles that orient these lexicographic decisions echo confluences of history, dialectology, and faith; they signal towards an array of presences, and ultimately they refract the meaning of the text, emitting reverberations of times, spaces, imagination, and other epistemic qualities that are still nested in this Jewish language in which *Ansina* is written. "Glossary" is one last stroke of radical proximity between strangers that Moscona has practised throughout her book. This time, the reader is called to introspection in search for the instance that both understands and does not know Judezmo. Grasping the beauty of the book is, for a Spanish-speaking reader, an obligation, a duty to the voices of those strangers who speak within the poems, echoes of which are the words of contemporary Spanish. What Judezmo teaches the reader of *Ansina* is the impossibility of co-opting the language's inalienable difference. This book demands aesthetic appreciation on the edge of linguistic competence.

The importance of placing *Ansina* in the historical perspective of Sephardic Jews and the cultural sequence of their Iberian vernacular and its variants lies in being able to understand that what happens in the microcosmos of each of Moscona's poems is an act in context, not a nostalgic revival of a partial identity. In other words, the poems affect the world of the readers, not the interiority of a lyric voice, for the enactment of the voice is based on intimacy's normative quality, both as one's innermost world and as one's relationship with another. The Mexican poet does not approach the memory of others. Rather, she stays close to her own amnesia, preparing the ground for bifrontal claims of justice, towards the past and future, self and other. The resonances of Sephardic history in Moscona's language enter the space of the poems, bringing together voices and stories for which learning anew is mandatory, for it is through the act of anagnorisis that justice can be done. A purposeful proximity that straddles times and geographies obliges the reader to listen to echoes of the agonistic dialogues that Judezmo carries out still, albeit posthumously. Silent others appear as linguistic caesurae that refract poetic memory, while new discursive trajectories strive for directionality.

Cynthia Gabbay considers the relation produced by contemporary Judezmo poetry in interstitial spaces as "evento epistémico" (2022, 74, 72, "epistemic event"): an act that sheds light on how history transcends the present. What is unique about *Ansina*, says the Argentine scholar, is that Moscona opens this space within Judezmo: an "espacio lúdico dentro del djudezmo contemporáneo" (Gabbay 2022, 84, "a playful space withing contemporary Judezmo"), where mysticism, poetry, and science come together (2022, 87). In this chapter, I have dealt with two things that Gabbay observes without pursuing: the actuality of ideological clashes within Judezmo-speaking communities over time, as the geography of the liminal space within; and what she names "ethos pedagógico" (Gabbay 2022, 83, "a pedagogical ethos"), by means of which Moscona reworks both language and poetics. Radical proximity obliges the reader to hear the fracture within, for it maps out the linguistic and aesthetic interstitial spaces in which this *tongue mother* of *Ansina* has been and continues to be used for dialogic struggles. The epistemic and moral conditions of intimacy in *Ansina* take up old reverberations; they buck against David Fresco's pessimistic view of Judezmo's eloquence. Moscona portrays the ethical quality of the lyric genre imprinted in the emblematic gesture of making the case for the word as the absent other. By using Judezmo, the language of around 400,000 speakers worldwide, and for which there is no new generation of native speakers, the poet pushes against the boundaries of the non-verbal from a place of linguistic posterity already besieged by silence.

The temporal and spatial paradox of word and silence creates a compelling map of what intimacy, laid out aesthetically in verse, means with regard to our relation with another. Moscona takes a linguistic, ethnographic, scientific, and philosophical stance towards Judezmo and its history. On one hand, she observes her topic as the structure of what she talks about, while on the other, she inhabits Judezmo in an extroverted manner, transforming it in order to encounter what there is to be said in a world of deadly quiet. The outer boundary of language, namely, its expressive quality, presses towards the inner space of words, expanding their generative possibilities. This aesthetic endeavour inside the text is a *mise-en-abîme* of the specular relationship the poet proposes to her readership, defined as any speaker of Spanish. To read *Ansina*, I operate paradoxically beyond linguistic competence; I enable the history of the word, the fading sounds of the past, silence inasmuch as words' afterlife; I occupy the *terra incognita* of utterances that sound and look like the most familiar but are at the same time the uncanniest. The poems of *Ansina* are simultaneously a discourse and the simulacrum of social enunciation, a tentative depiction of something that lies outside the word and its negative, silence. *Ansina*'s words are an exercise in duty against history and posterity.

# 3

# Breach of Intimacy

The experience of being alone while someone else is present appears to
be the paradoxical apogee of intimacy in Winnicott's example of the
pleasure of lovers after "satisfactory intercourse." Each "is alone and
contented to be alone ... able to enjoy being alone with another person ...
free from the property of withdrawal." We might recall that John Keats,
from whom Winnicott borrowed an epigraph for his famous essay on the
"right not to communicate," writes of finding a contented hermetic repose
"not in lone splendor" but "pillowed upon my fair's love ripening breast."
The capacity for this erotic solitude has a history, of course. Bollas
evokes the "silence of the small child before falling asleep," in reassuring
proximity to his parent, but also "alone in [his] bed, eyes open, imagining
[his] life." Not surprisingly, maternal attention is the principal metaphor
for the reliable yet unobtrusive presence upon which, or with which,
the capacity to be – silent, alone, alive – is realized.

Nancy Yousef, *Romantic Intimacy*

## TOWARDS *MIGRACIONES*

The discursive horizon on which the author of *Romantic Intimacy*
examines the relationship of lovers sketched in the epigraph is a combination of silence and word, where the former signals benevolence
and the latter thankfulness. Intimacy possesses an ethical content that
alleviates the suspicion of reification of one participant on whose
silence the speaking subjectivity is built (Yousef 2013, 128).
Irrespective of their specific verbal participation, the lovers are equally
responsible for the moral quality of their exchange, for it is compas-
sionate being that motivates repose and gratitude. If word expresses
thankfulness, silence means trust, two attitudes that feed into each

other. I maintain that the intimate relations mentioned are necessarily and systemically nuanced by justice; they are ethical agencies of radical proximity that destabilize hierarchical positions of authority, where authority refers to a principle and/or an author/creator. In this sense, intimacy appears to be a propitious environment for the virtue of virtues. I do not mean here that those capable of intimacy are necessarily righteous or favour equity, but rather that intimacy itself, be it the human landscape of two, or a social setting, demands that intimates be *good* to each other. In this regard, intimacy eidetically differs from other settings where human connection occurs, for while the act of getting together for the needs and joys of social or private life may or may not be honourable or virtuous, intimacy cannot exist outside of ethical praxis. Hence the parameter of justice appears as the condition *sine qua non* for radical proximity.

Though serene milieux seem ideal for intimacy, it is neither the secluded contact nor the serenity of love alone that warrants intimacy. Lauren Berlant and Michael Warner in their article "Sex in Public" refer to the following performance: at a leather bar, two male participants put on stage a session of feeding/eating. The one standing, whom the researchers call "top," fills the mouth of the one seated – correspondently "bottom" – with milk and different kinds of food.[1] The two men "carefully keep at the *threshold* of gagging ... From time to time a *baby bottle* is offered as a respite, but soon the rhythm intensifies" (Berlant and Warner 2000, 329, my emphasis). Such exhibition of the abject renders visible that the difference between torture/punishment and intimacy is a matter of a limit: virtue is the vital environment for any given act between people wide open to each other, with equal access to decision and praxis. Between the two men there is an agreement whose existence is exhibited and whose effectiveness is tested. In this spectacle, a fragile social praxis of intimacy is achieved on a threshold where equality and consent meet and counter subjection and violation. I maintain that this existence on edge is eidetically immanent to the condition of intimacy as justice, above and beyond the character and positionality of those proximate.

This same criterion of vicinity is performed also between stage and audience: "The crowd is transfixed by the scene of intimacy and display, control and abandon, ferocity and abjection ... [People] have pressed forward in a compact and intimate group" (2000, 329). Radical proximity shifts the border between performers and viewers. In fact, the delicate boundary at which the erotic vomiting is performed affects other frontiers: it draws closer those whose sense of personal space is swept away, at least inwardly. Intimacy alters the spatial distribution of agency, creating new time and space coordinates of action; it is contagious.

Surprised by the intensity of the spectacle, Berlant and Warner make a suggestive observation: "we have never seen such a display of trust *and* violation" (2000, 329, my emphasis). Furthering this assertion, I maintain that in intimacy the moral attitudes of the participants are not copulatively contiguous, but rather functionally complementary. One is the condition of existence of the other. One does not hold the place of cause and the other that of effect; the two are always already intertwined as ethically responsive stances. Intimacy, I suggest, is that particular condition of contact between two embodied or discursive instances, where there is no action and reaction, activity and passivity, top and bottom, but rather a harmony whose meaning derives from the agents' contiguity. Without a centre of gravity, just as successive musical sounds in atonal music, radical proximity is harmony with no effective teleology, a *de facto* parity by means of which positional asymmetries of power are effectively reworked towards fairness. This is the idiosyncratic struggle of intimacy as relational subjectivity and intersubjective sociability. Moreover, I propose to see the fragility of the limit between the related but self-standing moral attitudes – two notes, in Shoenberg's conception of non-hierarchical dissonances and consonances – as the touchstone upon which any given situation of human closeness is tested in terms of intimacy. This trial may be located in space, as material or imaginative fact, with another human, animal, or nature itself; or in time in the quality of memory. In the particular case of the erotic vomiting, for instance, while violation elicits an attitude of trust in order to shed its iniquity, hope imprinted in trust is challenged and affirmed in violation. Here intimacy is that quality, no matter how tenuous or defiant, that can tell sexual pleasure from violence, parity (as consent) from equality imbalance, benevolence from powerlessness, complicity from subordination.

The bottle in this scene of abject sexuality, pleasure, and applied force is invested with the semantic and moral values of trust, it carries the reminder of a kind of nurturing that thematically backs up complacency rather than compliance. After all, the display of pleasure outdoes the master/slave dynamic. Berlant and Warner see in what happens on stage a common fantasy of the maternal. "The top begins pouring milk down the boy's throat, then food, then more milk. It spills over, down his chest and onto the floor" (2000, 329). The bottle comes as a comfort despite the continuation of the stuffing. However, by means of the receptacle's spatial interposition, feeding obeys a rule. While the container serves as an intermediary in the association of the two erotic partners, it also controls the flow of food, measures its quantity, and even offers the fantasy of a beginning and end. In incarnating the limit, the receptacle and source of milk becomes a metonym for mother and/ or nurse, who enters the scene to accompany desire with a hope for safety. The bottle does not warrant hope, it plays out hope as a force within the aggression. The container introduces a form – trust – within the formless – violence – without eliminating gagging, measured also up against contention in a continuous process.

Gloria Gervitz's poetry does more than question a mother's role as the "reliable yet unobtrusive presence upon which, or with which, the capacity to *be* – silent, alone, alive – is realized," as Yousef claims in the epigraph of this chapter. It brings the symbolic locus of nurture, comfort, and trust under the light of radical proximity as fairness. The starting point for the daughter's lyric voice in *Migraciones* is a troubled reliance. The mother's blame is obscure, yet the reader is introduced in a proximity fraught with grievances. Throughout the long poem Gervitz will map out the regulatory functions of closeness: the rights and obligations it elicits from those near, the mechanisms and processes of reparation it makes available. Here, the maternal is the backdrop against which the daughter will treat intimacy as a problem of justice.

The grounds where intimacy and justice can be repaired, in *Migraciones*, are desire and language, two quests that rely on the mother, for she is the first object of desire and the source of linguistic acquisition. What makes such a quest within the maternal both arduous and possible is the quality of the malleable matrix whereby the mother shapes and is shaped by different agencies, lyrically depicted as changes in time and space, movements, migrations. The conspicuous maternal "Thou" hypostatizes the lover, the priestess, the grandmothers, the nurse, the oracle, the witness, the immigrant, the believer, those who are sad or raging. This variety of instances during which intimacy with the mother is pursued involve a broad horizon of inter- actions with different agents whom the maternal brings into relief and radical proximity so as to test the moral quality of relations that are possible when the self is defined by relationality learned with the mother. The conflicts within the locus-mother represent a spectrum of positionalities for self and other, by means of which Gloria Gervitz renders visible the ethical, institutional, and affective reach of fairness and injustice within intimacy.

In a brief review of Vivian Nice's 1992 book *Mothers and Daughters: The Distortion of a Relationship*, Mary Evans boldly concludes: "mothering – however complex – is perhaps the most important human social relationship" (1993, 193). What interests me in this quotation is the adjective *social*. Unless every human encounter is considered as such, which would produce an unnecessary flattening of distinct positionalities, the dimension of sociability attributed to child bearing and/or rearing by women creates, first, a differentiation between private and intimate. Second, it becomes apparent that the nature of intimacy with the mother is social beyond its spatial dimensions. Third, it appears that human perception of what is or is not fair finds a primal blueprint full of cognitive and affective nuances and capable of accounting for an array of bonds in early life within the maternal sphere.

In the particular case of mothers and daughters, feminist psychoanalysis has debated the Freudian model on the basis of a relational formation of selfhood. Daughters' sexual development does not become stagnated on account of attachment to the mother. Rather, proximity to the mother is "multidimensional, self-enhancing, and contentious from the very beginning" (Bernstein 2004, 608; see also 615, 617, 618). Furthermore, because the initial pattern of being together is one of necessary inequality, the sphere of the maternal is foundational to how we take in primordial experiences of rights and relationship to authority. In addition to its social dimension, motherhood belongs to the sphere of the corporeal. Whether it is the result of pregnancy, adoption, or fostering, it implies a wrapping of two bodies together, by the practices of nurture, cleanliness, sleep, vigilance, and, primarily, desire.[2] With regard to the public sphere, there is a sinuous but clear line from the house within which maternal intimacy is enjoyed and suffered every day, to the public space where lawmaking happens.[3] Yet the aesthetic reverberations of motherhood in thinking and achieving justice beg inquiry and need to be fleshed out.

In the next pages, I explore the multi-level nature of sociability that radiates from the elegiac relationship of a daughter and her mother. I also assess the influence this connection has in the sphere of the socially possible, plausible, and legitimate in Gloria Gervitz's long lyric poem *Migraciones*. "The essential human relationship," namely, the nexus between a child and a mother (Rich 1986, 119), is for the Mexican poet a rarified world where fragments of history, queer eroticism, heretic religious attitudes, and deep metapoetic reflections take place.[4] Moreover, it is with regard to this bond with the paradigmatic other that the daughter comes to be cognizant of her desire, rage, suspicion, resistance, care, companionship, memory, and oblivion. Within the maternal space, the lyric self confronts sexuality to the limits of incest and auto- and homo-eroticism, questions the religious institutions of her matrilineal heritage, retells the history of migrations, challenges the authority of the mother and the one that derives from motherhood. In stirring together eccentric desire and normativity, Gervitz demonstrations the moral reach of motherhood, the intimate relationship *par excellence*, albeit lived and understood differently from culture to culture, from epoch to epoch, from gender to gender. The poem rethinks the power differential that springs out of a most common human experience: the relation of self and the m/other, as desire and alïenation. Because of the key role of the maternal as primordial matrix of sociability, justice and intimacy are mutually illuminated in the poem. Affective failures, intellectual mishaps, violent deeds, passionate attachments, conscious responsibility for the other and the world, and nebulous processes of remembrance stand as indispensable inner stages that show the efficacy and limits of intimacy with regard to fairness, in concept, beauty, and praxis.

The first instalment of *Migraciones* was published in 1979 under the title "Shajarit" (Shacharit).[5] The title refers to the morning prayer in the Jewish ritual, and situates the poem in a memorial and autobiographical context, while tracing the linguistic boundary between Spanish and Hebrew. Once within "Shajarit" the reader straddles also the frontier between Judaism and Catholicism, religion and secularism. In 1986, a revised version of this text was published under a new title: "Fragmento de Ventana" (Fragment of Window). The change in the title draws attention to the fragmentary nature of the text, announcing its expansion to come, while capturing the opening of the lyric self towards within and without, by locating her on a threshold. In 1987, "Fragmento de Ventana" and "Yiskor" ("Yizkor"), the first addition to the poetic project, appeared together as one publication under the title *Yiskor*, from Esnard Editores. This title too refers to the Jewish religious tradition, this time to the evocation of the dead, especially of a departed parent, in which the mourners ask God to remember those who died. *Yiskor* opens with a painting by the Spanish artist

Julia Giménez Cacho depicting a woman sitting, dressed in white. Another three illustrations by the same painter depict women who mirror or duplicate each other. In the painting that closes the book, three women appear dressed in mourning.

In 1991, "Leteo" ("Lethe") was added to amplify the materials of Gervitz's poetic universe with the evocation of yet another ancestral tradition, that of classical mythology. The title comes from the Greek word λήθη (oblivion). The Greek tradition adds a new dialectical movement, for it inserts in the process of remembrance the catalyst of forgetfulness. In this edition by the Fondo de Cultura Económica, the title *Migraciones* serves as an umbrella to all three poems, endowing them with the quality of fragments belonging to a growing whole.

In 1993, Gervitz published *Pythia*, a book of poetry that features three collotypes by the photographer Luz María Mejía. The model is Lola Lince, a Mexican dancer, and the images show a naked woman in three fetal poses. Situated on a stage with unfinished and inhospitable walls, reminiscent of a well in which light comes from a single source up above, the female body contorts painfully. "Pythia" was later incorporated into *Migraciones* together with "Equinoccio" ("Equinox"), in 1996. In 2000, the book was further amplified with "Treno" ("Threnody"). An edition of 2002, again in Fondo de Cultura Económica, included all six sections. In 2003, Gervitz published "Septiembre" ("September"). In 2004, a bilingual edition of *Migrations / Migraciones* appeared, based on the 1993 and 2002 editions, with "Septiembre" as its seventh part. Mark Schafer's translation on many occasions sheds light on the original through linguistically and culturally sensitive interpretations. In two consecutive years, 2016 and 2017, first in Ediciones Paso de Barca and then in Mangos de Hacha, Gervitz published her poem in a version that grew from within, and in which there were no sections or partial titles. The two editions prepare the reader for the final text of *Migraciones*, published in 2020, from libros de la resistencia, in their collection *Poíesis*.[6] What seemed to continue the tradition of *Cántico*, by Jorge Guillén, and *La realidad y el deseo*, by Luis Cernuda, appeared now as a story lyrically told, in the vein of a much older tradition, such as the one rooted in *Las soledades* by Luis de Góngora.

Formally, the sustained dialogues bring *Migraciones* closer to a dramatic form, and its passages of prose poetry intensify metapoetic reflections. The extension of the line in some parts evokes the intonation of biblical versicles. *Migraciones* incorporates passages in English, especially in "Treno," extracts of Hebrew prayers, sentences in Yiddish, epigraphs from contemporary and classical literatures, ekphrastic episodes of photographic material, references to Jewish rites and marginally to Hindu spirituality, and classical mythology. Starting with the edition of 1991, Gervitz has placed at the end of her book a few laconic explanations of the titles of each section, as well as a "Glossary" translating and explaining religious terminology. Over years and editions, the poet has modified this appendix.[7] Starting in 2016, Gervitz added a previously much missed native imagery, making the poem vibrate with snapshots of *tianguis* – typical Mexican outdoor marketplaces – public squares, musical landmarks, and other references from her contemporary national and pre-Columbian culture. The poem creates a universe with special emphasis on the legacy of the past, also conceived as memory, based on family relics as well as on eroticism, art, and the body. All these topics are enveloped in constant metapoetic musings. Ethical debates, rumours, laments, eulogies, prophecies, promises, and confessions address and respond to a central inquiry revolving around proximity to the mother and the ethical quality of the poetic universe. Diverse endeavours to find love, religion, country, a voice and desire of her own characterize the daughter's struggle to repair wrongdoings within the jurisdiction of maternal authority.

To this day, critics have read *Migraciones* as a book of oppositions: the miracle of memory opposed to the wound sustained by remembering (Sefamí 2005); the individual against the community (Rodríguez 2006); history versus personal experience (Imboden 2012); the particularity of the body vis-à-vis cosmic spirituality (Brougham 2014).[8] In 2019, I argued that "Shajarit" is the complex dialogue of an array of forces, and the crossroads of what memories claim and desire demands (Karageorgou-Bastea 2019). Gervitz's sole creation unfolds in the historical context of diasporic movements before the Second World War and continues throughout the twentieth and twenty-first centuries. It follows the uprooting of a Jewish family from Eastern Europe and the establishment in Mexico of a matrilinear clan. There are two male figures in the poem. One is a husband/father who trades in dried fruits and goes to work in the morning while the wife, probably the grandmother who came from Kiev, cries alone in the house (Gervitz 2004, 38, 40). The other is a lover, who appears once in "Equinoccio" (Gervitz 2004, 110) and is a conspicuous figure from 2016 on. Outside the familiar imagery, the reader finds mythological allusions to the Sibylline emblem of Pythia. She is the source wherefrom the word springs, and as such the alter ego of the daughter-poet. The River Lethe personifies oblivion: "Era el Leteo" (Gervitz 2004, 72; "It was the River Lethe," 73). That river represents a radical migratory movement, one that awakens the need to materialize memory in words, but also to let go of the mother, who is accompanied by the transgressive Orphic figure of the daughter to the netherworld.

Women lead the poem: the lyric self, characterized everywhere as a daughter-granddaughter-poet; the omnipresent mother, site of desire and of the mother tongue; the Jewish grandmother who plays the piano, and the other, a devote Catholic from Puebla, owner of a mansion in the neighbourhood of Las Lomas (2017, 174); Lupe, the nanny, silent witness of the girl's first autoerotic adventures, about whom we know very little until the most recent editions, in which she plays a significant role representing class and race difference, in addition to providing elements that codify alternative *loci* of the maternal (Gervitz 2017, 174–6).

Regarding all these figures, Marc Schafer affirms:

> *Migraciones* is a universe of females: all the voices in the poem are female and the poem is populated by females – from the "I" and "you" to the girl, the mother, the grandmother, the nanny, the adolescent girls, the Ancient One, Our Lady, immigrant women, secretaries, maids, the she-wolf, the Pythia, girls of the frescos at Knossos, even memory and the word itself, both of which are feminine nouns in Spanish. (In Gervitz 2004, 157)

Such genealogy originates in the incandescent centre of *Migraciones*: "the most feared image of all ... that of the competent, omnipotent mother of infancy" (Bernstein 2004, 614). Although full of female presences, the poem is in fact an ongoing dialogue between the daughter and the mother by means of which the society of the poem is hypostatized. Self- and social formations in *Migraciones* are possible as passages across the limits of the personal and the historical, by means of the interpersonal and transgenerational. The plot of the poem is a sort of **gynaeodicy**, the story of women's justice.[9] I argue that *Migraciones* exemplifies the possibility of accessing parity by reworking the position from which motherhood is exerted. The poem follows the development of theoretical feminism from the relational model of identity that came to counter the paradigm of the autonomous individual, to intersectional feminism, which incorporated different and contradictory views of the relationship between the mother and the daughter. From the strong bond of a lifetime to rejection of the maternal prototype, from tenderness to desire, the mother of *Migraciones* is both adored and vilified. The daughter's struggle in the poem is to understand the exercise of mothering and to discern the possibility of building a fair society on principles drawn from and against motherhood.

A century ago, Sigmund Freud argued against the moral fortitude of women on the basis of genital physiology:

> For women the level of what is ethically normal is different from what it is in men. Their super-ego is never so inexorable, so impersonal, so independent of *its emotional origins* as we require it to be in men. Character-traits which critics of every epoch have brought up against women – that *they show less sense of justice* than men, that they are less ready to submit to the great exigencies of life, that they are more often influenced in their judgements by feelings of *affection or hostility* – all these would be amply accounted for by the modification in the formation of their super-ego. (1925, 256–7, my emphasis)

Unlike sons, whose fear of castration is a powerful incentive for abiding by the law of the father and abandoning attachment to the mother, a process that warrants full access to cathexis and sublimation of the object of desire, daughters, having no penis to lose, display a slower access to object-relations and a more permanent and unobstructed attachment to the mother. Furthermore, women need not negotiate psychically with the fear that amounts to heeding the prohibition of incest. Respect for the law as the limit that shall not be crossed is from this perspective a field in which women also manifest their difference, allegedly, as moral inferiority.[10]

Nancy Chodorow reworks Freud's idea:

> As long as women mother, we can expect that a girl's preoedipal period will be longer than that of a boy and that women, more than men, will be more open to and preoccupied *with those very relational issues that go into mothering* – feelings of primary

> identification, lack of separateness or differentiation, ego and body-ego boundary issues and primary love not under the sway of the reality principal. A girl does not simply identify with her mother or want to be like her mother. Rather, mother and daughter maintain elements of their primary relationship which means they will feel alike in fundamental ways. (Chodorow 1978, 110, my emphasis)

If we orient Chodorow's account of Freud's argument towards sociability, the moral stances of women prove to be opposite of what the father of psychoanalysis speculated, because of the emphasis given in their identity formation on relationships, a lesson learned through proximity to the mother, for it is in the sphere of togetherness that the concept of justice is born. Nonetheless, Chodorow locates the scope of women's ethos in motherhood and its reproduction, giving Freud's argument an obscure validation, one that carries ontological, moral, and political grievances for women (Johnson 1987, 142). From this perspective, a woman's identification with her mother appears as an endorsement of institutions of intimacy, in a society that takes heteronormativity and productivity as keys to the organization of economy and of desire.

In the 1990s, feminism proposed to understand its object of study within postcoloniality, as a critique and resistance in terms of race, ethnicity, sexual orientation, and class. This point of view places the object of study within social relations of power, while it attracts attention to different forms of oppression that apply to women in marginal positions (de Lauretis 1990, 138–9). At this point, women of colour and lesbians move away from (the feminist) home. In addition to the spatial dimension of this eccentricity, de Lauretis underscores its discursive effect, for textual and self-displacements, she argues, imply "a practice of language in the larger sense" (1990, 139). New epistemologies emerge from the diversification of feminist approaches to identitary circumstances of different groups within the category woman, as well as the ways they impact consciousness and subjectivity formation. Yet motherhood has not been doubted as the basis of a woman's identity until very recently.[11]

In an article from 1949, Donald Winnicott lists eighteen reasons why a mother hates her baby boy. The very length of that ominous list makes it a terrible thing to consider regarding mothers and their feelings towards their babies. Winnicott shows how a deeply and honestly felt sentiment of violent rejection may actually have a curative effect for difficult psychotic cases, as well as heuristic value for an analyst's introspective work. Among these poignant justifications for a mother's hatred, there are two that I consider especially relevant for understanding the specific relation between daughter and mother in *Migraciones*: "F. To a greater or lesser extent a mother feels that her own mother demands a baby, so that her baby is produced to placate the mother ... R. He [the baby boy] excites her but frustrates – she mustn't eat him or trade in sex with him" (1949, 355). The pattern of relationality here is certainly quite aggravating if it calls on a woman to offer a child in order to placate a demanding mother. The plea aims beyond procreation as survival. It touches upon the propagation of models of oppression that women sustain and impose on other women; it disseminates tacit forms of obedience where biological reason takes the form of teleology. Motherhood appears as a sacrifice of the daughter at the altar of mother/hood. Furthermore, such submission, framed within the taboos – "the oldest human unwritten code of laws" (Freud 2001, 22) – of cannibalism and incest, reaches back to ancestral times and primeval rites.

Winnicott is not alone in exposing the dark side of the territory that runs from Medea to the angel of the house. Feminists have spoken openly about it since the early stages of second-wave theorizations. Adrienne Rich in *Of Woman Born* starts by accepting that her experience of childrearing had been one of "pain and anger," "a ground which seemed ... the most painful, incomprehensible, and ambiguous I had ever traveled, a ground hedged by taboos, mined with false-namings" (1986, lxiii). While feminism did the foundational work of making visible women's affective ambivalence towards motherhood, contemporary social theorists have given a decisively political twist to the phenomenon. Women's identity based on the principle of responsibility for others has been criticized as a way of spreading social inequality and systemic injustice on the basis of gender, ethnicity, class, race, and citizenship within the capitalist labour economy. Emma Dowling observes that the cost of tending to the needs of others within the British health care system falls mostly on unpaid or underpaid women. She argues that women are exploited because they are identified as caregivers and because of the false consciousness of identity based on a woman's role as a mother. In *The Care Crisis: What Caused It and How Can We End It?*, Dowling points towards the political impact of such affective structures:

Against the idea of the autonomous individual whose concerns revolve around himself and is always hailed as the epitome of social progress and individual freedom, we can ask what this celebration of individual autonomy obfuscates: who does the work to allow for that individual to emerge and thrive? On whose assistive labour does this depend? How and why is this assistive labour so often rendered invisible? (2021, 53)

If, in the patriarchal economy of bodies and agencies, mothering of daughters is the fundamental experience on the basis of which women understand self and other, biological and symbolic reproduction of mothering partakes in the sustaining of gendered forms of exploitation. Oppression and invisibility are two effects of this form of staying close as experienced by women who raise their children and tend to their aging parents, as mothers, daughters, or underpaid workers.[12]

In Western societies the caring female figure is anchored in the fantasy of the mother/daughter continuum.[13] Daughters have exposed ambivalent feelings with regard to their mothers, especially related to erotic desire and pleasure (Marcus 2004, 700–1).[14] In 1979, Luce Irigaray published a lyrical reflection on the topic: "Et l'une ne bouge pas sans l'autre" ("And the One Doesn't Stir without the Other").[15] The French philosopher addresses her mother, refusing to follow the latter's lead in the chain of reproduction. Countering her mother's choice from the standpoint of a dissident daughter, she advocates for movement, errancy, nomadism, vis-à-vis the paralysis to which patriarchal power has condemned mother ([1979] 1981, 60, 73). Ambiguity surfaces when the daughter recognizes that the ancestral, dreamlike knowledge that seems to resist oppression is in itself opaque ([1979] 1981, 60, 64). One example of this alternative epistemology arises from one of mother's primordial abilities: sustenance. Dismantling this area of transcendence of maternal power starts with seeing feeding as stuffing and relating it to sexuality and aggression. Irigaray attacks the illusion of motherhood as nurturing, an act she presents as a cannibalistic feeding/eating by means of which mother/daughter separateness is erased, and their bodies are endlessly fed into reproduction:

Once more you're assimilated into nourishment. We've again disappeared into this act of eating each other. Hardly do I glimpse you and walk toward you, when you metamorphose into a baby nurse. Again you want to fill my mouth, my belly ...

I want no more of this stuffed, sealed up, immobilized body ...
You've disappeared, unperceived – imperceptible if not for
this flow that fills up to the edge. That enters the other in the
container of her skin. That penetrates and occupies the container
until it takes away all possible space from both the one and
the other, removes every interval between the one and the other.
Until there is only this liquid that flows from the one into the
other, and that is nameless. ([1979] 1981, 62–3)

Contrary to the intimacy on the public stage of the erotic vomiting
narrated by Berland and Warner, intimacy as sustenance is filled with
despair and suspicion. The material of oppression is the liquid nourishment that turns mother and daughter into two communicating
vessels who in the course of feeding become uncontained, lose their
boundaries, blend. Because of this obliteration of frontiers, the volume
of the liquid spills over the contours; it blurs the threshold of separation; it expands and erodes even ontological differences, erasing
everything in its passage. The overflowing impetus of the food invites
the formless into the dyadic relationship. Faced with such aggression,
Irigaray struggles to restore the two different bodies on the limit of
desire and word:

Haven't you let yourself be touched by me? Haven't I held your
face between my hands? Haven't I learned your body? Living its
fulness. *Feeling the place of passage – and of passage between
you and me.* Making from your gaze *an airy substance to inhabit
me and shelter me from our resemblance.* From your/my mouth,
an unending horizon. In you/me and out of you/me, clothed or
not, because of our sex. In proportion to our skin. Neither too
large nor too small. Neither wide open nor sutured. Not rent,
but slightly parted. ([1979] 1981, 66–7, my emphasis)

In the sensual exuberance of this passage, the daughter desperately asks
about and for boundaries, more so because the two women live in
paradoxical symbiosis, inhabiting even while sheltering each other.
This agonic struggle between *eros* and *thanatos* takes place by means
of the imagery of female genitalia, a fantasy that holds the key to the
radical proximity of daughter and mother because it escapes binary
oppositions as it becomes apparent in the elliptic sentences that
conclude Irigaray's thought.

The onset of longing in the maternal body at contact with her infant is one of the taboos that render mysterious and inaccessible the maternal body: "the child's mouth, caressing the nipple, creates waves of sensuality in the womb where it once lay" (Rich 1986, 18). In recent years, maternal yearning has been qualified beyond the sexualization of a woman's body. Cristina Traina examines the ethical implications of a mother's erotic arousal at the contact with her infant in terms of the inequality between the two, posing the question of this *eros* in political terms: "assuming that human society will always be composed of people of unequal power, and that less powerful people will always be to some degree in the care of the more powerful, how do we negotiate sensuality, desire, and pleasure in all relations between unequals?" (2011, 4). Evidently, this is a problem of justice, and Traina affirms it so by advancing the concept of "erotic attunement," as a hinge between sensuality and legitimate care in relations that lack parity.

This theoretical twist brings the scholar to a bold conclusion: "But if attunement is perceptive cultivation of *right relation* between persons, attunement is simply *justice approached from the direction of intimacy.* Considerations of justice and power are central" (Traina 2011, 242; my emphasis). The argument sets intimacy as a starting point from which societies can and must achieve justice. Through its musical metaphor of attunement, the recourse to sensuous adaptation to one another suggests that justice is a necessity that points towards the harmonious, as well as a possibility opened up by desire. In motherhood, this way of relating is not a tool of social teleology but a *de facto* ethical demand that, though it does not alter the positional inequalities of the dyad, it demands a constant moral deliberation between embodied authority – the mother – and incarnated exigency – the child.

In *Migraciones*, intimacy is achieved by way of receiving and relating to others inside the receptacle-mother. The daughter faces the relationship with the m/other within a broad cultural complexity, namely, as a historical, racial, gender, and class matter, whereby m/otherhood becomes a potentially polymorphic stage of pacts and antagonisms. Affects, knowledge, desires, embodied experiences of the world, voices of different pitch and calibre, intersect on the maternal ground; they take from it the character of closeness, and they imprint on it the foreign – language, desire, religion, experience, and so on – thus operating deep changes in the way m/other and daughter become aware of each other, beyond the exclusivity of their bond. Intimacy as justice in the face of m/other shapes anew the experience of togetherness with the world and the self. The relational appears thus as a combination of centripetal and centrifugal forces, on account of which what belongs to the sphere of another becomes an indispensable common ground for each of those involved so as to lay bare the mechanisms of mutual definition.

From a Jewish theological perspective, Mara Benjamin maintains that the proximity of a mother with her child possesses a particular aspect of legality: "The child for whom one takes responsibility becomes part of oneself. When that happens, it is impossible to know whether the law comes from outside of from within" (2018, xx). Benjamin examines the foundational bond of a parent with her child in light of the relation between God and Israel. Interdependence (xxi) allows for a swap of positions and analogies of power between the mother/God and child/Israel, and thus for the elaboration of a changing map where love and obligation, freedom and subjection, heteronomy and sovereignty, constantly change subject and object (2018, 4, 7, 12, 13, 24–5). The versatile positionality of the members in those binaries with respect to authority brings Benjamin to affirm that "God is not only loving parent but demanding baby" (2018, 13). Drawing also on personal experience, Benjamin states early in her book: "it was clear to me that there was a law, and the law applied to me by virtue of being my child's parent" (2018, 8). As mothers we are rectified anew by our children, by a law, a limit, a sense of moral being. This kind of relationality in which the daughter is defined by the mother and the latter is reshaped under a new law is achieved notwithstanding despair and a recurrent sense of defeat (2018, 23). The ambivalence stemming from the bond between mothers and daughters arises from the confusion of these entities within social environments that press towards the reproduction of motherhood. Ambiguity in emotional terms means that the sphere of the mother is symbiotic as much as it is fraught with need for radical separation. In addition, from a moral point of view, mother and daughter are tainted by responsibility and responsiveness, both as duties and burdens.

### MIGRACIONES

There are two main axes on which intimacy with the mother appears as a problem of justice in *Migraciones*. The first is guilt, transmitted from mother to daughter on the genealogical continuum that defines matrilineal legacy. The handing over of responsibility, inherent to gender identity and the identification between mother and daughter, blurs the existential frontier that separates the two and points towards the onerous quality of symbiotic relationality. In order to forgive and forget, the blame needs to be exonerated through a process of remembering that the daughter carries out in the name of the mother. The need for moral repair brings forth a double realization. On one hand, the legitimacy of accusations against the mother, in themselves never voiced in the poem, and the process of atonement that follows them, are effective due to a wider normative horizon of righteousness and wrongfulness. On the other hand, from the insight gained in the process of understanding guilt and making amendments, namely that "[t]he justice of law, justice as law is not justice. Laws are not just as laws. One obeys them not because they are just but because they have authority" (Derrida 1992, 12), there stems the second aspect of fairness that nests in the bond of the mother and the daughter in *Migraciones*: authority.

Gervitz refers explicitly to the topic of fairness in the context of memory, testimony, mercy, forgiveness, and the restoring of an ethical order. At various points throughout the poem, the lyric speaker touches on it: "Y te acuso / Pero de qué puedo culparte" (Gervitz 2004, 42); "Abísmame memoria para que pueda perdonar ... / Memoria ¿me oyes? / Creces como lo que se olvida / Y aquella que soy ofrece perdón a la que fui" (2004, 56); "Si pudiera aprender la compasión" (2004, 58); "Ahora ha quedado absuelta de la trama que fue su vida" (2004, 60); "Madre, no me juzgues. Tú también estás condenada al olvido" (2004, 68); "Sólo la compasión es infinita" (2004, 74).[16] There is also a brief simulacrum of a courtroom witness examination: "Testigo / Contesta / Contéstame" (2004, 56, "Witness / Answer / Answer me" 2004, 57). The gradual, staircase-like distribution of these lines on the page and the urgency echoed in the personalized "contéstame" imply an emphatic crescendo. This turns testimony into interrogation and takes the judge/lawyer and witness away from the public space of the courtroom, to the more personal sphere of a painful plea. There the positions of power get inverted: the voice that examines appears at the mercy of the power exercised by the silence of the witness. The affective tone with which the lines end points towards blind accusations that have no specific content aside from the emotional burden they denote.

The poem touches upon the question of a power by means of which law acquires its legitimacy. This happens throughout the lyric speaker's journey towards language and poetry, on one hand, and desire, on the other. These *loci* of passionate quest are directly related to authority, and to the mother:

Desde estas palabras te hablo
Desde el pensamiento y la idea del pensamiento
Desde lo que recuerdo
*Desde ti y el principio que emana de ti*
Desde el deseo de llegar a ti. (Gervitz 2004, 84, my emphasis)[17]

Marc Schafer translates the word "principio" as beginning. The term refers to both principle and start. I choose to emphasize the former in the sense of *arche* over the latter because of its allusion to time. "... I speak to you ... / From the principle that emanates from you" appeals to an originating rule that defines the quality of its source as generative of ethos and aesthesis. By using the verb *emanar*, Gervitz points to that root from which spring the daughter's word and desire, as the two faces of a sole drive.[18] This origin appears charged with ambivalent emotional tones in the poem.

For the daughter, the beginning of time represents the limit where silence and word split once and for all in the sphere of the maternal as source of speech. For the poet, this same movement gives access to a principle of representation. This reverse migration and projection manifest a desire to start over, to get in touch with the unknown at the root of the lyric speaker's being, and of course, to make possible a new destiny. At times this voyage takes the form of linguistic and existential slippages and falls. It relates to the remembrance of a lost homeland and culture, language and religion; to the yearning of the prophetess for the word as *incipit*; and to the poetic quest for the originary cry: "Me dejo caer. Regreso" (2004, 22); "Llego al lugar del principio donde comienza el comienzo," "Recomienzo" (2004, 26); "Recomenzado todo y siempre lejos la imaginación lo irreversible soñado / Remembranzas," "Era el regreso" (2004, 30); "En dónde estuve todo este tiempo? / Estoy anclada en el mismo lugar" (2004, 34); "(en realidad no pasa nada estoy en el mismo lugar)" (2004, 36); "Nunca más me embarcaré en aquel mar tan soñado" (2004, 38); "¿Hacia dónde regreso? (2004, 46); "Me muevo ahora cerca del silencio," "Duermo en la memoria" (2004, 48).[19] The place of return is hardly defined even when it has a name and by the context, we can infer the historical events to which it refers. The blurring limits of this *arche* allow for all

Breach of Intimacy

desires and purposes to fit in: from the aesthetic aspiration to poetry, to the quest for historical reparation through memory, and from the creative power of *eros* to the bodily yearning for the centre of women's sensuality. There is a disputable moral debt in the transcendence of the origin on the poetic adventure of the lyric self, one expressed as a twofold problem, of legitimacy and loyalty.

At the beginning of "Yizkor," Gervitz writes:

Como Jonás en el vientre de la ballena
Como la Sibila dentro de las paredes húmedas y negras
Sin saber qué decir      sin nada para decir
Por ti siempre para ti
Esta fidelidad debe haber sido a mí misma

Viejos sentimientos cuidadosamente olvidados rompen el olvido
Y sabes que te hablo a ti      sólo a ti      para siempre a ti

El aire inmóvil      Se llena de flores
La lluvia también se desplaza hacia el sueño
Lentamente recupera su sombra      se inclina como un sauce
                                                        Cae
Yo regreso a casa. (Gervitz 2004, 54)[20]

Homecoming is defined in Gervitz's poetic exodus by biblical piety (Jonah) and pagan prophetic apprehension (Sibyl), both nesting in figurative matrices. The place of return is identified as an encounter with the word to the extent that the word reveals in its articulation the meaning of existence and relocates loyalty from the duty towards m/other to the realm of obligations towards the singing self. Memory is one way to this end: a precipitation comparable to rain and the weeping foliage of a willow in its harmonious sloping towards the ground. Two analogous trajectories show what homecoming looks like: the destiny of the moral man and the visionary woman, both in captivity, is comparable to the law of gravity, the fall of rain and foliage – two synecdoches of crying – relentlessly obeyed in nature. Locations of pain and freedom exchange places and features. It is not clear where relief is possible and where pain is overcome. From these spiritual and natural landscapes, poetry emerges as a matter of lawfulness. The lyric self laments and rebels against the foundations of modern lyric poetry since Petrarch: *la voz a ti debida,* "the voice because of you," the quintessential modern lyric claim of debt to the female lover, celebrated in the Hispanic tradition from Garcilaso de la Vega to Pedro Salinas.[21] In *Migraciones*, the lover's place is occupied by the mother, a form of the hollow wherefrom the poet needs to pledge allegiance to her own word.

The troubled yearning for the origins is founded also in heretic religiosity. The titles of the two first sections, the references to Jewish holidays as landmarks of lyric events, lines of prayers, allusions to the Zohar and Kabbalistic mysticism, mourning for spirituality lost, speak to the prominent place of Jewish heritage in the poem. Adherence to this cultural world comes laden with consciousness of loss: the Jewish grandmother mourns the dead – "mis muertos" – in Russian and Yiddish (Gervitz 2004, 34) pointing to the heteroglossia of Jewish languages. Linguistic qualms have a religious aspect: women's lack of access to a world ciphered under the holy tongue. This exile needs to be exposed and healed in order for the lyric speaker to find answers to metaphysical anxieties and to questions about life and death. In *Standing Again at Sinai*, Judith Plaskow lifts the veil of silence from over the history of women within the Hebrew Bible and the rabbinic tradition of wisdom. She considers gender exclusion in specific theological terms as a matter of fairness: "the Jewish passion for justice did not extend to Jewish women," for "women are not perceived as normative Jews" (1991, 5). The parallel of what Plaskow perceives as being excluded from the justice of God is not far from Freud's view of women as less apt for secular justice and ethical life. To recast the scriptures' gendered meaning, it is necessary, posits Plaskow, to hear the intimations of these voices that tell the story of a matriarchal substratum shaping legal biblical stipulations. Such claim on memory is organic to being a Jew, argues Plaskow, because of the importance of remembering for a people whose identity is based on endlessly refunctionalizing the past in the cyclical reading of its history in the Torah (1991, 29–31). Excluding women's wisdom from Jewish epistemology is a form of exile that goes along with physical and linguistic diaspora bestowed upon Jewish women in mainstream religious practices. Access to memory through reading and interpreting is thus a path to fairness in spiritual life. In the case of *Migraciones*, Judaism, approached from the point of view of women in intimate dialogues, responds to the claim of such identity beyond matrilineal genealogy. The passion of this return, in itself heretic, for it diverges from orthodoxy, goes beyond disobedience.

Gervitz fills her poem – with particular intensity the two first instalments – with resonances of Jewish and to a lesser extent Christian liturgical moments: Shacharit, Kaddish (2004, 18), Yizkor (2004, 16), the transliterated and original Hebrew *incipit* of Shema Israel (2004, 50), and that of Yizkor (2004, 54), the reference to the festivities of Rosh Hashanah, the sound of the Shofar, the solemnity of Yom Kippur and the notes of Kol Nidrei (2004, 16), the Shabbat candles (2004, 6), and the sanctifications of God in this faith (2004, 120). Biblical Hebrew and Aramaic interrupt the flow of the Spanish text. The pious figure of the grandmother lights the candles from and for an eternal Shabbat (2004, 26), immobilizing time and memory, a stasis replicated in the same sonata she plays on the piano (2004, 14). However, neither the lyric speaker (2004, 16) nor the grandmother (2004, 40) can say Kaddish for their dead or upon their own lyric death. Women can barely access this world of "olvidadas plegarias, ásperas" (2004, 14, "raw, forgotten prayers," 2004, 15), wrapped in mourning and nostalgia. Catholicism is invoked through the incantations of the rosary, during the evening mass at the Plaza del Carmen (2004, 16), by the *milagros* that pile up on the walls of churches (2004, 18), and through various invocations of the Virgen de Guadalupe, also referred to as Señora de las rosas (2004, 78, Lady of the roses 2004, 79). The encounter of Judaism and Christianity is emblematic of the tensions depicted in the closeness and antitheses of the two monotheistic faiths, stemming from the same law of the Ten Commandments, antagonizing each other, however, on the grounds of history, ethics, and metaphysical aspirations.

The institutional and spiritual forces originate in the ceremonial atmosphere they establish within the poem through language, as well as in the principle – *arche* – to which they point: "Ciudades de hilo, carreteras que llevan siempre al principio" (Gervitz 2004, 18, "Cities of thread, highways that always lead to the beginning" 2004, 19), says the lyric voice, alluding to the thread of traditions located in diaspora, but focusing always on the return, the norm that gives coherence and meaningfulness to migrations. Judaism is identified with "Flores de tinta en un hebreo luido saliéndose de los rollos de la Toráh" (2004, 18, "Ink flowers in spent Hebrew dripping from the scrolls of the Torah" 2004, 19). In a similar way, Christian faith straddles the bodily and discursive dimension of spirituality wearing down the marbles of statues and the lips of the believers: "Las palabras están gastadas como esas piedades con el mármol gastado por los besos / Madre de Dios ruega por nosotros" (2004, 38, "The words are worn like the marble of those pietàs worn down by kissing lips / Mother of God pray for us" 2004, 39). Schafer translates the word "piedades" by the names of statues in Catholic churches, emblematic of mournful motherhood. The word "piedades" – pieties – appears to me as two-faced. It is an ekphrastic allusion to the homonym figures and a reference to the pious passion that the lips of the believers dispense on the immobile body of the mother the sculptures represent. The wasted mouths and worn-down volumes add corporeality and intensity to the connection between mother, mouth-kiss, and mouth-word. Spent on the hard surface of the mother's body, the lips translate spirituality into passion and eloquence into inorganic material.

Who can break this mournful existence of woman, do justice to a woman's life? When it comes to mourning the death of the grandmother, the lyric self states an imperative need, pointing towards those women who can bear mourning, because they can enunciate it:

> Alguien debería contratar a esas mujeres *que lloran por los otros*
> A esas que han criado hijos
> Amasado su pan
> Las que barren todos los días la puerta de su casa
> Aunque sea por dinero
> Que lloren contigo, que lloren por ti. (Gervitz 2004, 40, my emphasis)[22]

Schafer's translation of "que lloran por los otros" as "who cry for the dead of others," instead of "who cry for others," which would be the literal translation, marks a point of departure in order to think of the domestic sphere not as a form of destiny for women, but as a space of possible professionalization. The mourners' elegiac song can be detached yet effective; it patently maps out relationality beyond the limits of intimacy as affection. Poetry translates women's solidarity into a sort of trading with words devoted to another's pain. Professionalization of such radical proximity – assuming another's dismay and relation to death – or rearing children, feeding and cleaning, caring for others, bring women workers' specific claims into the terrain of justice. I do not imply that women domestic workers and nannies, or women paid mourners, have had fair work conditions in the past or now. On the contrary, I argue that in the specific case of the passage from *Migraciones*, because of a multifaceted oppression related to race, gender, and class, colonized women fight for equality, and they use as a weapon for their struggle elegiac poetry. To be sure, *Migraciones* breaks the bond of mothers and daughters by having women of paid labour carrying out a daughter's grief for her mother's death. Both the lyric nature of the song and the grief it conveys sever the immediate connection of dead and mourner while at the same time they produce solidarity among a gender group.

Gervitz returns to this aspect to amplify the role of the nanny, another woman of the working class, a mother in surrogacy. In the most recent versions of *Migraciones*, the Indigenous servant from Oaxaca is characterized by a certain muteness related to her poor Spanish. She breaks the laws of the house by introducing in the mind of the little girl doubts regarding the pre-eminence of a father-line godhead, through the cult of the Virgen de Guadalupe (Gervitz 2017, 175). Lupe infuses the poem with mythical, affective, and sensorial input. The nanny narrates stories about her *nahual*, her animal protector. Racial difference comes into play in the form of prohibition: upper-class white girls do not have *nahuales* (Gervitz 2017, 176). Instead they have Indigenous nannies to protect them, to chase away their fears, buy them candies, withstand their tantrums, satisfy their fancies (2017, 175). The nanny envelopes the girl in her *rebozo* (shawl) and in her scent, a world of sensations from which the lyric speaker will be expelled when Lupe elopes with the gardener. In the glimpse we catch of Lupe's life, despite her servitude, this woman exercises an agency of desire, and not only one of sacrifice, appropriate for traditional maternal figures. The price for this is death: "[Lupe] debe haber muerto hace mucho / a mí se me murió cuando me dejó y se fue" (Gervitz 2017, 176, "[Lupe] must have died a long ago / for me she died the day she left me and took off" Gervitz 2021, 173). The melancholic lyric speaker is not only a daughter of sorts who is unable to accept maternal desire, but also a young, upper-class white mistress who senses in the nanny's desire a kind of disobedience, and who chastises it with the capital punishment, oblivion. Lupe diverges from the position of the mother because she invests her eroticism on someone outside the dyad.

Vis-à-vis the laconic nanny, the two grandmothers endow the lyric speaker with a passion for language, all the way from the physicality of its articulation to its promise of beauty and redemption. Because of women's marginality in the Judeo-Christian religious tradition this longing is also filled with lament. Here the struggle is against an omnipresent silence. Elissa Marder contends that to speak from and about mother as the condition of language – the mother tongue – and of desire – a form of the abominable – is an endeavour through which one catches a glimpse of a monstrosity that cannot be put in words, one that structures the code from which we are expelled as speakers and desiring subjects: "The mother tongue is a foreign language. This language of desire is always already a foreign language from which its speaker is exiled and in which he or she is lost" (Marder 2012, 203). From this perspective, diaspora is the main parameter for existence within the mother tongue. One way to confront such principle is to adopt – or be adopted by – a properly foreign language.

Benigno Trigo examines this phenomenon in Rosario Ferré's fictional prose, poetry, and essays, where she transitions from Spanish to English. Passions, positive and negative, emerge from the relation with the mother and the mother tongue (Trigo 2006, 63–89). Rehearsed in men's voices, the struggle for separation is achieved by means of the mother's silence, a symbolic death, reversed into man's new birth (2006, 72), and an architectonic element in the construction of a man's world.[23] For daughters, writing matricide is a taboo also because of a daughter's attachment to the mother tongue. Ferré, Trigo argues, deals with the topic by means of self-translation: "For Rosario, writing in another language is a way of translating the abject mother tongue; it is a way of developing the second skin that is necessary to live. Not surprisingly, writing in another language is also identical with translating herself and coincides with self-exile" (2006, 77). Unlike self-translation's open door for a return to the mother, the presence of two different languages in the same text, in the same voice, traces a frontier of dissemination.

For Gervitz, English is the refuge of an orphan, adopted into a step-language, in an effort to belong and redefine the constant parameter of desire in the relation with the mother/tongue. The foreign language implicates a distance taken within radical proximity that allows relationality to emerge as different from identification with the mother, and from complete merging with her words:

y yo quería llegar a ti
pero *tú eras yo*
y tan oscura el agua
and the river is full of corpses
and she is so lonely
an orphan in the world of the dead

but this is not loneliness
*it is not sadness*
*this flow is pure joy*
though joy is always sad at its root. (2004, 120, English in the
original, my emphasis)[24]

The identity blurring between I/Thou, in Spanish, and joy/sadness, in English, creates an *ad hoc* parallelism between languages. Gervitz does not translate her poem; instead, she refracts the code in which she writes. The two languages resemble iridescent variations of light, stemming from reflection on the same surface yet oscillating between similitude and unlikeness. The poem returns to the River Lethe, to the body of water surrounding Hades, a boundary around death. The copulative conjunctures "y/and," the paronomasia of "and/an," their anaphoric repetition, all these elements create a bridge between two separate territories. The languages propagate a set of images by means of distortion, and expand the zones of contact, while avoiding precise resonance and reproduction. A rhetoric of discontinuity keeps each component standing alone. Because of such independence and commensurability, English and Spanish are two units of matching values, yet they are unable to further each other in terms of rhythm and acoustics towards a common aesthetic purpose.

The linguistic surface – the poem in two languages – corresponds to a deep discernment, a wilful separation in the structure of "tú eras yo." While the mournful apostrophe to the mother is a way to sustain the dialogue and thus the passion of togetherness, nested in the shared code, English breaks such a continuum by placing between the two women the silence of the mother's tongue and the linguistic excess of the daughter.[25] The "you," becomes a "she," removed from closeness, foreign to the lyric speaker. The daughter relinquishes access to the mother and vice versa, the mother withstands this reversed orphanhood. The child finds a stepmother-tongue where death is comforted and threnody can be articulate beyond nostalgia:

Step- Old English *steop-*, with connotations of "loss," in
combinations like *steopcild* "orphan," related to *astiepan,*
*bestiepan* "to bereave, to deprive of parents or children," ...
Old High German *stiof-*, German *stief-*), literally "pushed out,"
from PIE *steup-*, from root *(s)teu- (1) "to push, stick, knock,"

128 Beyond Intimacy

with derivatives referring to fragments (www.etymonline.com, s.v. tep-, emphasis in the original)

Hidden in the etymon of the prefix "step-" lies the possibility of change: the child is pushed out; it starts living in separation. The lyric speaker takes refuge in the stepmother-tongue, a breather from a relationality taught as sameness.

Another way to break the symbiosis with the mother is through desire. This force defines union at the same time that it makes the dissolution of the mother/daughter model of sociability possible. In *Migraciones*, emancipation and thus justice for women comes from the exercise of an exhibitionist, genital, auto- and homo-eroticism that resists the phagocytosis of motherhood. The end of this struggle is barrenness, while desire for the mother is its strategy. Desire is a force of convulsion and upheaval. It is omnipresent and directed towards an elusive "Thou." This chameleonic figure, directly out of the mould of motherhood, haunts every discreet speaking individuality. The grandmother, the lover, the image in the mirror, the place of return, the time of death, the source of the word, all seem to speak from the place of the mother at some point. Up against this oddly refracted object of desire, the daughter exercises a masturbatory and homoerotic sexuality. The lyric speaker's eroticized body is a landmark of defiance with regard to the insistent stasis in which the opening of the poem wants to fix her: "*En* las migraciones de los claveles rojos, donde revientan cantos de aves picudas / y se pudren las manzanas antes del desastre / *Ahí donde las mujeres se palpan los senos y se tocan el sexo*" (Gervitz 2004, 14, my emphasis, "In the migrations of the red marigolds where songs burst from long-beaked birds / and apples rot before the disaster / Where women fondle their breasts and touch themselves" 2004, 15). Different maternal embodiments prepare the way for the mother's appearance: the nanny, the Jewish and the Christian grandmothers, women depicted in photographs in black and white, an omnipresent female "Thou"- lover current, imagined, revoked in memory. At the end, when mother appears, she transitions between death and life, the past and the present. The transcendence of this figure in the shaping of the main voice goes beyond the liminality of death and gives the poem its elegiac character: "La muchacha que lloraba abrazada a su madre muerta sigue llorando dentro de mí" (2004, 34, "The girl who cried as she clasped her dear mother still cries inside me," 2004, 35).

Death marks the limit of the physical body. However sensuality, including violent passion, is lived through memory, another form of desire, for it stands *in lieu* of the beloved and moves the poem. Thus mourning as a signal of death meets sexual exuberance in a constant paradox. "Shajarit" lays down the body of the lyric voice, literally as discourse, and figuratively, as the locus of longing. The section profusely carries the ache of separation, while the lyric self strives for a return to an unspecified and variable place. Words originate there together with expressive dysphoria and erotic attachment:

*El polen* cubre aquella memoria de espejos
Apenas nos movemos
Pero aparta de mí tus ojos. Son terriblemente bellos
Todavía me arde, me toco, estoy sola
Alba desaguada. De otros diluvios
Querida, lejana
*Quiero llegar otra vez al lugar donde duermo*
La complicidad de la voz
*su persistencia*
Y yo soy *lo* que está cayendo (24, my emphasis)[26]

Pollen, the golden powder of plant reproduction, used earlier in the poem in a scene laden with self-erotization, is related to orgasmic fluids, compared to words, and anchored in passion. The mirrors invoke splitting and sameness even while they awaken the horror of beauty. Longing is born and satisfied in and by a body in reflection. The lyric voice refracts as it undergoes a syntactical and ontological transformation from subject to predicate/object ("*yo* soy *lo* que está cayendo"). Synchronized movement and stasis – "apenas nos movemos," "lugar donde duermo" – solitude and togetherness, self-eroticism and desire for another, beauty and horror: the memory recalled is of tantalizing ambiguity. Word and body, poetry and desire, go hand in hand:

En la vertiente de las ausencias al noroeste
En el estupor desembocan las palabras, la saliva, los insomnios
y más hacia el este me masturbo pensando en ti
Los chillidos de las gaviotas. El amanecer. La espuma en el
    azoro del ala

El color y el tiempo de las buganvilias son para ti. *El polen*
  quedó en mis dedos
Apriétame. Madura la lluvia, tu olor
de *violetas* ácidas y afiebradas por el polvo
las palabras que no son más que una oración larga
una forma de la locura después de la locura (2004, 16, my
  emphasis)[27]

Violets serve as an identifying element of the mother, though they also function as a bridge between the latter and the daughter in an episode in which the reader is introduced to a series of festive preparations: workers bringing their creative energy to the house, a room prepared for ablutions, women waxing their legs (Gervitz 2004, 42-4). The scene of effervescence before a gathering or a wedding is interrupted by ominous allusions that start with the description of a woman dressed in white, observed by the lyric voice:

Con blusa blanca y la falda *de aquel otro recuerdo*
Complácese ella en su cuerpo
Lejos del oráculo
Ensoñecida
Agarrada de la profundidad de las violetas
Ah, muchacha celosa
Sin oponer resistencia
En la espera
En la anunciación
En la quietud que antecede a la visita
Que antecede al nombre
En la belleza absoluta del regreso
En la fiebre
En la percepción anulada
En la fragilidad. (2004, 44, my emphasis)[28]

The apostrophe characterizes the young woman as envious and brings forth the emotions of the lyric voice. The passage recalls both the grandmother who came from Kiev (2004, 38) and the mother holding the violets (2004, 16, 44). Again the characterization of the matrilineal sequence of blurring figures structures desire as auto-erotic, and word as substance. The ontological weight of the "name" is interwoven with its sacredness because of the allusion to *HaShem* – The Name – a euphemism for God, that implies both the holiness of the word and the prohibition that lies within it, and which Gervitz repeats later on in the poem (2004, 90).

The daughter's erotic passion and mournful discourse are discussed with respect to fusion – belonging to/with the mother – and agonic struggle – individuation. Mother is invoked as a "tú" (you) throughout *Migraciones*. She fulfils different roles: she consoles, enrages, exercises violence, dies, abandons, eroticizes, teaches. The attachment of the lyric self to her is expressed unequivocally, but it is also a painful contradiction: "Siempre fuiste la más hermosa / Nadie más tuvo importancia / Oh maligna" (Gervitz 2004, 36, "You were always the most beautiful / No one mattered more / O maleficent one" 2004, 37); "Hermana madre no me permitas tu separación" (2004, 42, "Sister mother don't let me be separated from you" 2004, 43). Partner of fleeting, intense encounters, this incestuous, homoerotic, queer mother is elusively announced early on in the poem: "Y tus dedos como moluscos tibios se pierden adentro de mí" (2004, 14, "And your fingers, lukewarm mollusks, slip inside me" 2004, 15). She is the sum of immigrant women who accompanied the grandmother in her trajectory from Kiev to Mexico, and with whom the lyric self identifies in her desire for the word and the mission of forgiveness and forgetting: "Mi voz se confunde con la tuya" (2004, 62), "(bendíceme madre)," "Madre, no me juzgues / Tú también estás condenada al olvido" (2004, 68). The fusion of voices continues in the afterlife: "Como si fuese yo la que ha comenzado a morir y no tú" (2004, 72), until the dramatic invocation – "Ven entonces olvidada / Ven y dime / ¿Me reconoces en ti?" (2004, 76) – of a mythic healing figure – "Tú madre que curas" (2004, 78). Later on the mother is the prophetic woman of divine powers in search of the word: "la oficiante / vieja madre cómplice" (90).[29] The shared history takes a definite turn towards justice, when repair becomes possible close to the end of the poem. The absolute other appears, at this point, in body, word, and metaphysical hypostasis as a possibility of reciprocal pardon: "oh mother if I only could forgive you / o mother if only you could forgive me" (2004, 122, English in the original).

At the end, the dialogue between mother and daughter is voiced from inside and out, from voice and sight, from pleasure and being, as all hard limits of separation fade:

132                  Beyond Intimacy

> ese gozo
> míralo
>       no se dice
> es tú misma
>     tú
>     en ti (Gervitz 2004, 128)[30]

The mother identifies also with mythological figures like Pythia or with the personified oblivion of the River Lethe. She is often hiding behind this reiterative *tú*, evoked painfully.[31] Only on one occasion does a grammatically masculine *tú* appear in the 2004 *Migraciones*. In "Equinoccio," the lyric speaker affirms the blending and even overflow of otherness within: "y tú más oscuro que nunca / me *desbordas*" (2004, 110, emphasis added, "and you who surmounts me / darkest" 2004, 111). I propose to translate "desbordas" as "overflow" or "overwhelm" rather than as "surmount" in order to evoke the cramming of the inner space to the point of ejection/ejaculation, but also the affective impact of the spilling over the edge of a full receptacle. The poem continues:

> pero soy yo la que cruza los límites
>
>     como una mancha se extiende
>     como un puño levantado
> ardiéndose hasta lo más huérfano
>              gimiéndose
>
>     como una ceiba desgajada
>        la dolorosa pasión
> ...
>       de este silencio
> ábreme como un surco
>
>     loba. (2004, 110, my ellipsis)[32]

In migrating, the lyric self crosses frontiers, with her fist lifted as a sign of disobedience – " como un puño levantado" – assuming her power in the confrontation with fear. Here too the mother, the lover, and the word overlap in tentative appearances: the mother is desired from the position of orphanhood, the lover is depicted in painful passion, and the poetic word goes from silence to the furrow, a metonymy for the flow of writing, the line of the poem, the physiology of female genitalia.[33] In the most recent edition, Gervitz has revised the lines "y tú más oscuro que nunca / me desbordas," changing the gender of "darkest" from masculine to feminine: "y tú más oscura que nunca / me desbordas" (2017, 149), and almost at the end, she insists: "desbórdame // palabra" (2017, 261, "overwhelm me // word"). The different valences of the subject deconstruct the effect each has on the lyric speaker. Between the man-lover and the intimate word there stands the mother, a Janus-faced goddess, who opens the way for desire and language, imprinting on them the passion and the pain of her relationship with the daughter.[34]

Affliction originates in the mother and crosses the spheres of being and acting. Intimacy is constructed in disquiet. The all-encompassing mother enters forcibly, even though invoked, in the space of the daughter in a reverse pregnancy, a rape, as the opposite of literary creation: "Yo no inventé a esa muchacha, ella forzó su existencia dentro de mí" (Gervitz 2004, 30, "I did not invent that girl, she thrust her existence inside me" 2004, 31). It does not really matter who is talking nominally, the mother, the grandmother, the daughter, the lover, Pythia, or some other woman; they are all trapped into and condemned by the heritage of mother and motherhood. The exchanges between these instances acquire pitches of command, plea, rage ("Destiérrame / Déjame ir / Ten piedad de mí / Tú que me has consolado / Ayúdame a olvidarte / ¿Me oyes? / Estás todavía conmigo? / Eres acaso mi propio eco?" 2004, 36); but also of deep endearment ("Arrúllame / Envuélveme," 2004, 38); reproach ("Me haces daño / Suéltame / No me quites lo que he aprendido por mí misma," 2004, 38). Feelings of grief, anger, rebellion bring the protagonists to the same space: "No puedo hundirme más abajo de tu corazón" (2004, 42).[35]

In *Migraciones*, the intimate is tormented by relationality itself and vice versa. Justice is served on this stage through ending a kind of motherhood that within the logic of patriarchal violence is a deep structure of domination, as Catharine MacKinnon puts it: "it is only within a context where male power already exists that the relation between mother and child can be characterized as one in which the mother is seen as powerful in the sense that the relation becomes one of horror, anxiety, betrayal, cruelty, and – crucially – eroticism" (1987, 53). This origin is intrinsically laden with and defined by pain; home coincides with diaspora, birth is decay, sociability becomes ensnared in personal and social agony. The matriarch sets paradigms of spirituality, gender difference, sexuality, and above all ways of inhabiting the world through language.[36] The fierce endeavour of the daughter thus is to keep alive the promise of togetherness in equality in the context of an abusively intimate motherhood, where surrender and distancing are dealt with in tandem. Sexuality – exuberant, queer, provocative – is the foundation of this process of being woman within mother. Though heavily surveyed in the ambit of reproduction, in which motherhood is the fiduciary of gendered forms of domination, sensuality appears to be key for the separation of the dyad, as well as the weapon of choice the daughter embraces wholeheartedly. She will cross the limit of incest in variations of auto- and homo-eroticism in order to aspire to personhood within and against maternal rule.

Gloria Gervitz appropriates and reworks a polity after the *polis* ruled by the son's desire for the mother, and also against a matriarchal model of sociability. To do so she distances herself, on one hand, from the Freudian archetype of the society of brothers, and on the other, most importantly, from the model of the daughter's pre-oedipal attachment to the mother, repeated endlessly by the reproduction of motherhood, regarding which second-wave white feminism has claimed that "woman has always known herself both as daughter and as a potential mother" (Rich 1985, 110). In Gervitz's "Leteo" the daughter's quest for identity within the memory of matrilineal filiation emphatically attacks the continuum of daughterhood/maternity from within, giving birth to the mother as tongue: "Y te oía dentro de mí / Te oía en la *desembocadura* / Naciéndote" (Gervitz 2004, 86, my emphasis, "And I could hear you inside me / Could hear you at the *breach* / Being born" 2004, 87). The poetic word adumbrates sensuality as a woman's right. A paradoxical motherhood exhausts the law of succession in the chain of reproductivity. In short-circuiting this mirroring, the lyric self affirms a practical rejection of the uttermost juncture of intimacy, thereby infusing its institutions with the chill of insubordination in the form of poetry.

The daughter's endeavour will be to interrupt the harm in the cycle of repetition, for which she too takes responsibility: "Estamos unidas por las mismas culpas" (Gervitz 2004, 36, "The same guilt ties and binds us" 2004, 37), "y caemos por la msima pendiente / cómplices" (2004, 90, "and we tumble down the slope / complicit" 2004, 91), she admits, alluding to an original sin. Breaking free from the dominion of that law of the eternal return – "Porque siempre es la primera vez, porque hemos nacido muchas veces / y siempre regresamos" (2004, 20, "Because it is always the first time, because we have been born many times / and always return" 2004, 21) – requires a cleansing, which takes the form of a homecoming to silence: "Me muevo ahora cerca del silencio" (2004, 48, "I move towards the silence now" 2004, 49). The lyric speaker proposes to contest the continuity of women's roles as mothers/grandmothers and to inhabit the opaque root of words: "Una mujer en lo oscuro de sí / En lo sola de sí ... // Por qué no abrir los ojos en la oscuridad / En la propia oscuridad como al principio" (2004, 48, 50, "A woman in the darkness of herself / In her solitude ... // Why not open my eyes in the darkness / In my own darkness as in the beginning" 2004, 49, 51). In this genesis, there is no mother and no light, but one woman, and the old, synaesthetic, lost words: "las viejas palabras las largas palabras / Las oscuras las sumergidas" (2004, 84, "the old words the long words / The dark ones the sunken ones" 2004, 85). The consciousness of orphanhood announces the beginning of personal agency: "Entré al lugar entréme huérfana" 2004, 92, "I entered the place enter me orphan" 2004, 93). In the silent *name* and the dark *place*, where the *arche* is absent, word and woman are born parthenogenetically in water and light, as prophet and prophecy emerging from the Castalian Spring: "en lo abismal de su agua / la fuente se alumbra a sí misma" (2004, 94, "in the water's abyss / the spring sheds light on itself" 2004, 95).[37]

The speaker-seer is now capable of linguistically assaulting the *sancta sanctorum*:

y dije tu *nombre*
y el *lugar* era de aire

y la palabra
la *presa* (Gervitz 2004, 102, my emphasis)[38]

Words obey a law of immaterial incarceration within the name and the place, the two most common euphemisms for God in the Jewish tradition. Poetry is born enclosed in an immaterial space.[39] Gervitz sheds light on this panoptic fortification, where instead of emptiness she discovers a prisoner – *presa* – who is the prey – *presa* – within walls of contention – *presa*. Where man left a carcass, there is now a memorial to the domestication of natural forces, a totem of sorts, where alleged protection is offered, and contention is performed, for man's epic of society building. A mournful effort of salvation characterizes Gervitz's poetic voice in her struggle to convert this mother-dam to a dyke-matrix, unruly, unproductive. Gervitz defines anew the legacy of matrilineality, from genealogical succession in overlapping functions to the poetic self and her doomed destiny.

Queer sexuality intensifies this kind of resistance. From the beginning, the girl exhibits desire and satisfaction, with the nanny's silent complicity (Gervitz 2004, 14). The young woman masturbates in her bed and under the gushing water in the bathtub (2004, 16). She asks for satisfaction from her woman-lover. She evokes the perfume of women's sex (2004, 16, 22), the images of flowers open to penetration, while invoking erotic touching between women-friends and recalling her sex filled with animalistic energy (2004, 20, 22). She laments the fate of her grandmothers, who screamed of frigidity (2004, 34). The daughter begs: "Ven y bésame levemente apenas rozando el día / Ven Antiquísima ven y sácame de este silencio / ... / disuélveme en tu lengua como a una hostia" (2004, 78, 80, "Come and kiss me softly barely grazing the day / Come Ancient One come and take me from this silence / ... / dissolve me on your tongue like a host" 2004, 79, 81), inviting the mother to a symbolic union, a sacrilege of melting mouths, where words can actually break silence.

Eroticism, already a form of dissidence since the first publication of "Shajarit," finds its ideological plenitude in the later editions. Placed almost at the end of what in previous editions of *Migraciones* was "Septiembre," a new text bursts in effervescence. The poet riddles the page with long descriptive vignettes of life in Mexico, colourful images of *tianguis*, snapshots of desire, implorations of an open body. The lyric self is frantic with exuberance, expressed in extenuating polysyndeta that run more than thirty lines long at a time (Gervitz 2017, 168, 170, 171). The story of the daughter is recast in the key of an eroticized body. The little girl explores her genitals and takes pleasure even while harbouring and rewriting an ethical system that condemns lust. In "The Laugh of the Medusa," Hélène Cixous champions female auto-eroticism as a form of breaking the walls that contain woman. She ties together self-erotic explorations and writing, both subject to shame and fear (1976, 876–7). Cixous considers that this sexuality in the open belongs to the New Woman, who, through her body, breaks the chain that subjugates the Old one (1976, 878). Gervitz's effort seems to follow this line of emancipation. Part of this endeavour

# Breach of Intimacy

is to transform the moral valence of woman's self-eroticized body from filthiness to owned pleasure. The lyric self claims:

> me meto los dedos
> me exploro
> encuentro el punto del placer
> ...
> cierro los ojos y me digo –cochina
> decírmelo me excita
> y lo que siento se expande
> me invade toda
> me cubre toda
> y soy este cuerpo
> este rapto esta inmensidad
> estoy en el placer adentro del placer de darme placer
> y mi nana dormidísima en la hamaca de al lado. (2017, 165)[40]

In the word "cochina," resonates physical filthiness, moral depravation, and, in the Jewish tradition, religious abomination. The reprimanding effect of the law is wiped away in the voice of the New Woman, for whom moral sanction equals sexual arousal. Breaking the law of the mother with regard to practices of cleanliness avails an expansive and vibrant sexual experience. The law is physically defeated in this episode: the nanny, the Old Woman, sleeps incapable of stopping the masturbating girl taking pleasure in her body.

From this excitement, the poet goes on to build a parallel: the liveliness of the tropics. Fruits, vegetables, seafood, grains, textiles, objects of faith and magic, singing birds, music, populate the scene. Amidst such abundance, women from Tehuantepec and Juchitán stand out for their earthly, bodily existence, mothers and lovers of men, surrendered to excess of food, drink, and sex:

> mujeres de grandes tetas con pezones de amapola
> ...
> acostumbradas a darse placer frotándose el clítoris con aceite
> de coco
> acostumbradas a amamantar niños y a amamantar hombres
> acostumbradas a chupar el pene como si fuera un caramelo
> (Gervitz 2017, 169)[41]

The little girl dives into the eroticism of the surroundings, she gives in to auto-satisfaction, she overflows the public space with the fluids of her sex:

> y yo traigo los calzones mojados
> y el sexo pegajoso
> y en el baño sucio del mercado
> me toco y me vengo y me orino. (Gervitz 2017, 172)[42]

Female sexuality, organically related to the imagery of the pre-modern Mesoamerican culture and and tropical nature, invades the poem, and during a brief moment it seems able to sweep the mother, as erotic partner, along. Gervitz gives the erotic disobedience of her main protagonist a cultural dimension, which had been only marginal in previous instalments. Now woman does not submit to religion, she is not just dragged into exile and diaspora. She is the mistress of her fate; she inhabits her body by the same token that she articulates her word. But the Old Woman is not far away, and the law of motherhood is not dictated from outside but from within.

Overwhelming desire does not foil the ancestral fear, also boundless, to which the lyric self succumbs in obedience (Gervitz 2017, 191). The name of the fear is mother, and her law is the tyranny of biology:

> ¿y de qué madre huyo?
> ¿y qué madre huye de mí?
> dichoso aquel que huye de su madre
> dice Lezama Lima
> y yo de quién huyo *si traigo el útero dentro*
> *de quién si no puedo salir de esa matriz*
> *no puedo salir y la madre*
> está fría y está cumplida
> y yo allí hambreándome de su hambre
> *allí dentro de la madre que tuve*
> *allí dentro de esa madre que me inventé*
> y nos devoramos la una a la otra
> y no nos saciamos
> y la madre también soy yo (Gervitz 2017, 224, my emphasis)[43]

There is a painful identification with the mother's body through symbiotic proximity that allows for exchanging roles because both mother

## Breach of Intimacy

and daughter are attached to and through the uterus. The lyric self of *Migraciones* mourns a fruitless struggle to break free from the mirroring identification with the mother, the cultural destiny of woman as the gatekeeper of the future in her capacity to be mother. The daughter's horror comes from being imprisoned in the uterus, and this fright is matrilineal and ancestral, it follows woman in life and death (Gervitz 2017, 232), and it can only be atoned for in oblivion.

The lyric self needs to bury the maternal body in order to continue with creation that is not procreation. This moment comes when "la palabra" opens the desiring body. This word "no es el fruto de tu vientre" (Gervitz 2017, 251, "is not the fruit of your womb" 2021, 248), says the lyric voice self-dubbing and doubling, and with these words she ousts motherhood, she denies reproduction. There is no designated maternity here. "Palabra" is not a synecdoche for the tongue that ties the daughter with the mother, nor is it for that of a delirious cunnilingus (2017, 213), in which Pythia's plea for prophecy resonates (2004, 92).[44] Devoid of divine breath and magic power, empty just like god's name (2017, 251), this word "está en todos y es de nadie" (2017, 251, "is in everyone and belongs to no one" 2021, 248). Maternity of words moves away from possession. The long poem's quest against symbiosis sets the parameters for a new proximity: a poetic word that is neither mother nor daughter; neither productive nor reproductive; that starts and ends in its articulation each time, nesting always into the particular conditions of diction. "La palabra" puts forward a claim of non-ownership.

In this chapter, the problem of radical proximity as justice has been set up against intimacy between a mother and a daughter. Moving through different cultural and social settings, the daughter examines her relationship with the mother and her matrilinear cultural inheritance. The speaker finds herself imprisoned not only as the daughter of her mother, but also as the next in the reproductive line of motherhood, within a man's world. Almost condemned to paralysis in such space, she strives to escape a bond within which it is hard to discern where mother ends and daughter begins. The latter rebels through speaking the language of desire, a parthenogenetic code by means of which she enters in dialogue with the world outside the symbiosis, in search of agonistic closeness. Moments of triumph, such as the ones in which sexuality manifests itself either in the pleasure within – pleasure of the imagination – or those that bring the lyric self in radical proximity to her natural and social environment, are intertwined with passages of grief, where the daughter surrenders to symbiosis. The poet examines feminist thought and builds her own appeal for justice by dismembering the body of the mother through an impregnable stepmother tongue. Lament for what is lost – a delirious desire for maternal intimacy – is the face of what radical proximity as justice for woman brings about. Gervitz's lyric process of frontier discernment is still far from resolved, in the penultimate edition of a long series of migrations. Nonetheless this being together in the eroticized space of the word that is not born from a mother and that belongs to everybody, this dialogic and promiscuous poetic possibility of togetherness, is at least a step towards equality.

# Conclusions

## *Radical Proximity*

¡Alejarse! ¡Quedarse! ¡Volver! ¡Partir! Toda la mecánica social cabe
en estas palabras.

César Vallejo, "Algo te identifica"[1]

Intimacy has been the trademark of lyric poetry ever since
Romanticism. Traditionally the genre moved in the territory of self
and other(s) as the proverbial overheard utterance that delves into the
complexities of thoughts, emotions, and spiritual anxieties. The turn
towards reading for ideology and ethics started with deconstruction
and Marxist literary theory. More recently, gender and postcolonial
studies have turned long-standing formal approaches to poetry towards
new horizons. In Latin America, the Romantics' involvement in the
cultural configuration of the nation-state, the *Modernista* lyric voices
of resistance with regard to the insertion of the sub-continent into
processes of modernization, the rebellion of the avant-garde that targeted the bourgeois cultural establishment, and the movements of
*poesía de compromiso* (committed poetry) from mid-twentieth century
on, have made plain that lyric poetry is never too far from history, the
public sphere, and social struggles.[2]

Caught in the opposition between the private and public spheres,
intimacy has had its defenders in the humanities and social sciences,
for it is considered a privileged vantage point for gauging the transcendence of the personal over the political. Within this field of study,
the rise of the affective and the private in late capitalism has also been
attacked. The paradoxical dualism of intimacy, its extreme inward
focus on the one hand and, through mass media, its intense public
exposure on the other, has been considered a new form of despotism
(Béjar 1987, 69), and even a way of life with "a stupefying effect
politically" (Sennett 2017, 424).[3] Nevertheless, through race theory

and feminist and postcolonial critique it has become more and more evident that although *difference* is lived in the terrain of identity and in the confrontation between self and other within, it is also always a struggle deployed and performed in the social and epistemic arenas.

The spatial oppositions of identity politics became more intricate with the rise of intimacy as a theorical category, especially as it became clear that the intimate was crucial in writing history – for instance, in the case of historical trauma. Argentine literary scholar Nora Catelli defines intimacy with regard to history as follows:

> en lo íntimo no reside la verdad de la Historia, sino la vía –
> hoy privilegiada – para comprender la Historia como síntoma …
> Lo íntimo es el espacio autobiográfico convertido en señal de
> peligro y, a la vez, de frontera; en lugar de paso y posibilidad de
> superar o transgredir la oposición entre privado y público. Es un
> espacio pero también una posición en ese espacio; es el lugar del
> sujeto moderno – su conquista y su estigma – y al tiempo es algo
> que permite que esa posición sea necesariamente inestable.
> (2007, 9–10)[4]

In late modernity and postmodernity, intimacy has been a space opened up for the individual that straddles identity and politics, precisely because it allows for a two-faced existence: towards personalized knowns *and* unknowns as interdefined instances. Moreover, because intimacy destabilizes the emphasis on individuality as identity, it shows that the meaningfulness of even the innermost self is dependent on bonds with others whom we welcome into us. In that same act in which we feel that others welcome us into the world, intimacy gains terrain as a critical category, especially in relation to affects and particularly to love.[5]

In an interview to Nicolas Truong later published as a book titled *In Praise of Love*, Alain Badiou considers love to be a practice through which a new world is invented, for love changes the perspective from identity to the standing point of difference, from singularity to plurality. Those who love each other are this virtual and potential society, where all the functions of the social shape and are modelled by the conditions of intimacy. Love is the event of constructing "a world from a decentered point of view other than that of my mere impulse to survive or re-affirm my own identity," affirms Badiou (2012, 25). Although utterly slanted, for Badiou refers to the love between two

Conclusions    143

people, a man and a woman, to marriage and procreation, and to love as the expansion of a lesser impulse, namely, desire, what interests me in his account is the commensurability highlighted between politics and art by means of intimacy. This relation shifts the stress from identity as a personal adventure to sociability. Loving intimacy is, for Badiou, pivotal in order to establish a critical parallelism between family and the state: love has in family, the institution of intimacy *par excellence*, what thought and administration of power find in the auspicious institution of the state. As a political act, intimacy approaches poetry, for both take huge risks with regard to language (Badiou 2012, 42). This aesthetic twist places the interest of the connection between self and other – lovers, citizens, and poetic interlocutors – on the basis of imagination and representation, thus expanding the focus of art onto social realities. In the end, the French philosopher affirms: "Art has a very powerful point, in the sense that *it does justice to events*. That could even be a possible definition of art: art is what, at the level of *thought*, does complete justice to the event" (2012, 78, my emphasis). In other words, art and especially what art produces as thought is *de facto* justice.

Contrary to affects in general, love is a feeling that *can* be commanded and one that holds legal consequences and taxonomic efficiency. Paul Ricoeur considers that it is possible to establish a relationship between love and justice within the Judeo-Christian rhetoric of praise. Interestingly, the philosopher turns to poetry in the Hebrew Bible and explores the imperative mode that the lover uses to address the beloved in the Song of Songs. Ricoeur suggests a crucial moment in which the foundational law of all laws – the command to love – relies on the poetic value of morphology: "This poetic use of the imperative [Love me!] has its own connotations within the broad range of expressions extending from the amorous invitation, through pressing supplication, through the summons, to the sharp command accompanied by the threat of punishment" (1995, 27). Part of Ricoeur's argument is also based on a rhetorical analysis of "the command of love," by which an identification between law and love and the equality of the lovers are inferred: "the commandment to love is love itself, as though the genitive in the 'commandment of love' were subjective and objective at the same time" (1995, 27). In this context, the order is "love" and love is the instance that commands every act – a basic law, a premise constitutional to the lawfulness of an act. The right word is the foundation of this bond of love and lawfulness.[6]

Both the juridical edifice of the Mosaic law, based on the relentless command to love God over all things, and the golden rule of Christianity, to love one's neighbour as oneself, bespeak love's normative applicability. This relation between love and the law is playfully and poignantly presented in W.H. Auden's poem "Law, say the gardeners, is the sun." After several attempts to clarify the meaning of law with regard to who talks about it, the lyric self submits a definition based on sentiments, sensations, and intellectual competence:

And always the loud angry crowd,
Very angry and very loud,
Law is We,
And always the soft idiot softly Me.

To the equally sectarian perceptions of law based on "we" or "me" entitlement, Auden opposes lovers' positions in order to make law a matter of negotiation in the space between two, and of the knowledge, morality, and aesthetics that stem from intimacy. The challenge of the poem is to create a "we" that is different from the crowd's multiplicity of selves and that depends on personal, different instances in radical proximity to one another. The poetic voice concludes the attempt to define law in a catachrestic simile:

If *we, dear,* know we know no more
Than they about the Law,
*If I no more than you*
Know what we should and should not do
Except that all agree
Gladly or miserably
That the Law is
And that all know this,
If therefore thinking it absurd
To identify Law with some other word,
Unlike so many men
I cannot say Law is again
*No more than they can we suppress*
The universal wish to guess
*Or slip out of our own position*
*Into an unconcerned condition.*

Although I can at least confine
Your vanity and mine
*To stating timidly*
*A timid similarity,*
*We shall boast anyway:*
*Like* Love I say.

*Like* love we don't know where or why,
*Like* love we can't compel or fly,
*Like* love we often weep.
*Like* love we seldom keep. (Auden 1969, 154–6, my emphasis)

By means of enjambment, simile, anaphora, paronomasia, antithesis, and paradox, the lover's concept of law, one that implies a previous dialogue or understanding with a "dear" other, takes precedence momentarily over the rest of the definitions. At the beginning of the passage, the law stands for hermeneutic equality ("If we, dear, know we know no more / Than they about the Law, / If I no more than you"), while its normativity derives from the word ("Like Law I say"). Yet a definition of what the law is via metaphors or metonymies falls short ("I cannot say Law is again"). The alternative of not being able or willing to find a definition leaves the lyric speaker with the hard choice represented in "an unconcerned condition." Civic inertia gives way to a final attempt to define not the idea but the function of law/love, not because the I/you love each other, but because they share a space under the premise of some kind of responsibility to know, accept, suffer, rejoice, and do away with both unruliness and norm. Love and law are fragile aspirations, withstanding contradictions, uncertainties, margins of failure. The former wraps the latter in "the queer, the oblique, the incoherent, and indeed, the erotic" (Huffer 2013, 177).[7] Notwithstanding the tender adjective that accompanies the pronoun "we," in the end, the lesson learned in love for law admits the frailty of both ideals.

Where do we, readers and citizens, go from here? How can poetry take up where Auden left off in the search of social justice through intimacy? I have proposed radical proximity as that poetic closeness created by words that tend to another, in which others shape the limits of self, embrace, and are encompassed within self, and respond to a world created in the contact of those who come close. The collections

146                    Beyond Intimacy

of verse I have read tell stories of humans under threat and thus of
human relations that come about in danger, whose existence represents
a difficult access to justice. The lyric speakers face injustices such as
social death within an epidemic, the denigration-to-death of a language
and its speakers, and women's subjugation to the reproduction of
motherhood as the condition of survival of humankind. They thus take
refuge in desire for and in imagination with others.

In their poetic trajectories, the lyric speakers become visible and
audible to the extent that they position themselves with regard to
others, to movements of closeness and alienation. Imagining and
desire for togetherness and justice, doomed as they may be because
of death (*Poesida*), historical demise (*Ansina*), or affective impair-
ment (*Migraciones*), show the way to a fair praxis. In dialogue with
opacity, death, and history, *Poesida* and *Ansina*, and (in negative
dialectics) *Migraciones* mark a way of being *as if* self and other are
always bound together, always mutually responsible for one another.
On the threshold, one's words are articulated in dual tones, rendering
audible the claims and laments of others. The self is discovered in
the material of imagination, rather than in that of identity. From the
time and space of the posthumous, Bohórquez and Moscona's lyric
speakers enunciate that "what is most human is not rationality but
the uncontrolled and uncontrollable continuous surge of creative
radical imagination in and through the flux of representations,
affects, and desires" (Castoriadis 1990, 128). This is the world in
which damage has been perpetrated and justice needs to be restored.
Gloria Gervitz follows the opposite trajectory: she discovers the
conditions of proximity in which justice is not possible, and she
chooses childlessness as a form of extenuating the body within, as
the material of a lament, the only justice a poet has access to for the
exploited maternal body.

In the poem whose verse serves as epigraph of this section, César
Vallejo writes:

Algo te identifica con el que se aleja de ti, y es la facultad
común de volver: de ahí tu más grande pesadumbre.
    Algo te separa del que se queda contigo, y es la esclavitud
común de partir: de ahí tus más nimios regocijos.
    Me dirijo, en esta forma, a las individualidades colectivas,
tanto como a las colectividades individuales y a los que, entre

# Conclusions    147

unas y otras, yacen marchando al son de las fronteras o, simplemente, marcan el paso inmóvil en el borde del mundo.

Algo típicamente neutro, de inexorablemente neutro, interpónese entre el ladrón y su víctima. Esto, así mismo, puede discernirse tratándose del cirujano y del paciente. Horrible medialuna, convexa y solar, cobija a unos y otros. Porque el objeto hurtado tiene también su peso indiferente, y el órgano intervenido, también su grasa triste.

¿Qué hay de más desesperante en la tierra, que la imposibilidad en que se halla el hombre feliz de ser infortunado y el hombre bueno, de ser malvado?

¡Alejarse! ¡Quedarse! ¡Volver! ¡Partir! Toda la mecánica social cabe en estas palabras. (Vallejo 1978, 206)[8]

What I have exposed as the effort of Bohórquez, Moscona, and Gervitz towards poetic responsibility in the face of injustice, a kind of conscious activism of the imagination whereby we inhabit this world always in togetherness, is poignantly delivered in the Peruvian's poem as the space between, the frontier on which we are defined. Vallejo straddles bitterness and mercy. In the third versicle he mocks and convokes individualities and collectivities similar to those of "me" and "we" in Auden's poem. The convex half-moons we are to one another resemble, on the one extreme, the thief with their victim, and, on the other, the doctor with their sick patient. The nuanced indifference between those brought together by acts of theft and cure materializes in the objectified stolen good and the imperfection of the cured organ. Solar clarity shines over these separate positions that Vallejo scorns by comparing them to monolithic happiness and virtue. The reader knows that it is the simplest thing for an exultant human being to be or become gloomy, and for the righteous to be evil. The movements of closeness and separation in the last versicle are mechanical. They represent whimsical spatial oscillations and correspond to geometrical traces, ordered by a voice from nowhere. The location of departure – the self – and arrival – the other – are only points in space. Radical proximity is the condition of being that can convert this map into a representation of social movements where the quality of positions depends on the interaction itself, and therefore not on who initiates it, where it comes from, and where it concludes. No matter how far or how close we are, and no matter how instrumental our contact is to who we are, what defines our interactions as fair – justice is always relational – in time and space, that is in our history together, is what we become with one another on the inner and outer borders, and this is exactly what Bohórquez, Moscona and Gervitz deliver with regard to the lyric genre, the aesthetic verbal form par excellence of the relational.

# Notes

### INTRODUCTION

1  Throughout the book I use *radical proximity* and *intimacy* almost as synonyms, for it is the latter, inasmuch as the intersubjective condition of relationality, that provides the basis for poetry's desire and possibility to partake in fairness. The difference I see in radical proximity is that this condition of sociability sustains a will of active togetherness beyond time and space, which is not an ingredient of intimacy.

2  One of the criteria that make possible a compound inquiry of *Poesida*, *Ansina*, and *Migraciones*, is the quest for justice for two marginalized and persecuted groups. Janet R. Jakobsen has established a relation between homosexuals and Jews beyond comparison and analogy. She proposes the term "twinning," thus orienting the connection she observes towards creating and sustaining political, ideological, and social alliances, in the context of social justice, without collapsing the differences in conditions from which homophobia and antisemitism stem (2003, 79–80).

3  In a very common catachresis, Mei uses the term poetical as a synonym for literary and even as another word for narration.

4  Américo Castro and Leo Spitzer point to perspectivism as a sign of modernity that Miguel de Cervantes (Spain 1547–1616) makes current. Rather than a generic feature of narrative prose, such a strategy stems from cultural resistance against recalcitrant forces developed in the historical context of the *Contrarreforma* and the Council of Trent (1545–63), during the first Spanish *Siglo de Oro*. Américo Castro in *El pensamiento de Cervantes* repeatedly establishes the prismatic aesthetic vision of the author of *Don Quixote*, construed as "geometría literaria con múltiples dimensiones" (1925, 295, "literary geometry of multiple

150 Notes to pages 8–10

dimensions"). Departing from Castro's contribution, Leo Spitzer establishes linguistic perspectivism as a dialectic between refracted images of the world and the unique and central position Cervantes holds before his text (1945, 41–85).

5 Along the same line, poetry also converges with social justice in the context of protest. Franco (Bifo) Berardi locates such possibility in the lyric word's correspondence to and expression of affects, and thus in its human situatedness (2012). In 2018, the Italian thinker returns to poetry as a social practice of resistance, in *Breathing: Chaos and Poetry* (2018). Here it is the ethical valence of the poetic use of language that opposes concepts of value borrowed from the financial sphere. Concretely, Berardi affirms: "Poetry is the excess of language, the signifier disentangled from the limits of the signified. Irony, the ethical form of the excessive power of language, is the infinite game that words play to create and to skip and to shuffle meanings. Poetry and irony are tools for semiotic insolvency, for the disentanglement of language from the limits of symbolic debt" (2018, 32).

6 Jacques Derrida challenges the immediate relation of responsibility and justice. He points to the inherent and pragmatic bias of any decision related to the fairness of an action, and thus to the impossibility of univocally just deliberations: "If I conduct myself particularly well with regard to someone, I know that it is to the detriment of *an other* [sic]; of one nation to the detriment of another nation, of one family to the detriment of another family … This is the infinitude that inscribes itself within responsibility … And this is why undecidability is not a moment to be traversed and overcome" (1996, 89).

7 There are cases of close vicinity in which fairness and responsibility are lost, one such being the case of torture. Elaine Scarry has masterfully analyzed this context of shared spatiality, making apparent that in these extreme circumstances there is a cognitive gap between those involved, one that leads to the invisibility of the victim and their pain. "How is it possible," the scholar asks, "that one person can be in the presence of another person in pain and not know it – not know it to the point where he himself inflicts it, and goes on inflicting it" (1985, 12). The answer to this question is radical distancing: "The most radical act of distancing resides in [the torturer's] disclaiming of the other's hurt" (1985, 57). Radical proximity is the opposite of the spatial and ethical positioning of the torturer and the person tortured, one in which both body and language enter in process of annihilation. I will return to this difference in the third chapter, to show that the at times fine line between intimacy and violence depends on fairness.

Notes to pages 11–16

8 Young proposes and defends a paradigm of social acting through which to understand and confront social injustices in a systemic manner. The model of strict liability used to judge who has caused a damage that someone else suffers is important in order to achieve answerability for an act of wrongdoing, individual or not. However, it cannot account for systemic injustices, where no single person may be guilty of unlawful acts that cause harm. Systemic injustices point to outcomes caused by many agents, throughout time and via social institutions, within the margins of the law (Young 2003, 9).

9 The topic of responsibility can also be accessed through the relation between love and respect. Following Martha Nussbaum's review of this dialectic in the achievement of justice, Henry Richardson assesses: "[L]ove underwrites a discernment of particulars that amounts to *an intimate form of respect*. Respect, by contrast, demands of us a response to distant people that is less tepid than a general and distance-diluted philanthropy" (1998, 259, my emphasis). Love and respect are attitudes that warrant an interest and a semantic approach to others, framed by our immediate relation to them. Radical proximity goes beyond the paradox of an *intimate form of respect* for it does not depend on the ontological status of another or on who she, he, or it affectively represents for the self.

10 "We will not be limited, mean-spirited, mediocre, when we access intimacy," because "what intimacy ... makes us discover, consequently but discreetly, without alerting, is nothing less than what suddenly, by the possibility it opens up, undermines the conception of an I-subject blocked in its solipsism."

11 Schopenhauer exemplifies these forces through the parable of the porcupines, who come close due to the cold and distance themselves because of the pain felt by each because of the other's quills: "One cold winter's day, a number of porcupines huddled together quite closely in order through their mutual warmth to prevent themselves from being frozen. But they soon felt the effect of their quills on one another, which made them again move apart. Now, when the need for warmth once more brought them together, the drawback of the quills was repeated so that they were tossed between two evils, until they had discovered the proper distance from which they could best tolerate one another" (1974, 651–2). The quills enact the basic principle of fear and its derivative need for protection, through which the dialectics of vicinity and separation bring forward awareness. To the extent that Schopenhauer's porcupines understand their physical existence as limits and protective mechanisms to which each one is at the same time the victim and the cause of pain for self and other, they come into being

152 Notes to pages 17–22

socially. An expansive self, one that considers recognition of another as self, is thus the centre of the protective mechanism of the law, and the respect due to it is that which safeguards self and other. Needless to say, there is no provision for limit, respect, and acknowledgment for those not assigned a selfhood identical or comparable to any species imposing the legitimacy of its own limit. In this setting, radical proximity and the self-consciousness that derives from it turn out to be supposedly reckless practices that counter the dominant model of sociability based on law.

12 Harmony is the one characteristic held in common by theories of justice as heterogeneous as those of Plato, Aristotle, David Hume and John Rawls (Hampshire 2000, 22). Hampshire favours a view of justice as debate and "adversary argument" (29).

13 Oriental philosophy too advocates for a society and an individual organized and ruled with harmony: "[I]n Confucianism, a truly fair society is essentially a society of great harmony ... [T]he path to social harmony is ... a conscious self-rectification of each social institution, practice and individual" (Chen 1997, 503, 504). In both systems of thought and political organization, acceptance of social hierarchy is a precondition for justice because the differences between people are thought of as part of natural law.

14 By contrast, Aristotle affirms that imitation, the basis of dramatic poetry and an innate inclination of human beings, is conducive to knowledge (2005, 1448b), because literature is able to grasp the connection between particulars and universals (1451b). The poet is a mimetic artist, thus "he must represent [says Plato's student] the kind of things which were or are the case; the kind of things that people say or think; the kind of things that ought to be the case" (1460b). The Stagirite's defence is built on literature's ethical and cognitive merits. These elements also justify the end point of his definition of tragedy: "and through pity and fear accomplishing the catharsis of such emotions" (1449b). The benefits of dramatic poetry for life are not limited solely to rationality; they extend to affects.

15 Johnston considers reciprocity to be the cornerstone of every concrete materialization of the principle of justice, with the exception of Kant's metaphysics continued in some ways by John Rawls's configuration of justice as fairness. The author of A Brief History of Justice criticizes both systems of thought.

16 Scarry counters the legacy of classical humanism, for which love is a propagator of the search for beauty and, consequently, of goodness. The idea involves again Plato and a concept of love as an irrepressible impulse of the body and the soul towards what dominates the senses and serves

Notes to pages 25–7

as a first step towards the knowledge of virtue harboured in beauty. The eventual movement away from feeling and materiality puts in the places of beholder and beheld virtue and idea.

17 Whitman founds the American modern nation-state citizenry on his poetic and ethnographic endeavour; it is he who writes (γράφειν) the nation (ἔθνος) and spiritually legitimates the borders within which a particular kind of sociability is plausible (1881, 195–7).

18 Critical theorists as well as literary scholars have rehearsed different explanations of the prose poem and its timeliness in the nineteenth century. LeRoy Breuning considers that Rimbaud, one of the first poets to use the prose poem, cast in it his rebellion against the social and literary establishment (1983, 8). Lawrence Lipking suggests that the main feature of modern poetry, and probably of modern art, namely, the importance given by artists to the process of creation as the core quest of modern aesthetics, is best represented by the prose poem (2000, 462). For Jonathan Monroe, the prose poem is a starting point with elite standing that brings about the discursive appearance of historical changes in class and gender issues; in this sense, the moulding of this paradoxical creature proves to be at the same time ideological and utopian (1987, 24–5). The genre itself presents the specialist with thrilling questions on dialectics and identity. Marvin Richards affirms that the prose poem is a privileged vantage point from which one can understand that "a synthetic union [of identity and alterity] can be obtained on a speculative level, but such a valorization of unity comes at the expense of the constituent alterity." For Richards, the deep ambivalence of prose defined as poetry and poetry identified as prose "aptly describes the thrust of the prose poem as a genre" (1998, 103, 107). The critical literature on the subject tends to focus more on the transgression of conventions than on a set of answers that could help us understand the prose poem as an aesthetic problem within historical dimensions and cultural parameters that have to do with law and justice.

19 "The trial is then the theater of a tension between, on the one hand, the pre-existing legal qualification of the facts which reduces their singularity, and, on the other hand, the backdrop against which they stand out ... [T]he action of the trial takes place in the present tense. Its purpose in this sense is to abolish time ... to nullify the regularization that time seemed to have provided ... [Justice] limits the story, it symbolically stops the course of evil. [Justice] has two principal functions: tell what is right and adjudicate a sentence."

20 In both French and Spanish, "pein" signifies sentence/punishment and sorrow.

# CHAPTER ONE

1 "There are many ways of being virtuous. Love is one of them." Pedro Castera, *Mines and Miners*.

2 Cathy Jrade pointed out for me this interpretive possibility.

3 "*Poesida* / Ye are dead. However / ¿Are ye truly dead /promiscuous homosexuals? / DEAD ALWAYS OF LIFE: / Says Vallejo, / THE CAESAR." All of Bohórquez's translations are mine.

4 "To be human, Vallejo believed, was 'To have been born in order to live in our death!' while time 'marches barefoot / from death toward death' … In 'Sermon on Death,' Vallejo lamented: 'It's for this, that we die so much? Just in order to die, / we have to die at every instant?'" (Lebovits, 2020, https://symposeum.us/writing-silence-cesar-vallejos-poetry-of-exile).

5 In *Trilce* LXXV, Vallejo writes: "Estáis muertos. // Qué extraña manera de estarse muertos. Quienquiera diría no lo estáis. Pero, en verdad, estáis muertos. // Flotáis nadamente detrás de aquesa membrana que, péndula del zenit al nadir, viene y va de crepúsculo a crepúsculo, vibrando ante la sonora caja de una herida que a vosotros no os duele. Os digo, pues, que la vida está en el espejo, y que vosotros sois el original, la muerte. // Mientras la onda va, mientras la onda viene, cuán impunemente se está uno muerto. Sólo cuando las aguas se quebrantan en los bordes enfrentados y se doblan y doblan, entonces os transfiguráis y creyendo morir, percibís la sexta cuerda que ya no es vuestra. // Estáis muertos, no habiendo antes vivido jamás. Quienquiera diría que, no siendo ahora, en otro tiempo fuisteis. Pero, en verdad, vosotros sois los cadáveres de una vida que nunca fue. Triste destino. El no haber sido muertos siempre. El ser hoja seca sin haber sido verde jamás. Orfandad de orfandades. // Y sinembargo, los muertos no son, no pueden ser cadáveres de una vida que todavía no han vivido. Ellos murieron siempre de vida. // Estáis muertos" (Vallejo 2015a, 103–4). "You are dead. What a weird way of being dead. Anybody would say you're not. But, really, you be Dead. You voidly float behind that membrane which tick-tocking from zenith to nadir journeys from sunset to sunset, throbbing before the music box of a painless wound. I tell you, then, that life is in the mirror, and that you are Death. The original. While the wave goes, while the wave comes, with impunity one is dead. Only when the waters burst upon the facing shores curling and churning do you then transfigure and, believing you're dying, sense the sixth chord that's no longer yours. You are dead, not having ever lived before. Anyone would say, not being now, in another time you were. But, really, you are the cadavers come from a life that never was. Sad fate. Not

Notes to pages 31–7 155

having been anything but dead, always. To be a dry leaf, without ever having been green. Orphanhood of orphanhoods. And nonetheless the dead are not, cannot be cadavers of a life they've not yet lived. They died of life. You are dead" (Vallejo 2015b, 151–2).

6  Whether in the context of philosophy, literature, performance, or therapy, in *Romantic Intimacy*, Nacny Yousef insists that neither epistemic sufficiency nor affective recognition of the other is necessary for intimacy. The grounds on which intimacy thrives are far from reciprocal or based on recognition and respect, but rather are based on "indeterminate and undetermined modes of attention and appreciation" (2013, 24).

7  There is a consistent discrepancy around the year of Bohórquez's birth: the poet affirms that it is 1937, while almost everybody else considers it to be 1936. In "Carta," the poet writes: "[mi calavera] alumbrando desde el doce de marzo / del treinta y siete" (2000, 33, "my skull illuminating since March twelve / of the year thirty-seven"). On this topic, see also Munguía Zatarain (1994, 70).

8  Unfortunately, as happens with most of online criticism about Bohórquez, de la Cadena does not document his sources, and his writing style makes it difficult at times to follow his narrative and critical trains of thought.

9  See articles by Bruno Ríos Martínez del Castro, Ana Álvarez, and Avril Blanco (2013) in the *Tierra Adentro* homage eighteen years after the poet's passing. See also Ríos (2014a, 2014b) and Bustamante Bermúdez (2015).

10 For a particularly enlightening view of the African American community's response to AIDS health care and the prevention campaign around the end of the 1980s, see Dalton (1989). The scholar exposes five reasons for that community's resistance to AIDS control practices issued by the American medical establishment: overemphasis on the African origin of the disease in a campaign launched mainly by white centres; suspicion regarding those centres' interest in the African American community's well-being; deep-rooted homophobia; the problematic link between that community and drug abuse; and, finally, the resentment felt by many African Americans "at being dictated to once again" (1989, 211). This last reason is key to Bohórquez's attitude toward institutional efforts to prevent the spread of AIDS.

11 Regarding the ideological climate of the public sphere in which the virus was represented and in which the scientific research on it was developed, see Watney, "Moral Panics" ([1987] 1997, 38–57, *passim*) for the UK and (partly) Canada, and Bersani (1987, 198–9, *passim*) for the United States.

12 The attitude of the justice system toward the health crisis was antagonistic and hostile: "It was, after all, the Justice Department of the United States

156 Notes to pages 39–43

that issued a legal opinion stating that employers could fire employees with AIDS if they had so much as the suspicion that the virus could be spread to other workers, regardless of medical evidence. It was the American Secretary of Health and Human Services who recently urged Congress to defer action on a bill that would ban discrimination against people infected with HIV, and who also argued against the need for a federal law guaranteeing the confidentiality of HIV antibody test results" (Bersani 1987, 201).

13 "I apply myself in remembering me / in remembering you / to death." (Bohórquez 2000b, 33).

14 "From the author. AIDS showed up within the other, everyday violence against gay men, a bloody spectacle assumed without much scandal or hypocrisy even now ... and gay men, astonished and subdued, face to face with the anxiety of the unknown, found themselves mightily harassed, dragged violently to the gas chambers of the most accredited and malignant spellbinds, and the tentacles of the abyssal horror of *unemployment, shamelessly demonized by the press and the ministers of the church*, because A I D S was a divine punishment. Later on, there were many characters in this plot of death: the same citizens and the concubines of the citizens, and the secretaries and the drivers of the citizens and the tamed chimpanzees of the women of the citizens and the heated dogs of the bedrooms of the wives of the citizens and the lovebird and the glutton cat. Then the AIDS institutes and those who preached in favor of condoms became trendy, the problem started seasoning and ripening, and the phantasmagoric speculation gave way to worried efforts for prevention ... So many individuals, public and private, disappeared, dead of archangelical death, nymphomania, fear, because A I D S was the death that did not dare speak up its name; so many people, public and private, went tinny tiny, bald, and died from sweet Spring death; from hay fever, because their guts betrayed them, but never from A I D S, as the Convenor would have it. I am bringing forth this *document*, cruel yet in solidarity in order to claim infinite understanding for the citizens of the world, dead of this end of the millennium cancer; and to beg for kindness towards these poems of paradise lost, which one day, unpredictable to my imagination, we will discover again for ourselves: 'Poesida,' testimonial poetry by the one who could write it with all the words a man is capable of, in Hermosillo, Sonora, on March twentieth nineteen ninety-one." (emphasis added).

15 With regard to the exclusionary mode of modern national identities, see Watney's chapter on moral panics, in which he exposes and analyzes the

Notes to pages 43–9                                    157

concept and its limitations regarding the spread of AIDS in the 1980s. On the incompatibility between gay and national identities, forged by the media in that era, see Watney ([1987] 1997, 43–6).

16 "It is not ... a descent into hell, but, in any case, a desperate assault on paradise. A paradise that must continue precisely at the moment that the forbidden fruit is tasted ... This paradise supposes a peculiar morality based on a strictly bodily spirituality, which translates into a certain banal and inconsequential idleness, a fragmented emotionality with rapid and random ridges, penetration without rapport, agitated but brief breath, vitality without fertility."

17 "[When] AIDS is a slogan of the 80s / I want to see what I'll be saying / from where I am: / Lazarus resurrects every day."

18 "So, there was a day when the GOOD neighbor / premiered the movie, like a wheat field in flames: / AIDS IS COMING / AIDS IS HERE."

19 "Horror came upon / *the happy birthday of dear DEATH TRACY*; / one / then, / still in love with the obscure things / turned the eyes to the left, to the / right, / behind, before / longing for mirrors in which to touch a fertile face, / but what came was in enmity, / splitting and life is not the same: / *because to die for AIDS is different / from what anyone supposed*; / and relentless horror came upon / of living essentially dead now or in the future / or we are dead, / and we obstinately / persevered: dead-drunk / rock, / dead-end / rock, / deadfall / rock, / deadly gone world / rock, /o yeah, / *because to die for AIDS is different* / and there we go, carnal bro / becoming less and less, / piss off, pass bye / don't fuck with me, motherfucker death, / *because to die for AIDS is different / like to spit on olden olden God*, / rock / rock / rock'n rolling, / despite that day."

20 Arenas committed suicide on 7 December 1990. It is not clear when Bohórquez finished *Poesida*. He signed the prologue in March 1991, yet the last poem of the book, "Envío" ("Dispatch"), dedicated to Carlos Eduardo Turón, refers to the death of this Mexican poet on 3 April 1992.

21 "But yes against you, urban faggots, / tumescent flesh and unclean thoughts. / Mothers of mud. Harpies. Sleepless enemies / of the love that bestows crowns of joy. // Always against you, who give boys / drops of foul death with bitter poison. // Always against you, / *Fairies* of North America, / *Pájaros* of Havana, / *Jotos* of Mexico, / *Sarasas* of Cadiz, / *Apios* of Seville, / *Cancos* of Madrid, / *Floras* of Alicante, *Adelaidas* of Portugal" (García Lorca 1988, 161 and 163).

22 "Because there were shameless days / in which we were so lewd / so mobile / so fertile / so placid / so sordid."

158 Notes to pages 50–60

23 "On the TV: / AIDS, AIDS, AIDS, AIDS / and there I am dead again; / I shake my head / and it is now / that I breathe moved / moved that you lift me up / from the dust / 'causethislove this / ¿love? / one day one day one day / of those days / on the streets."

24 "Rise up to be born with me, brother / Give me your hand from the deep / zone of your disseminated sorrow. // You'll not return from the bottom of the rocks. / You'll not return from the subterranean time. / Your stiff voice will not return. / Your drilled eyes will not return. // Behold me from the depths of the earth, / laborer, weaver, silent herdsman" (Neruda 1991, 41).

25 Bohórquez's faith does not go through any religious institution, yet his rapport with God acquires at times a mystical tone, especially because it is established in strictly personal and mostly sacrilegious terms.

26 "Why this ailment of death in this old beach / itself a loveless graveyard / in this old scab / day to day lifted and lived again / in this poor faminine / in itself impoverished and extenuated / by the barren race. Being / AIDS. / What a deep word / it cringes our heart / and squeezes it!"

27 "Outside, in the sun, / the children play, / bitter wind, / with a small boat / in rough sea."

28 "I always saw them die of this other urban death. / Never of natural transition. / Maybe they fade out from kiss to kiss ... / under the showers of public baths / or blindly in the heat of movie theatres, / performing fornication / in shadowy caves / or in fetid bars / ... / skeletons of that Spring / suddenly leafless, / without the delicta carnis until yesterday / blooming green with AIDS / tiny wrinkled men, damned, / while a crazy howling of terror: / why? / comes out of their exhausted mouth / at the end. / I've never seen anyone die, lucky me, / but they still do."

29 "I stand here in mourning / because I can. / Because if I do not speak up / I / poet of my hour and my time, / my soul would sink of shame, / for I kept silent."

30 "Alas almost-perfect transvestites of the carnivals, / leading ladies of the gyms, soaring asses, / fags of the sacristy, / poor things of the small village / stoned by the neighbors / sieged by the dogs, / hanged and burnt in the relentless night."

31 "in-between, / chiaroscuro, / hail-catcher, / queer / because of that I know that now / I know what / my song is about."

32 "This one was Braulio Yesterdays, / who contracted overnight, from the root, / exhausted magnolias, / who managed to see junk / after having spilled fragrances, / and fearless embers after having crossed the fire // without becoming a saint, / who reached a record of not having been / as he could have / his own unforgettable character, / burning smuts after

having given / delightfully into misfortune, / signs that one time he tasted / evanescently / the abundant honey of love, / the irrefutable proofs of bad luck / of bad death / in the darkness of the hospital."

33 "When the dawn flaps her wings again / and clarity comes back to the world, / and maybe I am not here, / and the youth assume once again / the whatsoever power of love / in whichever gender, / and AIDS is but a slogan of the 80s, / I have to see what to say / from wherever I am: / Lazar resurrects every day / from the minerals of manure, / and the dove of the massacre / will make young pigeons / under the sky."

## CHAPTER TWO

1 "How is it possible to cultivate the spirit of this people? Talk to them about physics, traction, optics, acoustics; talk to them about chemistry, of the equivalent, of cohesion and affinity, of what is incalculable, and impenetrable; tell them all this, and this people will not be able to understand because this does not exist in its language."

2 According to Tapani Salminen, "since the Middle Ages, Judezmo [has been] the traditional language of Sephardic Jews" (2007, 251). This chronological comment implies that the language of the Sephardim, though critically related to the exile from Spain, belongs to its community before the expulsion, as an identity mark. David Bunis supports also this opinion: "Ottoman Judezmo developed into a single, independent, self-contained linguistic system characterized by some phonological, morphological, lexical and semantic features shared by all of its regional varieties, in opposition to the complex linguistic system constituted by the diverse dialects of Spanish in all of its regional diversity" (Bunis 2011b, 30).

3 In the late eighteenth century, a literature of mostly secular content appears in Jewish communities of the Balkans and the Ottoman Empire. Three publications in Judezmo, from 1778, 1823, and 1845, respectively, mark important moments in the use of the language for educational and entertainment purposes: *La guerta de oro* (Garden of Gold), by David Attias, in Livorno; *Otsar aHayim* (Treasure of Life), by Israel Hayim, in Vienna; and *Shaare Mizrah* (Gates of East), the first periodical in Judezmo, published in Izmir by Raffael Uziel. Attias was born in Sarajevo, and *La guerta de oro* is a book composed of different sections about which David Bunis affirms: "His own work was an innovation: a manual of non-rabbinic orientation, offering information of diverse kinds, including a brief introduction to Italian, an essay criticizing Eastern fatalism, and advice for Sephardim in the East who intended to visit Western Europe" (Bunis,

160        Note to page 67

Chetrit, and Sahim 2003, 107). In the diversity of materials found in the book, the author tacitly expresses his desire to inform and educate, but also he accounts for the cognitive and intellectual needs of the communities he is addressing. Attias attributes to Judezmo a lesser status relative to the Castilian version of his contemporary Spanish and thus shows "probably the first expression in Judezmo literature of the 'enlightened' (i.e., self-denigrating) attitude" towards this language, even though he is "one of the earliest writers to suggest that its speakers could derive pleasure from reading a work that had a true taste of authentic spoken language" (Bunis, Chetrit, and Sahim 2003, 106). *Otsar haHayim* is an anthology of thematically different materials, that addresses the educational needs of young Jewish boys. Its importance lies in "its adhesion to the 'write as you speak' principle and the introduction of nomenclature in Sephardic communities as a tool to understand Hebrew texts through Judeo-Spanish and German" (Quintana 2013, 36). Hayim's book treats the language of the Sephardic communities as a fertile field of deliberation at the crossroads of religious education and secular life. It touches upon the topics of biblical knowledge for religious instruction and for practising translation, of geography and arithmetic. It also includes a trilingual glossary: Hebrew, Judezmo, and German (Quintana 2013, 37). In *Ansina*, Moscona re-enacts a version of the linguistic awareness that is key in the composition and the readership's use of both *La guerta de oro* and *Otsar haHayim*. As education moved away from the exercise of memory toward broader access to printed materials, *enladinar*, the oral practice that preserved both faith and orthodoxy through strategies of memorization, became a reason for attention to orthographic rules and thus to linguistic normativity and homogenization.

4   "I permit myself, you professors, who spend your days burping upside-down, to tell you that you do not know our language… you study stories, and listen to phrases, but you've got it all backwards… from outside you want to judge what's inside? // a lot can be said / in this language / I can enlarge myself in it / even be born again / and write of love and science // you don't come upon language / just for use / in poems or in tying brothers / and sisters together // language is / for counting / the stars / for studying / insects / for trapping / thieves / and raising children / and birds / on the roof / of the houses / (for the cleaning of teeth / language /retreats far / back in the mouth) // you don't just find it / in the university / language is more than / a revival / it is an ingathering // of this / and of that // it is not the sum / but the remainder / of the sum / the divisor and the dividend // it is the evening / when the eyes / close / upon themselves /

Notes to pages 67–70

and from within / open in clarity" (all *Ansina* translations are mine in collaboration with Nissim Lebovits).

5 For the classification of Judezmo as an endangered language, see Salminen (2007). Judezmo is considered a Jewish language together with Italkian, Juhur, Krimchak, and Yiddish, vis-à-vis a variety of dialects spoken by Jewish communities in diaspora that do not have the same status for they do not comply with the operational definition of language found in the *Encyclopedia of World's Endangered Languages* (Salminen 2007, 214).

6 *dibaxu* is also the title of a collection of poems in Judezmo by the Argentine author Juan Gelman, published in 1994.

7 Haïm Vidal Sephiha affirms: "au Moyen Age, et au-delà, les tenants d'une religion étaient considérés comme les tenants d'une seule nation, d'où des designations comme la *nation chrétienne*, la *nation musulmane* ou la *nation juive*" (1977, 18, "in the Middle Ages and beyond, adherents of a religion were considered to be adherents of a single nation, hence designations such as the Christian nation, the Muslim nation or the Jewish nation," my translation).

8 On the importance of Ladino as a factor that shaped the relationship between religious textuality and oral tradition, see also Sephiha (1977, 19–20).

9 For women's education, two prayer books (*siddurim*), a manuscript dating from the fifteenth or sixteenth century, and a book printed in Salonica in 1565, testify to the contact with material culture that Sephardi women also achieved through Ladino. Ora Schwarzwald's linguistic perusal dates the manuscript to the sixteenth century; others, though, date it to the fifteenth (2010, 38). The need for these *siddurim* – and others in Yiddish or Judeo-Italian – shows the gnoseological distance of members of the community – men and women alike – from Hebrew as the liturgical language of Judaism by the sixteenth century (2010, 37–8).

10 The idea goes back to Aristotle, who, in proving memory's relation to imagination (in Bloch 2007, 450a 22–5), connects both faculties to the primary realm of the sense: "Memory will belong accidentally to the mind, but essentially to the primary faculty of sense" (2007, 450a 13–14), affirms the Stagirite. In classical antiquity, the connection of memory and imagination gave way to the art of memory, which involved the use of a spatial layout of images to assist a rhetor in developing an argument. As the rhetor addressed the public in the agora, he would embark on a mental stroll around an imaginary map in which every part of the natural and human landscape evoked a meaning. In the context of the Renaissance, Frances Yates connects this kind of recollection to art and

162 Notes to pages 71–4

aesthetics because of memory's didactic efficiency, put to work especially in the artistic expression of religious content (1974, 81). More recently, Harold Bloom extended the reach of remembrance to the ideological formation of the canon, boldly affirming that "my literary memory has relied upon the Canon as a memory system" (1994, 37).

11 Moscona probes Judezmo's oral flare with an ear trained in the literary tradition of Guillermo Prieto, Ramón López Velarde, Mariano Azuela, José Revueltas, Elena Garro, Rosario Castellanos, Juan José Arreola, and of course, Juan Rulfo. Inhabiting the positions of the postcolonial citizen, woman, and oralist, she combines Judezmo's cultural resonances with her national, continental, and linguistic traditions. As a Latin American intellectual, she approaches the language of her ancestors from a peripheral position of resistance; as a woman poet she finds in Judezmo a path to assert cognitive and affective difference. Her epistemic predicaments are thus related to past, present, and future, as well as to Mexican culture and the Sephardic world.

12 Julia Cohen revises the myth of the special bond between the Ottoman Empire and its Jews in order to show the rich historical content of a process of proximity and distance, throughout which "patriotism had to be taught and learned, and, later, maintained and managed" (2014, 4).

13 In their compilation of documents of the Sephardic communities in the Ottoman Empire, Cohen and Stein include a text by Isaac Akrish, in which this rabbi condemns the contact of youth with foreign languages in secular schools (2014, 123–5). Akrish refers to a decision of the elders "not to allow any Israelite to send his son or his daughter to the school where they learn any one of the languages of the gentiles" – a resolution that all members rejoiced over when it was announced in the synagogues of Istanbul (Cohen and Stein 2014, 125).

14 Most scholars locate the beginning of Judezmo's written literary tradition in this work that Rabbi Khuli started and others furthered after his death in 1732. However, Olga Borovaya advocates for a sixteenth-century date: the publication of Moses Almosnino's (Salonica 1515–Constantinople 1580) *Regimiento de la vida* (Salonica, 1564), traditionally considered to have been written in Castilian Spanish. The scholar makes the case for a longer history of written and material culture in Judezmo; she also points to the controversial demarcations that define language itself as an evolving arsenal of expressive possibilities (Borovaya 2017, 47–51).

15 Moscona will use this same word to talk about the emotional ailment of the lyric self in *Ansina* and the linguistic comfort that Judezmo offers to her illness (cfr. Moscona 2015, 28–9).

# Notes to pages 75–80

16 Throughout the controversy surrounding Judezmo at the end of the nineteenth century, different attitudes created a horizon of debate. Some Sephardim defended folk Judezmo, written in Rashi script; others urged their coreligionists to adopt French, Italian, or German; still others hoped to reform Judezmo by following Castilian norms and script; many proposed the use of Hebrew for religious reasons or in furtherence of Zionism. Each of these positions carried an ideological weight related to the language's place in society, history, and the economy. Thus, it is no coincidence that among those who supported Judezmo, the lively language of the proletarian masses, we find Avraam Benaroya, a Bulgarian Jew, and a socialist worker and syndicalist, who was active in Ottoman and later Greek Salonica, where he created the first socialist workers' federation, published the newspaper *Solidaridad Obradera* in Judezmo, and later helped found the Greek Communist Party (KKE). For more on these attitudes and their representatives, see Bunis (1996a).

17 On the topic, see Lockhart (1997); Sefamí (2002); Halevi-Wise (2012), and Luna (2018, 119–63).

18 The linguistic soil of Spanish and Portuguese in Latin America is especially receptive to the expressive richness of Judeo-Spanish, to the point that Edna Aizenberg speculates about the possibility of creating a new language she calls "Spanyit," "a new Judezmo" (2012, 36).

19 Monique Balbuena hears Juan Gelman's Judezmo as "a more tender, even feminine, language [that the writer uses] to address both his dead son and his dead mother ... Similarly, Gelman's choice to use Ladino brings him one step closer to feminizing his language, when he seeks to embrace his loved ones" (2016, 153–4).

20 "The other language that was 'that of the family,' of the 'secret,' the fear and – probably – of shame. It had turned us 'invisible.' In addition, compared to French it seemed to me lacking nobility, without grammar and without ... literature." Translations of Nicoïdski's text are mine.

21 Cynthia Gabbay also points toward this timely orientation of *Ansina* as historical present (2022, 68).

22 "Myriam Moscona ... expresses her culture through references to the Kabbalah, to Jewish tradition in a broader sense, to the wise men of rabbinic spirituality, or to contemporary Jewish poets, and not through a nostalgic inwardly movement, or through the recollection of her ancestors, and the recourse to the topics or style of medieval poetry. On the contrary, her style is prosaic, casual, and coloquial." My translation.

23 After documenting methods of simultaneous oral translation from Hebrew to Ladino, David Bunis concludes: "All such translations are ultimately

164 Notes to pages 81–4

founded in the *orally-transmitted Ladino translation system,* rather than in any written prototype which may or may not have existed in the Middle Ages. While basically ignored by *Ladino* Bible scholars for 100 years, this fact is hardly surprising when one considers that, among the Judezmo-speaking *Sephardim,* literature has always been predominantly oral (taking the form of songs, ballads, stories, proverbs and riddles), and only secondarily printed" (1996b, 355, emphasis in the original).

24 Isaac Abravanel (1437–1508), Portuguese statesman, biblical scholar, philosopher, treasurer to Afonso V, King of Portugal. He was exiled after the king's death. He established his household in Toledo, where he collaborated with the Catholic monarchs, Isabel and Ferdinand. After the Edict of Expulsion, he resided in different cities in Italy. He is known to have spent much of his fortune to save Jews from enslavement in Morocco, in 1471, and from exile from the Iberian Peninsula in 1492. He was the father of Leo the Hebrew, author of *Dialogues of Love.*

25 "By means of such strategy, kinship between the two languages is reevaluated at the same time that ... a proper space is given to Judezmo within Latin American literature." My translation.

26 "Imbroglio in Fortaleza" // where can i find the flowers / that loose breaths of honey / from their lips? // are you thinking dirty thoughts? // now i am speaking / of the countryside / and an orchard / fine / to look / I am not speaking of the body / that belongs to you // do you feel me? // suddenly i'm thinking / of the flowers / of brazil / facing a shattered / africa // i am speaking of your body / but as a body politic organized / into countries / that cultivate / stems by which to raise / the language // this little bit of writing meant to speak / of all of this / but only speaks of you."

27 In a deeply moving passage, Marcel Cohen describes the small handful of Salonican Jews who survived the Holocaust: "Se akordan ke, fin al siglo veynte, los exiliados de Espagna no tuvieron ni el gusto de aprender realmente al grego o al turko, seguros ke stavan de avlar la más precioza lingua del moundo, una lingua jalis sakrada, *dulce komo la miel*" (2006, 81, "They remember that well into the twentieth century, those exiles from Spain had no interest in learning either Greek or Turkish, sure that they were speaking the most beautiful language in the world, a deeply sacred language, sweet as honey," my translation and emphasis). The Salonican community of roughly 56,500 Sephardim was decimated between March and August 1943. They were deported to the concentration camps on nineteen trains, along with most of the Greek Jews of Larissa, Ioannina, Athens, and Rhodes. The only Greek Jewish community that was saved in its entirety was the one on the Ionian island of Zakynthos (Sephiha 1977, 52).

Notes to pages 84–8 | 165

28 Regarding the politics of linguistic homogeneity that affected the preservation of Judezmo among Sephardim who immigrated to Israel before and after the Holocaust, Balbuena writes: "To build the nation-state and promote a national culture, Jews had to be unified around a single language and forget their native diasporic languages" (2016, 62).

29 "Everything is open and can be studied. Behind the wall of the bet, there is nothing that a living creature can probe, and because of this silence the poets write and because of this silence the prophets translate their prophecies and because of this silence the geometricians of the skies perform algorithms, and because of this silence there are chains of prayers."

30 A few differences exist between the two versions: upper versus lower case letters at the beginning of each line; one line – "Lo sabia de antes" (I already knew it) – added in the version of *Ansina*; different versification arrangements to achieve a sense of list in the sequence of "mi padre? / mi partero? / mi entierrador?" (my father? / my man-midwife? / my grave-digger?); spelling; the addition of "i miel" (and honey) to the "Kantika" line "en los kaminos de letche" ("on the ways of milk").

31 "I should probably explain [to rabbi Samuel and his wife] that we [the narrator and her companion] are not religious, that we are not pure, that we mix dairy and meat, that on Saturdays we go out and party, that we adore our gentile friends, that, in addition, we venerate the tawny Virgin of Tepeyac, and that we would be happy to march in a *goy* pride parade, but we are Jewish and love our condition." "Goy" – "גוי" – means gentile in Hebrew. The word has negative connotations, which are playfully dissolved in the context of pride parades of the LGBTQ+ communities. Moscona's narrator offers ideological alliances that cross and queer identity.

32 Moscona playfully raises here an issue that is central to modern Jewish studies: identity and how it relates to the category of authenticity. Who is Jewish, and how does Jewishness manifest itself? Jonathan Boyarin offers an alternative to essentialist and/or constructivist identity. Instead of asking who a Jew is, he directs his attention to *things* that are Jewish: food, music, sacred iconography, the book, circumcision, historiographic reconstructions of emblematic events, pilgrimages, memorial monuments, Hassidism, among other material and symbolic cultural instances. In each case, he argues that these identity landmarks are semiotically evolving, at times ambivalent and often contradictory (2017, 947–54).

33 "He confesses to us that, actually, he is not a learned rabbi … *In my youth I started learning Hebrew with my father. After the war there was nobody who could chant the prayers and do the rituals, and so I said 'here I am.' I belonged to the communist party but now I became the rabbi of Plovid.*

166                    Notes to pages 90–4

And the uproar of one more loud laugh makes the surface of the Turkish
coffee move on the wavelength of his laughter."

34  "Crazy About the Stranger" // next to me / a man drinks Turkish coffee /
green tie and a sick eye / I imagine he knows my thoughts // in the time
machine / he might be my father? / my man-midwife? / my gravedigger? /
black birds ascend towards the foliage // – good evening – I greet him //
it's me who speaks inside / of his little cup of coffee // I want us to meet
outside / on the trails of milk and honey / I still don't know who he is / but
I want to kiss him // I already knew / I am not a very trustworthy woman."

35  "The answer" // *Did you know / that in my notebook I found / a sort of
fractal design? // The answer and the question were twins / and made
complete sense… // (Like that Japanese movie / that made me cry / as I
had my mother's kimono on // It was the kimono / she had used in
Madame Butterfly) // At the beginning of everything / I fasten it round my
body / as if the body of my mother / were the little girl out there //* Oh, the
two of us / coming from a / long illness / of sweet speaking manner / two
mouths / two sick people / bite on the clef of… / with the key / of what? /
what are you talking about? / about expanding through these mouths? /
about offering your life to curing / abracadabra / although it's better to be
one-eyed rather than dead // oh the two of us / coming / from a prolonged
infirmity / did we find reasons to kill or die / take a closer look / here are
the facts / like a fern that refracts / embellished in the kimono of mother /
did you always know it, *janum* // the impregnated answer returns as a
question" (emphasis in the original)." "Janum" is a Turkish word meaning
"woman," also used as a term of endearment for women and girls.
"Abracadabra" is considered of Latin origin (*Oxford Dictionary of Word
Origins*, s.v. abracadabra). However, another source claims a Hebrew
root: "It's from the Aramaic phrase avra kehdabra, meaning 'I will create
as I speak.' The source is three Hebrew words, *ab* (father), *ben* (son),
and *ruach acadosch* (holy spirit). It's from the Chaldean *abbada ke dabra*,
meaning 'perish like the word.' It originated with a Gnostic sect in
Alexandria called the Basilidians and was probably based on Abrasax,
the name of their supreme deity (Abraxas in Latin sources)" (Quinion
1999, s.v. abracadabra). This etymon resonates with esoteric views of
the power to heal attributed to words.

36  Fractal: "any of various extremely irregular curves or shapes for which
any suitably chosen part is similar in shape to a given larger or smaller
part when magnified or reduced to the same size … This term was coined
in 1975 to describe shapes that seem to exist at both the small-scale and
large-scale levels in the same natural object. Fractals can be seen in

Notes to pages 95–107

snowflakes, in which the microscopic crystals that make up a flake look much like the flake itself. They can also be seen in tree bark and in broccoli buds. Coastlines often represent fractals as well, being highly uneven at both a large scale and a very small scale. Fractal geometry has been important in many fields, including astronomy, physical chemistry, and fluid mechanics. And even some artists are benefiting, creating beautiful and interesting abstract designs by means of fractals" (*Merriam-Webster Dictionary*, s.v. fractal).

37 "I come about a city / i remember / that there lived / my two mothers / and i wet my feet / in the rivers / of these and those waters / that arrive to the place // *tell me the story once more* // and I hear / my two mothers talk // in different rhymes / these two speak."

38 "Questions // in such a way john asked me to tell you / 'come and marvel still at the stealing you stole' / in such a way john told me to ask / in such a way all the birds flew away // in childhood / when it was time to ask / I drank / from the fountain of the voice // who pulls her hair in mourning without being in pain? / to God's departure I am already entering / each one of us is standing / open, gobble up, mouth of mine / 'cause I don't want to talk to myself just for talking's sake."

39 "For you were a robber / who left me for death. / Why not take with you / the plunder you sought" (John of the Cross and Kathleen Jones 2001, 27).

40 In *The Sovereignty of Good*, Iris Murdoch describes in these terms her process of learning a foreign language – Russian, in her case.

CHAPTER THREE

1 Unlike the verticality Berlant and Warner imply, I will argue that the notions of power in spatial distribution, from politics to sex, are a problem that radical proximity, material or symbolic, addresses and reorients toward relations of horizontality, and thus parity.

2 Paula Bernstein claims that a woman integrates "the sensual memories of her mother's body into her own pleasure ... The mother representations within become a component of sexual excitement. Feeling in one's own body the ability to give pleasure and arouse desire evokes the dim memory of the cherished sensual softness of the mother's body and the desires once felt for her" (2004, 620–1).

3 In *The Purchase of Intimacy*, Viviana E. Zelizer examines the different aspects and domains of intimacy as they are structured in terms of economic activity and thus regulated by the legal system. The scholar shows that the principles of hostile worlds, separate spheres, and nothing-but

168 Note to page 108

categorizations, all depending on the assumption that economy and intimacy are at odds with each other, lack practical and conceptual accuracy. Zelizer removes general misconceptions with regard to the economic and legal aspects of intimacy (2005, 209–86 and 287–308). At the intersection of economy and the sphere of private life, the scholar observes that "the law changes as general practices of intimacy change, legal decisions affect intimate practices, and participants in legal processes bring their own experiences and understandings of intimacy to bear on legal decisions" (2005, 293–4). To be sure, the definition of intimacy in Zelizer's book is eminently sociological, and despite recognizing intimacy's affective, sensual, and moral aspects, Zelizer deals mainly with institutions of intimacy – marriage, childrearing, labor division within private settings, and so on.

4  It is especially second-wave feminism that underscores the importance of the dyadic relation. For a revision of maternal transference from a psychoanalytic point of view, see the monographic issues of *Psychoanalytic Inquiry* from 2004 and 2006. Third-wave feminism distances itself from the idea that the girl accesses object-relations through separateness from the mother, in order to obtain autonomy and sexual maturity. This revision leads to emphasis on women's sexuality based on the bodily attachment to the mother. On this topic, see especially Marcus (2004). Regarding the process of writing the matrilineal memory, see Dalsimer (2004), where the scholar reflects on how a writer such as Virginia Woolf gets to forget or silence her own mother's writing. In a movement imbued with active residues of phallogocentric oppression, Dalsimer argues, Woolf distances her writer's self from Julia Stephen's fate. Contrary to that, there is vast support for the bond and identification in the dyadic relation mother-daughter among scholars working on minority groups; on this, see the edited volume by Brown-Guillory (1996), as well as Kuwabong (1998) and Anzaldúa (1987). For a mythical recast of the relation mother-daughter, see Rabuzzi (1988). Within the Hispanic poetic tradition, motherhood is a topic in the production of Concha Méndez (Spain 1898–1986), defined as "both female centered and female generated," thus negotiating the binary mother–daughter as repetition but also creation and change (Bellver 1998, 321). An essay on Olga Orozco (Argentina, 1920–1999) touches upon mourning for mother's death (Brougham 2019). This topic resonates in the elegy of *Migraciones*. However, Gervitz's poetic grief for the mother contains an array of emotions and thoughts absent from the Argentine poet's lines. In "Si me puedes mirar" ("If you can look at me"), by Orozco, Brougham observes the reference to the mother as "shelter, safety, and

Notes to pages 108–9

unconditional love" (2019, 38). The problematic of the house is also a bridge between the Argentine and the Mexican poet, yet in the latter's work there is an ambivalence regarding origin and destiny, home and exile, sedentary memories and nomadic desire. A recent account of the duty, love, and hatred with which motherhood has been charged in Western societies can be found in Jaqueline Rose (2018), where the renowned scholar also seeks justice for mother.

5 Throughout the chapter I will be quoting *Migraciones* from the bilingual edition of 2004, unless otherwise noted. The decision to quote from this among the consecutive versions of the long poem stems from a variety of reasons, the most prominent of which being that in the 2004 edition I see the culmination of an effort to sustain the fragmented nature of the poem, at the same time that I perceive the structuring presence of a centre that allows for each one of the singular stories in the text to find its own completion. This is a fundamental difference from later editions, where an all-encompassing centripetal structuring force prevails over the previously differentiated parts and centrifugal singularities of lyric lines and figures.

6 The three books differ in details of typography: italics for words in foreign languages that Gervitz dropped or added; some corrected typos – a question mark missing at the end of poetic phrase beginning with an inverted question mark, an accent that transforms the word "tránsito" from a noun (2016, 87, and 2017, 85, "transit") to the verb "transito," (2020, 88, "I transition"); words she added or erased – "y el amor estaba ahí para ser herido" (2016, 185, and 2017, 182, "and love was there to be wounded") becomes "y la herida allí para ser herida" (2020, 185, "and the wound there to be wounded," 2021, 179) or "lo hace y me lo hace" (2016, 196, "he does it to himself and he does it to me"), which she rephrases as "hace lo que le pido" (2017, 194, and 2020, 197, "does what I ask him to do"). The two major changes have to do with two short series of lines that she rearranges or erases at the beginning of the poem and that are the same in 2016 (14) and 2017 (12), but change in 2020: (a) "mientras todavía pueda sentir que siento /mientras todavía me obligue a seguir sintiendo / y el miedo me obligue a salir del miedo / y yo me obligue a salirme de mí" (14, "though I still can feel that I can feel / though it still makes me keep on feeling / and fear makes me break out of fear / and I make myself break out of myself" 2021, 8); and (b) "quisiera rezar y no sé rezar / ni siquiera sé qué es lo que quiero decir / todo está anegándose / no hay bordes / hay apaciguamiento / hay lo que no entiendo / y es que yo no inventé a esa muchacha / ella forzó su existencia dentro de mí / oscurísimas rosas germinándose en la memoria / las mujeres trenzándose los cabellos

Notes to pages 110–15

perfumándose las axilas / el olor del sexo madurándose" (2020, 16–17, "I wish I could pray and I don't know how / I don't even know what I want to say / everything is inundated / there are no edges / there is quietude / there is all I don't understand / and I did not invent that girl / she thrust her existence inside me / darkest roses sprouting in memory / the women braiding their hair scenting their armpits / the smell of sex ripening" 2021, 10–11). Both passages recycle ideas and parts of lines that Gervitz had developed in different places in 2016 and 2017.

7 In the 2004 bilingual version of the poem, the explanations have been partly eliminated or incorporated into the glossary, and the terms "milagro," "pietà," "quetzal," and "saudades" have been added. This points to the type of public that Gervitz anticipates: non-Jewish Spanish-speaking readers. In the 2017 edition, Gervitz adds geographical, culinary, herbalist, and everyday terms of the Mexican idiolect of Spanish, potentially appealing to readers outside of Mexico.

8 For further revision of the extant bibliography, see Karageorgou-Bastea (2019, 101–2).

9 I use the word as a calque of *theodicy*, the theological belief in divine justice despite the acceptance of evil's existence.

10 The law of the father and the prohibition of incest are symbolic spheres that are almost irrelevant for women's subjectivity. In the context of *Totem and Taboo*, Freud's main text of psychoanalytic anthropology, woman appears only in the role of the mother, the central location of sexual dispute between father and sons.

11 For a view of this issue in Latin American literature, see Anna Castillo (2019).

12 Regarding the representation of immigrant women domestic workers in Hispanic postcolonial contexts, see Murray (2018).

13 Feminism has pointed to the heterogeneity of materials and affections that build the mother/daughter compound, but the problem of their separation has remained at the centre of women's identity, as a phase in daughter's identity development; on this see Irigaray ([1979] 1981, *passim*), Gallop (1982, 116), and Whitaker (1992, 37, 38). Recent observations in the field of psychoanalysis have driven scholars away from this monolithic perspective in favour of a process of continuous oscillations and constant recasting of the positions occupied by the members of the binary (Bernstein 2004, 615, 617, 619).

14 Barbara Marcus offers a view of the complex links between sexuality, subject formation, and the relation of a daughter with her mother: "the capacity of the mother to be represented as a libidinal subject and

Notes to pages 115–20

to appreciate and participate in the daughter's bodily esteem has a central role in conferring the privilege of passion to the daughter" (2004, 687). From this recognition and integration of passion in the psychological development of women we derive a claim in agency (Marcus 2004, 684). Michelle Boulous Walker analyzes the line of feminist thought that connects identification with the mother to a return to the origin through a process of birth and rebirth specifically related to writing. Although a fundamental piece in a woman's sense of selfhood and of new epistemologies, the bond with the mother is highly fraught and ambivalent. Drawing on Freud, Nietzsche, de Beauvoir, Kristeva, Deleuze, as well as on feminist readings of these sources, Walker comes to a first conclusion: the moving epistemological perspectives of nomads, of those who do not aspire to a return to the origin-mother, but rather obey centrifugal forces of wandering, liberate them from the reproduction of thought. In a second movement, Walker analyzes Luce Irigaray's perspective on the mother/daughter relation as a basis for contradictory knowledge and integration beyond reproduction of mothering (Walker 1998, 162–70). Even though there are moments when the nexus of mother/daughter rids itself from the weight of paralysis, Walker reads Irigaray's proposition as doomed: "The promise of mobility gives way to the re-establishment of paralysis. The sensuous bond of mother and daughter is once again reduced to the lifeless representation of the mirror image" (1998, 173).

15 Irigaray's text, published the same year as "Shajarit," addresses many of the same claims that Gervitz's lyric speaker works on throughout four decades.

16 "And I accuse you / But what can I blame you for" (Gervitz 2004, 43), "Plunge into me memory that I might forgive ... / Memory do you hear me / You grow like that which is forgotten / And the woman I am offers to forgive the woman I was" (57); "If I only could learn compassion" (59); "Now she has been absolved of the plot that was her life" (61); "Don't judge me, mother. You too are doomed to be forgotten" (69); "Only compassion is infinite" (75).

17 "I speak to you from these words / From thought and the idea of thought / From what I remember / From you and the beginning that proceeds from you / From the desire to reach you" (Gervitz 2004, 85). Later on in the poem, the voice repeats: "hablo para ti / hablo desde ti" (2004, 96, "I speak for you / I speak from within you," 97). This dislocation of the singing voice that comes out of the maternal body, like a sound from a soundbox, is constant and culminates in "Septiembre," where the dialogue of love with the mother involves the production of the word (128–44).

172            Notes to pages 120–6

18 Earlier on, Gervitz writes: "El agua en su silencio de raíz / En su oscura lentitud de raíz / Se abre temblando / ... / Quedan las palabras" (2004, 80, 82, "Water in its silence of roots / In its dark slowness of roots / Parts trembling / ... / the words remain," 2004, 81 and 83). From darkness to light and from water to the growth of plants, the consecutive transformations of the physical world give way to a new genesis: the word. For an analysis of the passage as the poetic principle of *Migraciones*, see Karageorgou-Bastea (2019, 96–8).

19 "I let myself fall. I return" (2004, 23); "I come to the place of origins where the beginning begins," "I begin again" (2004, 7); "Everything begun again and imagination forever remote these irreversible dreams / Remembrances," "I was the return" (2004, 31); "Where was I all this time? / I am anchored to the same spot" (2004, 35); "(actually nothing happens I haven't moved)" (2004, 37); "Never again will I set sail on that long-dreamt-of a sea" (2004, 39); "¿Where do I return? (2004, 47); "I move toward the silence now," "I sleep in memory" (2004, 49).

20 "Like Jonah in the belly of the whale / Like the Sibyl within the damp, black walls / Not knowing what to say having nothing to say / Yours, always for you / I must have been faithful to myself // Old carefully forgotten feelings shatter forgetting / And you know I speak to you // no one but you always to you // The air is still it fills with flowers / The rain glides into sleep as well / Slowly regains its shadow leans like a willow/ Falls // I return home" (2004, 55).

21 I am referring here to the second stanza from Garcilaso's *Égloga III* (c. 1535), and its modern lyric re-enactment in *La voz a ti debida* (1933) by Pedro Salinas.

22 "Someone should hire those women who cry for the dead of others / Women who have raised children / Kneaded their bread / Women who sweep their front stair every day / they should weep with you, weep for you / Though they're paid to do it" (2004, 41).

23 Interpreting Ferré, Trigo affirms: "Similar to Theseus, in 'Requiem,' man conjures the monster again in the poem 'Fable of the Wounded Heron.' He needs the monster's labyrinths, its echo chambers, and its towers of wrath for support. *He needs a threshold, a hole, or an opening to be born.* He will build the architecture for his entrance and the dead mother is his lintel: 'perfect lintel of the dead mother / her body is marked by movement.' In his imaginary, as well as in the social imaginary, the mother is conceived as a dead certainty, *a fixture for movement*. The fortifying operation is defensive, and being defensive it is relentless in setting the stage for the equally implacable return of the repressed. Man builds a psychic wall

Notes to pages 127–30

around a void to protect himself from the ambiguity of a shared desire and an equally intense separation and prohibition" (2006, 72). In this quote, the three elements that interest me are spatial limit (threshold), movement (separation), and ambiguity.

24 "And I wanted to reach you / but you were me // and the water so dark" (Gervitz 2004, 121).

25 Cfr. "Mi voz se confunde con la tuya [...] / Ella sólo escribió cartas que no se atrevió a enviar y quedaron allí arrumbadas escritas / en un yiddish que ya nadie habla / No tuvo palabras para decir lo que sentía [...] // El silencio es un trabajo que durará toda su vida. Ocurre en lo más profundo / en lo más oscuro como una enfermedad mortal // ¿Yo? ¿Esa mujer soy yo?" (2004, 62; "My voice mingles with yours [...] / She only wrote letters she didn't dare mail. Cast aside they gathered there written / in a Yiddish no one speaks any longer / She lacked the words to say how she felt [...] // Silence is a task that will last her whole life. Like a fatal disease / it transpires in the deepest and darkest place // Me? Is that woman me?" 2004, 63). There is a striking difference in the two cases of heteroglossia in the text: silence haunts the letters in Yiddish, while the silence of Spanish in the passage in English and vice versa is an invitation to one's space, a flexible limit of dialogical eloquence.

26 "Pollen coating that memory of mirrors / We barely move / Do not look upon me. Your eyes are terrible and beautiful / I still feel the burning, I touch myself, I am alone / Dawn, drained by other floods / Beloved, distant one / I want to return to the place where I sleep / The complicity of voice / its persistence / And I am what is falling" (2004, 25). In the lines that follow, the lyric voice insinuates a sexual encounter with an exalted other: "Muévete más. Más / Pido mucho. Eres más bella, más aterradora que la noche / Me dueles / Fotografías casi despintadas por la fermentación del silencio" (2004, 16, "Move. More, more / I ask for a lot. You are more beautiful, more terrifying than the night / You ache in me / Photographs nearly faded in the fermentation of silence" 2004, 17).

27 "Words, saliva, insomnia pour / into the northeast edge of absence, into the stupor / and farther to the east I masturbate thinking of you / Screech of sea gulls. Dawn. The froth in the dazzle of the wing / The color and the season of bougainvilleas are for you. The pollen stuck to my fingers / Hold me tight. The ripening rain, your scent / of sour violets feverish with dust / words that are nothing but an extended prayer / a kind of madness after the madness" (2004, 17).

28 "Wearing a white blouse and the skirt from that other memory / She takes pleasure in her body / Far from the oracle / Clutching the depths of the

174 Notes to pages 131–4

violets / Ah, jealous girl / Without resistance / In the anticipation / In the annunciation / In the stillness that precedes the visitation / That precedes the name / In the utter beauty of the return / In the fever / In the annulated perception / In the fragility" (2004, 45).

29 "My voice mingles with yours" (2004, 63); "(bless me mother)," "Don't judge me, mother. / You too are doomed to be forgotten" (69); "As if it were I who had begun to die and not you" (73); "Come now forgotten one / Come and tell me / Do you see yourself in me?" (77); "You healing mother" (79); "the officiant / complicit old mother" (90).

30 "That joy // look at it // it is unspoken // it is yourself // you // in you" (Gervitz 2004, 129).

31 The mother is at times also a third person, placed in independent contexts: "Mi madre y algunas amigas juegan al bridge," (2004, 24; "My mother plays bridge with some friends" 2004, 25); "La madre enjuaga su cabello en la palangana azul" (2004, 44; "The mother rinses her hair in the blue basin" 2004, 45). In both cases the mother appears in her own world, rather than in relation to the daughter.

32 "But it is I who pass all limits // like a lengthening stain / like a raised fist // burning to the orphan's core / howling // like a split ceiba // the grievous passion ... // in this silence / open me like a furrow // she-wolf" (2004, 111).

33 In "Pythia," the erotic undertone becomes more evident as the lyric speaker begs: "ábreme con tu saliva / empújate hasta mi hondura hasta el desamparo // recíbeme como si fuese un puñado de tierra // tránsito yo misma" (Gervitz 2004, 92; "open me with your saliva / plunge into my depths my desolation // receive me like a fistful of dirt // I myself the passage" 2004, 93).

34 In "Pythia," the daughter begs the mother-Sibylline figure: "Tócame adentro de ti / con esa contención que se desborda" (2004, 96; "Touch me inside yourself / with that overflowing restraint" 2004, 97).

35 "Banish me / Let me go / Have pity on me / You who have comforted me / Help me forget // Do you hear me? / Are you still with me / Could you be my echo?" (2004, 37); "Rock me / Shelter me" (2004, 39); "You are hurting me / Let me go / Don't take from me what I have learned myself" (2004, 39); "I can sink no farther beneath your heart" (2004, 43).

36 The kind of motherhood whose analysis and reorientation the lyric self in Gervitz's poem painstakingly strives for corresponds to Julia Kristeva's view of maternal authority, based on "repetition of the *laws* of language. Through frustrations and prohibitions, [maternal] authority shapes the body into a *territory* having areas, orifices, points and lines, surfaces and hollows, where the archaic power of mastery and neglect, of the

Notes to pages 135–9

differentiation of proper-clean and improper dirty, possible and impossible, is pressed and exerted ... Maternal authority is the trustee of that mapping of the self's clean and proper body" (Kristeva 1982, 72; emphasis in the original).

37 Adjacent to the sanctuary of Apollo in Delphi, the Castalian Spring offered in antiquity its waters to the pilgrims visiting the oracle as well as the priests and Pythia herself for ritual cleansing. The name recalls the nymph Castalia, who transformed into spring coming out of the rocks in Mount Parnassus to escape Apollo. In the Roman era the fountain was a metonym for poetic enthusiasm.

38 "And I spoke your name / and the place was air / and the word / prey" (2004, 103).

39 Benigno Trigo interprets man's fortress-self as a construction based on symbolic matricide: "a psychic wall *around a void* to protect himself from the ambiguity of a shared desire and an equally intense separation and prohibition" (2006, 72, my emphasis).

40 "[I] slip my fingers in / explore / find the pleasure spot / ... / I close my eyes and say filthy girl/ saying it excites me / and the feeling spreads / takes me completely / covers me completely / and I am this body / this rapture this vastness / I am in the pleasure within the pleasure of pleasuring myself / and my nanny sound asleep in the hammock nearby" (2021, 162).

41 "Great-breasted women with nipples of poppies / ... / used to pleasuring themselves rubbing their clitoris with coconut oil / used to suckling men as well as children / used to sucking penises like hardy candy" (2021, 166).

42 "And my panties are wet / and my sex sticky / and in the dirty market bathroom / I touch myself and come and pee on myself" (2021, 169). The eschatological taints sexuality with carnivalesque nuances. Prohibition is crossed and no limit, no law, restrains the body of the girl who finds pleasure to be intense, morbid, sweet, and uncontrollable (see also Gervitz 2017, 200).

43 "And from what mother do I flee? / and what mother flees from me? / happy is he who flees from his mother / says Lezama Lima / and whom do I flee when I carry my uterus inside me / from whom if I can't leave that womb / can't leave and mother / has grown cold and is done / and I'm hungering there for hungering hunger / there inside the mother that was mine / there inside that mother I invented / and each of us devours the other / and our hunger is never sated / and I am the mother too" (2021, 221).

44 "La lengua metiéndose en la hendidura del sexo / y tú dejándote dándote / y él llevándote a más y a más y tú dejándote más y más / y más y más" (Gervitz 2017, 213, "and his tongue thrusting into the crevice of my

176                           Notes to page 141

sex / and you letting yourself go giving yourself / and he taking you
farther and farther / and you letting yourself go farther and farther /
and farther and farther" 2021, 210).

CONCLUSIONS

1   "To leave! To remain! To return! To depart! The whole social mechanism
    fits in these words." "Something identifies you" (Vallejo 1978, 206, 207).
2   With regard to Romanticism, I am referring to the contributions of
    Guillermo Prieto (1818–1897) and Ignacio Manuel Altamirano (1843–
    1893), for instance, in shaping the cultural profile of nineteenth-century
    independent Mexico. In terms of *Modernismo*, I have in mind the emblem-
    atic opposition of Rubén Darío (Nicaragua, 1867–1916) and José Martí
    (Cuba, 1853–1895) to the political influence of the United States in the
    region. The *Estridentista* group in México is one of many examples of
    vanguardists who advocated for art as social critique. Finally, personalities
    such as Ernesto Cardenal (Nicaragua, 1925–2020) and Roque Dalton
    (El Salvador, 1935–1975) championed with their lives a key role for their
    poetry in the history of political movements in their countries.
3   Two elements in Sennett's considerations relate to my topic: first, the
    fact that he separates, as John Rawls does too in theorizing justice (see
    "Introduction"), the territory of the intimate from justice and the tran-
    scendence of the law; and second, that he relates the rise of the private to
    the institution *par excellence* of intimacy, the family: "The public realm
    has morphed in its specifics over the course of time. What has endured
    relatively unchanged is *its legal meaning*; we still conserve from the
    Roman era the idea that 'public' stands for laws which apply to everyone
    while 'private' concerns deals of doing which are particular and on which
    *no legal light shines*. Socially, the distinction between public and private
    became more mobile with the dawn of the modern era," located by the
    sociologist in the Middle Ages and defined by relations "whose inner life
    mattered ever more, as did the very idea of '*inner*' and '*intimate*'" (2017,
    421, my emphasis). The way in which the public sphere is defined in its
    relation to the law appears stable and almost transhistorical, whereas
    intimacy suffers from legal obscurantism, and thus is unfathomable with
    regard to justice as social reality. For an early defence of the sphere of the
    personal in relation to the social, through performance, see Judith Butler
    (1988). In the field of anthropology, Michael Herzfeld (1997) uses the
    concept of "cultural intimacy" within the frame of homogenization in the
    historical process of nation-state consolidation. He finds that dissenting

Notes to pages 142–3

ways of intimate cultural being – culinary, dressing practices, and so on –
are not at odds with people's sense of citizenship and national belonging.

4 "The truth of History does not reside in intimacy, however intimacy is the
path – privileged nowadays – to understanding History as symptom ...
The sphere of the intimate is the autobiographical space turned into a
sign of danger, and at the same time as that of a frontier; into a place of
passage and of the possibility to overcome and transgress the opposition
between private and public. It is a space but also a position in space; it is
the locus of the modern subject – their conquest and stigma – and at the
same time it is something that causes that this position be necessarily
unstable" (my translation).

5 In his comment on Hannah Arendt's thought about how to make the
world a livable place for humans, fragile beings subjugated to a temporary
existence marked by uncertainty both regarding the origin and the teleology of being, Ronald Beiner underscores the importance of judgment as
a way to understand history in the German philosopher's thought. He
concludes: "We have argued that *judging* provides for affirmation of our
worldly condition by allowing us to draw pleasure from reflecting on the
past. But the aim is not really to *justify* the world but something more like
'confirming' our place in it; that is, *establishing contact with the reality of
our world or, perhaps, justifying this reality by asserting our connection
to it*. This formulation is suggested by a phrase that recurs several times in
Arendt's unpublished lectures; it is Augustine's 'Amo: Volo ut sis': to love
is, in effect, to say 'I want you to be.' Because of 'the sheer arbitrariness
of being,' because of the fact that 'we have not made ourselves,' we 'stand
in need of confirmation. We are strangers, we stand in need of being welcome.' It is by judging that 'we confirm the world and ourselves'; with
the faculties given us, 'we make ourselves at home in the world.' The
self-chosen company of shared *judgment* secures an otherwise tenuous
historicity" (in Arendt 1992, 154–5, my emphasis). In addition to the
pre-eminent place of doing justice as theoretical reason, in this passage,
I would like to draw attention to the bond with others necessary for us,
strangers, to substantiate who we are.

6 For a secular approach to the topic, one that is explicitly based on the
artistic form, Iris Murdoch argues that the unity of living is based on the
search for "good," and that the place where this can be seen clearly is in
art, which, contrary to chance and death, which define human life as part
of a chaotic universe, gives unity to the disconnected and incomplete
(1996, 97). It is beauty in art that appeals to love and brings the participant closer to good. Art is, for Murdoch, "a kind of goodness by proxy"

178 Notes to pages 145–7

(87), and the artistic form is where the relation between justice and beauty takes place. Unlike Ricoeur, Murdoch considers that the energy of beauty's dual nature, its artistic form and attachment to virtue, counters the horror of a purposeless universe.

7 Huffer defines as such the utopian remainder of an ideal ethical self, this "modern, moral, Western subject that lurks behind most everything we do, even when we try to dismiss him" (2013, 179).

8 "Something identifies you with the one who leaves you, and it is your common power to return: thus your greatest sorrow. // Something separates you from the one who remains with you, and it is your common slavery to depart: thus your meagerest rejoicing. // I address myself, in this way, to the collective individualities, as well as the individual collectivities and to those who, between them both, lie marching to the sound of frontiers or, simply, mark time without moving at the edge of the world. // Something typically neuter, inexorably neuter, stands between a thief and his victim. This, likewise, can be noticed in the relation between a surgeon and his patient. A horrible halfmoon, convex and solar, covers them all. For the stolen object has also its indifferent weight, and the operated-on organ, also its sad fat. // What on earth is more exasperating, than the possibility for the happy man to become unhappy, and the good man to become wicked? // To leave! To remain! To return! To depart! The whole social mechanism fits in these words" (Vallejo 1978, 207).

# References

AA. VV. 1995. *XIV Coloquio Nacional de las Literaturas Regionales.* Hermosillo: Universidad de Sonora.

Agamben, Giorgio. 1998. *Homo Sacer: Sovereign Power and Bare Life.* Translated by Daniel Heller-Roazen. Stanford: Stanford University Press.

Aizenberg, Edna. 2012. "Nuevos mundos halló Colón, or What's Different about Sephardic Literature in the Americas?" In Berajano and Aizenberg 2012, 31–7.

Akrish, Isaac. 2014. "A Rabbi of Istanbul Condemns the Teaching of European Languages." In Cohen and Stein 2014, 123–5.

Álvarez, Ana. 2013. "Abigael Bohórquez: La sagrada cotidianidad." https://www.tierraadentro.cultura.gob.mx/abigael-bohorquez-la-sagrada-cotidianidad.

Anzaldúa, Gloria. 1987. *Borderlands: The New Mestiza. La frontera.* San Francisco: Spinsters/Aunt Lute.

Arenas, Reinaldo. 1992. *Antes que anochezca.* Barcelona: Tusquets.

Arendt, Hannah. 1992. *Lectures on Kant's Political Philosophy.* Edited and with an interpretive essay by Ronald Beiner. Chicago: University of Chicago Press.

Arfuch, Leonor. 2004. "La visibilidad de lo privado: nuevos territorios de la intimidad." *Mundo Urbano* 12. http://www.mundourbano.unq.edu.ar/index.php/ano-2001/60-numero-12/107-3-la-visibilidad-de-lo-privado-nuevos-territorios-de-la-intimidad.

Aristodemou, Maria. 2000. *Law and Literature: Journeys from Her to Eternity.* Oxford: Oxford University Press.

Aristotle. 2005. *Poetics.* Edited and translated by Stephen Halliwell. Cambridge, MA: Harvard University Press.

180 References

– 2014. *Nicomachean Ethics*. Translated by H. Rackham. Cambridge, MA: Harvard University Press.

Arnould-Bloomfield, Elisabeth, and Suzanne R. Pucci. 2004. "Introduction." *L'Esprit Créateur* 44, no. 1: 3–8.

Auden, W.H. 1969. *Collected Shorter Poems, 1927–1957*. London: Faber and Faber.

Ayala, Amor, Rebekka Denz, Dorothea M. Salzer, and Stephanie von Schmädel, eds. 2013. *Zeitschrift der Verreinigung für Jüdische Studien*. Potsdam: Universitätsverlag Potsdam.

Badiou, Alain, and Nicolas Truong. 2012. *In Praise of Love*. Translated by Peter Bush. New York: New Press.

Bakhtin, Mikhail M. 1984. *Problems of Dostoevsky's Poetics*. Edited and translated by Caryl Emerson. Minneapolis: University of Minnesota Press.

– 1993. *Towards a Philosophy of the Act*. Translated and notes by Vadim Liapunov. Edited by Michael Holquist and Vadim Liapunov. Austin: University of Texas Press.

Balbuena, Monique R. 2016. *Homeless Tongues: Poetry and Languages of the Sephardic Diaspora*. Stanford: Stanford University Press.

Barret-Ducrock, Françoise, ed. 1999. *Pourquoi se souvenir?* Paris: Bernard Grasset.

Beinart, Haim, ed. 1992. *Moreshet Sepharad = The Sephardi Legacy*. Volume 2. Jerusalem: The Magnes Press/The Hebrew University.

Béjar, Helena. 1987. "Autonomía y dependencia: la tensión de la intimidad." *Reis: Revista Española de Investigaciones Sociológicas* 37, no. 1: 69–90.

Bejarano, Margalit. 2012. "The Sephardic Communities of Latin America: A Puzzle of Subethnic Fragments." In Bejarano and Aizenberg 2012, 3–30.

Bejarano, Margalit, and Edna Aizenberg, eds. 2012. *Contemporary Sephardic Identity in the Americas: An Interdisciplinary Approach*. Syracuse: Syracuse University Press.

Bellver, Catherine G. 1998. "Mothers, Daughters, and the Female Tradition in the Poetry of Concha Méndez." *Revista Hispánica Moderna* 51, no. 2: 317–26.

Benjamin, Mara H. 2018. *The Obligated Self: Maternal Subjectivity and Jewish Thought*. Bloomington: Indiana University Press.

Berardi, Franco "Bifo." 2012. *The Uprising: On Poetry and Finance*. Cambridge, MA: MIT Press.

– 2018. *Breathing: Chaos and Poetry*. Cambridge, MA: MIT Press.

# References

Berlant. Lauren, ed. 2000a. *Intimacy*. Chicago: University of Chicago Press.
– 2000b. "Intimacy: A Special Issue." In Berlant 2000a, 1–8.
– 2007. "Slow Death. (Sovereignty, Obesity, Lateral Agency)." *Critical Inquiry* 33, no. 4: 754–80.
Berlant, Lauren, and Michael Warner. 2000. "Sex in Public." In Berlant 2000a, 311–30.
Berman, Marshall. 2011. "'Mass Merger': Whitman and Baudelaire, the Modern Street, and Democratic Culture." In Seery 2011, 149–54.
Bernstein, Paula P. 2004. "Mothers and Daughters from Today's Psychoanalytic Perspective." *Psychoanalytic Perspective* 24, no. 5: 601–28.
Bersani, Leo. 1987. "Is the Rectum a Grave?" *October* 43, AIDS: Cultural Analysis/Cultural Activism (Winter): 197–222.
Bianchi, Emanuela. 2001. "Receptacle/Chōra: Figuring the Errant Feminine in Plato's *Timaeus*." *Hypatia* 21, no. 4: 124–46.
Blanco, Avril. 2013. "Caborca es una fiesta. La poesía de la frontera marginal: Abigael Bohórquez." https://www.tierraadentro.cultura.gob.mx/caborca-es-una-fiesta.
Bloch, David. 2007. *Aristotle on Memory and Recollection*. Leiden: Brill. https://doi.org/10.1163/ej.9789004160460.i-276.
Bloom, Harold. 1994. *The Western Canon*. New York: Riverhead Books.
Bohórquez, Abigael. 2000a. *Las amarras terrestres. Antología poética (1957–1995)*. Edited, with notes and introduction, by Dionicio Morales. Mexico City: Universidad Autónoma de México.
– 2000b. *Poesida*. Hermosillo: La voz de Sonora.
– 2005. *Heredad. Antología provisional (1956-1978)*. Foreword by Carlos Eduardo Turón. Hermosillo: El Colegio de Sonora/Instituto Sonorense de la Cultura.
– 2015. *Acta de confirmación y Canción de amor y muerte por Rubén Jaramillo y otros poemas civiles*. Edited by Gerardo Bustamente Bermúdez. Mexico City: Universidad Autónoma de la Ciudad de México.
Borovaya, Olga. 2017. "How Old Is Ladino Literature?" In Şaul and Hualde 2017, 43–52.
Boyarin, Daniel, Daniel Itzkovitz, and Ann Pellegrini, eds. 2003. *Queer Theory and the Jewish Question*. New York: Columbia University Press.
Boyarin, Jonathan. 2017. "In Search of Authenticity: Issues of Identity and Belonging in the Twentieth Century." In Hart and Michels 2017, 942–64.
Brennan, Bernadette, ed. 2008. *Australian Authors Writing for Justice*. Brisbane: University of Queensland Press.

Breuning, LeRoy C. 1983. "Why France." In Caws and Rifaterre 1983, 3–20.

Brougham, Rose Marie. 2014. "Yoga en 'Septiembre': una meditación por Gloria Gervitz." *Confluencia* 29, no. 2: 70–80.

– 2019. "Olga Orozco's Elegy." *Hispania* 102, no. 1: 35–44.

Brown-Gillory, Elizabeth. 1996. *Women of Color: Mother-Daughter Relationships in 20th-Century Literature.* Austin: University of Texas Press.

Bunis, David M. 1992. "The Language of the Sephardim: A Historical Overview." In Beinart 1992, 399–422.

– 1996a. "Modernization and the Language Question among Judezmo-Speaking Sephardim of the Ottoman Empire." In H.E. Goldberg 1996, 226–39.

– 1996b. "Translating from the Head and from the Heart: The Essentially *Oral* Nature of the *Ladino* Bible-Translation Tradition." In Busse and Varol-Bornes 1996, 337–55.

– 2011a. "Judezmo Glossaries and Dictionaries by Native Speakers and the Language Ideologies behind Them." In Busse and Studemund-Halévy 2011, 339–47.

– 2011b. "Judezmo: The Jewish Language of the Ottoman Sephardim." *European Judaism* 44, no. 1: 22–35.

– 2016. "Talk about Judezmo on the Ladinokomunita." In Miller and Norich 2016, 321–60.

– 2017. "The Lexicography of Sephardic Judaism." In Hanks and Schryver 2017, 1–25.

– 2019. "The Autobiographical Writings of the Constantinople Judezmo Journalist David Fresco as a Clue towards his Attitude to Language." In Herzog and Wittmann 2019, 105–98.

Bunis, David M., Joseph Chetrit, and Haideh Sahim. 2003. "Jewish Languages Enter the Modern Era." In Simon, Laskier, and Reguer 2003, 102–23.

Burt. E.S. 1999. *The Appeal of Literature: Nineteenth-Century French Lyric and the Political Space.* Stanford: Stanford University Press.

Busse, Winfried, and Michael Studemund-Halévy, eds. 2011. *Lexicología y lexicografía judeoespañolas.* New York: Peter Lang.

Busse, Winfried, and Marie-Christine Varol-Bornes, eds. 1996. *Sephardica. Hommage à Haim Vidal Sephiha.* Berne: Peter Lang.

Bustamante Bermúdez, Gerardo. 2015. "Abigael Bohórquez: para que 'no olvides mi nombre casi angustia.'" *Casa del tiempo* 2, no. 22: 49–53. http://www.uam.mx/difusion/casadeltiempo/22_nov_2015/index.html.

## References

Butler, Judith. 1988. "Peformative Acts and Gender Constitution: An Essay in Phenomenology and Feminist Theory." *Theatre Journal* 40, no. 4: 519–31.

– 1997. *Excitable Speech: A Politics of the Performative*. New York: Routledge.

Cadena y Aragón, Omar de la. 2015a. "Ciento volando. Una biografía intelectual de Abigael Bohórquez III." http://www.cronicasonora.com/ciento-volando-una-biografia-intelectual-de-abigael-bohorquez-iii.

– 2015b. "Letras segundas (Primera etapa). Una biografía intelectual de Abigael Bohórquez VI." http://www.cronicasonora.com/letras-segundas-primera-etapa-una-biografia-intelectual-de-abigael-bohorquez-vi.

– 2015c. "Letras segundas (Segunda etapa). Una biografía intelectual de Abigael Bohórquez VII." http://www.cronicasonora.com/letras-segundas-segunda-etapa-una-biografia-intelectual-de-abigael-bohorquez-vii.

– 2015d. "Muerto en vida. Una biografía intelectual de Abigael Bohórquez." http://www.cronicasonora.com/muerto-en-vida-una-biografia-intelectual-de-abigael-bohorquez-i-2.

– 2015e. "Primeras letras. Una biografía intelectual de Abigael Bohórquez V." http://www.cronicasonora.com/primeras-letras-una-biografia-intelectual-de-abigael-bohorquez-v.

– 2015f. "Siento volando. Una biografía intelectual de Abigael Bohórquez IV." http://www.cronicasonora.com/siento-volando-una-biografia-intelectual-de-abigael-bohorquez-iv.

– 2015g. "Terceras letras (Primer ciclo). Una biografía intelectual de Abigael Bohórquez VIII." http://www.cronicasonora.com/terceras-letras-primer-ciclo-una-biografia-intelectual-de-abigael-bohorquez-viii.

– 2015h. "Vivo en Muerte. Una biografía intelectual de Abigael Bohórquez II." http://www.cronicasonora.com/vivo-en-muerte-una-biografia-intelectual-de-abigael-bohorquez-ii.

Cassani, Alessia. 2019. *Una lengua llamada patria. El judeoespañol en la literatura sefardí contemporánea*. Foreword by Michael Studemund-Halévy. Barcelona: Anthropos.

Castillo, Anna. 2019. "Crear o criar: Maternity and Choice Feminism in Meruane's *Fruta podrida* and *Contra los hijos*." *Hispanic Review* 87, no. 3: 355–76.

Castoriadis, Cornelius. 1990. *World in Fragments: Writings on Politics, Society, Psychoanalysis and the Imagination*. Edited and translated by David Ames Curtis. Stanford: Stanford University Press.

Castro, Américo. 1925. *El pensamiento de Cervantes*. Madrid: Imprenta de la Librería y Casa Editorial Hernando.

184 References

Catelli, Nora. 2007. *En la era de la intimidad. El espacio autobiográfico.* Rosario: Beatriz Viterbo.

Caws, Mary Ann, and Hermine Rifaterre, eds. 1983. *The Prose Poem in France: Theory and Practice.* New York: Columbia University Press.

Chen, Xunwu. 1997. "Justice as a Constellation of Fairness, Harmony, and Righteousness." *Journal of Chinese Philosophy* 24, no. 4: 497–519.

Chodorow, Nancy. 1978. *The Reproduction of Mothering: Psychoanalysis and the Sociology of Gender.* Berkeley: University of California Press.

Christakis, Nicholas. 1989. "Responding to a Pandemic: International Interests in AIDS Control." *Daedalus* 118, no. 2, Living with AIDS part 1: 113–34.

Cixous, Hélène. 1976. "The Laugh of the Medusa." Translated by Keith Cohen and Paula Cohen. *Signs* 4, no. 1: 875–93.

Cohen, Julia Phillips. 2014. *Becoming Ottomans: Sephardi Jews and Imperial Citizenship in the Modern Era.* Oxford: Oxford University Press.

Cohen, Julia Phillips, and Sarah Abrevaya Stein, eds. 2014. *Sephardi Lives: A Documentary History, 1700–1950.* Stanford: Stanford University Press.

Cohen, Marcel. 2006. *Letra a Antonio Saura: In Search of the Lost Ladino: Letter to Antonio Saura.* Bilingual edition. Translated by Raphael Rubinstein. Jerusalem: Ibis Editions.

Cornell, Drucilla, Michel Rozenfeld, and David Gray Carlson, eds. 1992. *Deconstruction and the Possibility of Justice.* New York: Routledge.

Corral, Fortino. 1995. "El paraíso terrenal de Abigael Bohórquez." In AA. VV. 1995, 234–41.

Cover, Robert M. 1983. "Foreword: Nomos and Narrative." *Harvard Law Review* 97, no. 1: 4–68.

Dalsimer, Katherine. 2004. "Virginia Woolf: Thinking Back through Our Mothers." *Psychoanalytic Inquiry* 24, no. 5: 713–30.

Dalton, Harlon L. 1989. "AIDS in Blackface." *Daedalus* 118, no. 3, Living with AIDS part 2: 205–27.

Deleuze, Gilles, and Félix Guattari. 1986. *Kafka: Toward a Minor Literature.* Translated by Dana Polan. Foreword by Réda Bensmaia. Minneapolis: University of Minnesota Press.

Derrida, Jacques. 1992. "Force of Law: The 'Mystical Foundation of Authority.'" Translated by Mary Quaintance. In Cornell, Rozenfeld, and Carlson 1992, 3–67.

– 1996. "Remarks on Deconstruction and Pragmatism." Translated by Simon Critchley. In Mouffe 1996, 79–90.

*Diccionario de la Real Academia Española.* www.rae.es.

# References

Dolven, Jeff. 2001. "Spenser's Sense of Poetic Justice." *Ratitan* 21, no. 1: 127–40.

Dowling, Emma. 2021. *The Care Crisis: What Caused It and How Can We End It?* London: Verso Books.

Evans, Mary. 1993. "Mothers and Daughters: The Distortion of a Relationship." *Sociology* 27, no. 1: 192–3.

Feldstein, Leonard C. 1979. "Toward Integrity and Wisdom: Justice as Grounding Personal Harmony." In Kelbley 1979, 59–76.

Fischlin, Daniel. 2003. "Queer Margins: Cocteau, *La Belle et la bête*, and the Jewish Differend." In Boyarin, Itzkovitz, and Pellegrini 2003, 365–94.

Foster, David, ed. 1994. *Latin American Writers on Gay and Lesbian Themes: A Bio-Critical Sourcebook*. Westport: Greenwood Press.

Frank, Jill. 2018. *Poetic Justice: Rereading Plato's Republic*. Chicago: University of Chicago Press.

Freedman, Jonathan. 2003. "Coming Out of the Jewish Closet with Marcel Proust." In Boyarin, Itzkovitz, and Pellegrini 2003, 334–64.

Fresco, David. 1901a. "La lingua de los israelitas de Turkía." In Bunis 2019, 176–9, and Herzog and Wittmann, 105–98.

– 1901b. "Un puevlo mudo." In Bunis, 2019, 174–6, and Herzog and Wittmann 2019, 105–98.

Freud, Sigmund. (1913) 2001. *Totem and Taboo: Some Points of Agreement between the Mental Lives of Savages and Neurotics*. Translated and edited by James Strachey. London: Routledge Classics.

– 1925. "Some Psychical Consequences of the Anatomical Distinction between the Sexes." Translation and Edition by James Strachey. Preface by Peter Gay. *The Standard Edition of the Complete Psychological Works of Sigmund Freud*. Vol. 19, 1923–1925: *The Ego and the Id and Other Works*. New York: W.W. Norton. 241–58.

Gabbay, Cynthia. 2022. "Neodjudezmo en la lírica latinoamericana disidente: la construcción de registros intersticiales entre la autotraducción y el glosario." *Mutatis Mutandis. Revista Latinoamericana de Traducción* 15, no. 1: 65–94.

Gallop, Jane. 1982. *The Daughter's Seduction: Feminism and Psychoanalysis*. Ithaca: Cornell University Press.

Garapon, Antoine. 1999. "La justice et l'inversion morale du temps." In Barret-Ducrock 1999, 112–23.

García Lorca, Federico. 1988. *Poet in New York*. Translated by Greg Simon and Steven F. White. Edited and with an introduction and notes by Christopher Maurer. New York: Farrar, Straus and Giroux.

## References

Gelman, Juan. *dibaxu*. 1994. Biligual edition. Buenos Aires: Epudlibre.

Gervitz, Gloria. 1987. *Yiskor*. Illustrations by Giménez Cacho. Mexico City: Esnard Editores.

– 1993. *Pythia*. Mexico City: Mario del Valle.

– 2002. *Migraciones*. Mexico City: Fondo de Cultura Económica.

– 2004. *Migrations/Migraciones*. Bilingual edition. Translated by Mark Schafer. San Diego: Junction Press.

– 2016. *Migraciones. Poema 1976–2016*. Barcelona: Ediciones Paso de Barca.

– 2017. *Migraciones. Poema 1976–2016*. Mexico City: Mangos de Hacha.

– 2020. *Migraciones. Poema 1976–2020*. Colección Ποίησις [Poíesis] 15. Madrid: Libros de la resistencia.

– 2021. *Migrations. Poema, 1976–2020*. Translated by Marc Schafer. New York: New York Review of Books.

Goldberg, Florinda. 2013. "'Carta de naturalización': particularidad y universalidad en la poesía de Myriam Moscona." Special issue, *Chasqui: Revista de Literatura Latinoamericana* 4: 192–202.

Goldberg, Harvey E., ed. 1996. *Sephardi and Middle Eastern Jewries: History and Culture in the Modern Era*. Bloomington: Indiana University Press/the Jewish Theological Seminary of America.

Graubard, Stephen R. 1989. "Preface." *Daedalus* 118, no. 3, Living with AIDS part 2: v–xvi.

Halberstam, Jack (Judith). 2011. *The Queer Art of Failure*. Durham: Duke University Press.

Halevi-Wise, Yael. 2012. "A Taste of *Sepharad* form the Mexican Suburbs: Rosa Nissán's Stylized Ladino in *Novia que te vea* and *Hisho que te nazca*." In Bejarano and Aizenberg 2012, 184–201.

Hampshire, Stuart. 2000. *Justice is Conflict*. Princeton: Princeton University Press.

Hanks, Patrick, and Gilles-Maurice Schryver, eds. 2017. *International Handbook of Modern Lexis and Lexicography*. Berlin and Heidelberg: Springer.

Hart, Mitchell B., and Tony Michels, eds. 2017. *The Cambridge History of Judaism*. Vol. 8, *The Modern World, 1815–2000*. Cambridge: Cambridge University Press.

Hatty, Suzanne, and James Hatty. 1999. *The Disordered Body: Epidemic Disease and Cultural Transformation*. Albany: SUNY Press.

Herzfeld, Michael. 1997. *Cultural Intimacy: Social Poetics in the Nation-State*. New York and London: Routledge.

# References

Herzog, Christoph, and Richard Wittmann, eds. 2019. *Istanbul-Kushta-Constantinople. Narratives of Identity in the Ottoman Capital, 1830-1930*. New York: Routledge.

Huffer, Lynne. 2013. *Are the Lips a Grave?: A Queer Feminist on the Ethics of Sex*. New York: Columbia University Press.

Ibsen, Kristine, ed. 1997. *The Other Mirror: Women's Narrative in Mexico, 1980–1995*. New York: Greenwood Press.

Imboden, Rita Catrina. 2012. *Cuerpo y poesía. Procesos de presentificación del cuerpo en la lírica mexicana del siglo XX*. Peter Lang: Berne.

Irigaray, Luce. 1981. "And the One Doesn't Stir without the Other." Translated by Hélène Vivienne Wenzel. *Signs* 7, no. 1: 60–7.

Jakobsen, Janet R. 2003. "Queers Are Like Jews, Aren't They? Analogy and Alliance Politics." In Boyarin, Itzkovitz, and Pellegrini 2003, 64–89.

John of the Cross and Kathleen Jones. 2001. *The Poems of St John of the Cross*. Translated, with an introduction, by Kathleen Jones. London: Burns and Oates.

Johnson, Barbara. 1987. *A World of Difference*. Baltimore: Johns Hopkins University Press.

Johnston, David. 2011. *A Brief History of Justice*. Oxford: Wiley-Blackwell.

Jones, Gail. 2008. "Speaking Shadows: Justice and the Poetic." In Brennan 2008, 76–86.

Juan de la Cruz, San. 1989. *Poesie*. Critical edition by Paola Elia. L'Aquila and Roma: Japadre Editore.

Julien, François. 2013. *De l'intime. Loin du bruyant Amour*. Paris: Bernard Grasset.

Karageorgou-Bastea, Christina. 2006. "Abigael Bohórquez o la voz sobre la frontera." *Romance Quarterly* 53, no. 2: 144–60.

– 2019. "En lo más íntimo: recuerdo y anhelo en 'Shajarit' de Gloria Gervitz." *Iztapalapa. Revista de Ciencias Sociales y Humanidades* 86, no. 1: 93–118.

Katsaros, Laure. 2012. *New York-Paris: Whitman, Baudelaire, and the Hybrid City*. Ann Arbor: University of Michigan Press.

Kelbley, Charles A., ed. 1979. *The Value of Justice*. New York: Fordham University Press.

Kostelanetz, Richard, Joseph Darby, and Matthew Santa, eds. 1996. *Classic Essays on Twentieth-century Music: A Continuing Symposium*. New York: Schirmer Books.

Kristeva, Julia. 1982. *Powers of Horror. An Essay on Abjection*. Translated by Leon S. Roudiez. New York: Columbia University Press.

Kullavanijaya, Pranee. 2000. "Power and Intimacy: A Contradiction in a Thai Personal Pronoun." *Oceanic Linguistics Special Publications* 29: 80–6. www.jstor.org/stable/20000142.

Kuwabong, Dannabang. 1998. "Reading the Gospel of Bakes: Daughters' Representations of Mothers in the Poetry of Claire Harris and Lorna Goodison." *Canadian Woman Studies* 18, no. 2: 132. https://www.proquest.com/scholarly-journals/reading-gospel-bakes-daughters-representations/docview/217468581/se-2.

"La epidemia del VIH y Sida en México. Hoja informativa – 01." 2015. Gobierno de México. 30 November. https://www.gob.mx/censida/documentos/la-epidemia-del-vih-y-sida-en-mexico.

Lares, Ismael. 2012. *Abigael Bohórquez. La creación como catarsis.* Mexico City: FETA.

Lauretis, Teresa de. 1990. "Eccentric Subjects: Feminist Theory and Historical Consciousness." *Feminist Studies* 16, no. 1: 115–50.

Lebovits, Nissim. 2020. "Writing Silence: César Vallejo's Poetry of Exile." https://symposeum.us/writing-silence-cesar-vallejos-poetry-of-exile.

Lehmann, Matthias B., 2017. "The Balkans and Southeastern Europe." In Hart and Michels 2017, 104–32.

León, Denise. 2008. *Poemas de Estambul.* Córdoba: Alción Editora.

– 2011. *El saco de Douglas.* Buenos Aires: Paradiso.

Lipking, Lawrence. 2000. "Poet-critics." In Litz, Menand, and Rainey 2000, 439–67.

Litz, A. Walton, Louis Menand, and Lawrence Rainey, eds. 2000. *The Cambridge History of Literary Criticism.* Vol. 7, *Modernism and the New Criticism.* Cambridge: Cambridge University Press.

Lockhart, Darrell B. 1997. "Growing Up Jewish in Mexico: Sabina Berman's *La bobe* and Rosa Nissán's *Novia que te vea.*" In Ibsen 1997, 159–74.

– 2018. "The Semiotics of Djudeo-Espanyol in Recent Works by Myriam Moscona." *iMex. México Interdisciplinario/Interdisciplinary Mexico* 2: 110–21. http://doi.org/10.23692/iMex.14.9.

Luna, Ilana Dann. 2018. *Adapting Gender: Mexican Feminisms from Literature to Film.* Albany: SUNY Press.

MacKinnon, Catharine. 1987. *Feminism Unmodified: Discourses on Life and Law.* Cambridge, MA: Harvard University Press.

Marcus, Barbara F. 2004. "Female Passion and the Matrix of Mother, Daughter, and Body: Vicissitudes of the Maternal Transference in the Working through of Sexual Inhibitions." *Psychoanalytic Inquiry* 24, no. 5: 680–712.

Marder, Elissa. 2012. *The Mother in the Age of Mechanical Reproduction: Psychoanalysis, Photography, Deconstruction*. New York: Fordham University Press.

– 2014. "From Poetic Justice to Criminal 'Jouissance': Poetry by Other Means in Baudelaire." *Yale French Studies* 125–6: 69–84.

Matitiahu, Margalit. 1988. *Kurtijo Kemado/Ḥatser ḥarukhah: shirim*. Bilingual edition. Tel-Aviv: 'Eḳed.

– 1992. *Alegrika/Alegrikah: shirim*. Bilingual edition. Tel-Aviv: 'Eḳed.

Mbembe, Achille. 2003. "Necropolitics." Translated by Libby Meintjes. *Public Culture* 15, no. 1: 11–40.

Medina, José. 2013. *The Epistemology of Resistance: Gender and Racial Oppression, Epistemic Injustice, and Resistant Imaginations*. Oxford: Oxford University Press.

Mei, Todd. 2007. "Justice and the Banning of the Poets: The Wayaod Hermeneutics in Plato's Republic." *Review of Metaphysics* 60, no. 4: 757–78.

*Merriam-Webster Dictionary*. 2022. www.merriam-webster.com.

Miller, Joshua, and Anita Norich, eds. 2016. *Languages of Modern Jewish Cultures: Comparative Perspectives*. Ann Arbor: University of Michigan Press.

Milne, Heather. 2014. "Dearly Beloveds: The Politics of Intimacy in Juliana Spahr's 'This Connection of Everyone with Lungs.'" *Mosaic: An Interdisciplinary Critical Journal* 47, no. 2: 203–18.

Monroe, Jonathan. 1987. *A Poverty of Objects: The Prose Poem and the Politics of Genre*. Ithaca: Cornell University Press.

Morales, Dionicio. 2000a. "Las amarras terrestres de Abigael Bohórquez." In Bohórquez 2000a. 11–60.

– 2000b. "Los resquebrajamientos del alma." In Bohórquez 2000a, 7–11.

Moscona, Myriam. 2015. *Ansina*. Madrid: Vaso Roto.

– 2016. *Tela de sevoya*. Mexico City: Acantilado - Quaderns Crema/ Penguin Random House.

Moseley, Christopher, ed. 2007. *Encyclopedia of the World's Endangered Languages*. New York: Routledge.

Moody-Adams, Michele. 2022. *Making Space for Justice: Social Movements, Collective Imagination, and Political Hope*. New York: Columbia University Press.

Mouffe, Chantal, ed. 1996. *Deconstruction and Pragmatism*. London: Routledge.

Munguía Zatarain, Martha. 1989. *Ya no estoy para rosas. La poesía en Sonora (1960–1975)*. Hermosillo: Universidad de Sonora.

## References

- 1994. "Abigael Bohórquez." In Foster 1994, 70–2.

Muñoz, José Esteban. 2009. *Cruising Utopia: The Then and There of Queer Futurity*. New York: NYU Press.

Murdoch, Iris. 1996. *The Sovereignty of Good*. London: Routledge, 1996.

Murray, Michelle. 2018. *Home Away from Home. Immigrant Narratives, Domesticity, and Coloniality in Contemporary Spanish Culture*. Chapel Hill: North Carolina University Press.

Nehamas, Alexander. 2007. *Only a Promise of Happiness: The Place of Beauty in a World of Art*. Princeton: Princeton University Press.

Neruda, Pablo. 1991. *Canto general*. Translated by Jack Schmitt. Introduction by Roberto González Echevarría. Berkeley: University of California Press.

- 1997. *Canto general*. Edición Enrico Mario Santí. Madrid: Cátedra.

Nicoïdski, Clarisse. 2014. *La culor dil tiempu. Poezia kompleta. El color del tiempo. Poemas completos*. Edición bilingüe. Traducción Ernesto Kavi. Mexico City: Editorial Sexto Piso.

Nussbaum, Martha C. 1995. *Poetic Justice: The Literary Imagination and Public Life*. Boston: Beacon Press.

Ortiz Domínguez, Efrén. 2004. "Sublime abyección: La poesía de Abigael Bohórquez y de Juan Bañuelos." *Ciberletras. La literatura mexicana de fines del siglo XX* 11. https://www.lehman.cuny.edu/ciberletras/archives.php.

*Oxford Dictionary of Word Origins*. 2010. Edited by Julia Cresswell. Oxford: Oxford University Press.

Pardo, José Luis. 2004. *La intimidad*. Valencia: Pretextos, 2004.

Plaskow, Judith. 1991. *Standing Again at Sinai: Judaism from a Feminist Perspective*. San Francisco: HarperCollins.

Plato. 2000. *The Republic*. Edited by G.R.F. Ferrari. Translated by Tom Griffith. Cambridge: Cambridge University Press.

Quinion, Michael. 1999. *World Wide Words. Investigating English Language across the Globe*. https://www.worldwidewords.org/qa/qa-abr1.htm.

Quintana, Aldina. 2013. "Israel bar Hayim de Belogrado, the 'Write as you speak' Principle, and the Nomenclature in the Sefer Otsar Hahayim (1823)." In Ayala, Denz, Salzer, and Schmädel 2013, 35–55.

Rabuzzi, Kathryn Allen. 1988. *Motherself: A Mythic Analysis of Motherhood*. Bloomington: Indiana University Press.

Rawls, John. 1999. *A Theory of Justice*, rev. ed. Cambridge, MA: Harvard University Press.

Rich, Adrienne. 1986. *Of Woman Born: Motherhood as Experience and Institution*. New York: W.W. Norton.

## References

Richards, Marvin. 1998. *Without Rhythm or Reason*. Gaspar de la Nuit *and the Dialectic of the Prose Poem*. Lewisburg: Bucknell University Press.

Richardson, Henry S. 1998. "Nussbaum: Love and Respect." *Metaphilosophy* 29, no. 4: 254–62.

Ricoeur, Paul. 1995. "Love and Justice." *Philosophy and Social Criticism* 21, nos. 5–6: 23–39.

Ríos Martínez del Castro, Bruno. 2013. "La soledad de un poeta. Abigael Bohórquez." https://www.tierraadentro.cultura.gob.mx/la-soledad-de-un-poeta-abigael-bohorquez.

– 2014a. "Abigael Bohórquez, obra en orfandad crítica." https://www.excelsior.com.mx/expresiones/2014/11/30/995054.

– 2014b. "¿En verdad estáis muertos?: la (in)certidumbre del deseo en *Poesida* de Abigael Bohórquez." *Gaceta Frontal*.

Rodríguez, Blanca Alberta. 2006. "El cuerpo de la escritura. Una mirada a la obra de Gloria Gervitz." *Tópicos del Seminario* 16: 93–117. https://www.redalyc.org/articulo.oa?id=59401604.

Rose, Jaqueline. 2018. *Mothers: An Essay on Love and Cruelty*. New York: Farrar, Straus and Giroux.

Rosenberg, Charles E. 1989. "What Is an Epidemic? AIDS in Historical Perspective." *Daedalus* 118, no. 2, Living With AIDS Part 1: 1–17.

Rowe, Noel, "Just Poetry." 2008. In Brennan 2008, 46-61.

Salminen, Tapani. 2007. "Europe and North Asia." In Moseley 2007, 212–80.

Scarry, Elaine. 1985. *The Body in Pain. The Making and Unmaking of the World*. New York and Oxford: Oxford University Press.

– 1999. *On Beauty and Being Just*. Princeton: Princeton University Press.

Schoenberg, Arnold. (1941) 1996. "Twelve-Tone and Serial Composition." In Kostelanetz, Darby, and Santa 1996, 233–64.

Schopenhauer, Arthur. (1851) 1974. *Parerga and Paralipomena: Short Philosophical Essays*. Vol. 2. Translated by E.F.J. Payne. Oxford: Clarendon Press.

Schwarzwald, Olga. 2010. "Two Sixteenth-Century Ladino Prayer Books for Women." *European Judaism* 43, no. 2: 37–51.

Seery, John Evan, ed. 2011. *A Political Companion to Walt Whitman*. Lexington: The University Press of Kentucky.

Sefamí, Jacobo. 2002. "Memoria e identidad en la literatura sefardí y mizrahi en Latinoamérica." *Sefarad* 62, no. 1: 143–67.

– 2005. "La herida y el milagro en las 'Migraciones' de Gloria Gervitz." *Confluencia* 20, no. 2: 13–24.

Sennett, Richard. 2017. *The Fall of Public Man*. New York and London: W.W. Norton.

Sephiha, Haïm Vidal. 1977. *L'agonie des Judéo-Espagnols*. Paris: Editions Entente.

Simon, Reeva S., Michael M. Laskier, and Sara Reguer, eds. 2003. *The Jews of the Middle East and North Africa in Modern Times*. New York: Columbia University Press.

Sontag, Susan. 2001. *Illness as Metaphor and Aids and Its Metaphors*. New York: Picador USA.

Spitzer, Leo. 1948. *Linguistics and Literary History Essays in Stylistics*. Princeton: Princeton University Press.

"A Timeline of HIV and AIDS." 2022. HIV.gov. Last updated 29 April. https://www.hiv.gov/hiv-basics/overview/history/hiv-and-aids-timeline.

Tomain, Joseph P. 2009. "Narrating Justice." *University of Cincinnati Law Review* 77, no. 3: 783–98.

Traina, Cristina L.H. 2011. *Erotic Attunement: Parenthood and the Ethics of Sensuality between Unequals*. Chicago: University of Chicago Press.

Trigo, Benigno. 2006. *Remembering Maternal Bodies: Melancholy in Latina and Latin American Women's Writing*. New York: Palgrave Macmillan.

Vallejo, César. 1978. *The Complete Posthumous Poetry*. Translated by Clayton Ashleman and José Rubia Barcia. Berkeley: University of California Press.

– 2015a. *Obra Poética Completa*. Edited, with prologue and timeline, by Enrique Ballón Aguirre. Colección Clásica 58. Caracas: Biblioteca Ayacucho.

– 2015b. *Selected Writings of César Vallejo*. Edited by Joseph Mulligan. Translated by Joseph Mulligan et al. Middletown: Wesleyan University Press.

Volger, Candace. 2000. "Sex and Talk." In Berlant 2000a, 48–85.

Walker, Michelle Boulous. 1998. *Philosophy and the Maternal Body: Reading Silence*. London/New York: Routledge.

Watney, Simon. 1997. *Policing Desire: Pornography, AIDS, and the Media*. 3rd ed. University of Minnesota Press.

Waxler, Robert P. 2008. "Changing Lives through Literature." *PMLA* 123, no. 3: 678–83.

Whitaker, Linda. 1992. "Healing the Mother/Daughter Relationship through the Therapeutic Use of Fairy Tales, Poetry, and Stories." *Journal of Poetry Therapy* 6, no. 2: 35–44.

Whitman, Walt. 1881. "The Poetry of the Future." *North American Review* 132, no. 291: 195–210. http://www.jstor.org/stable/25100937.

## References

Winnicott, Donald W. 1994. "Hate in the Counter-Transference." *Journal of Psychotherapy Practice and Research* 3, no. 4: 348–56.

Yates, Frances A. 1974. *The Art of Memory*. Chicago: University of Chicago.

Young, Iris Marion. 2003. *Political Responsibility and Structural Injustice*. Kansas City: University Press of Kansas.

Yousef, Nancy. 2013. *Romantic Intimacy*. Stanford: Stanford University Press.

Zelizer, Viviana A. 2005. *The Purchase of Intimacy*. Princeton: Princeton University Press.

Zirker, Angelika. 2015–16. "Poetic Justice: A Few Reflections on the Interplay of Poetry and Justice." *Connotations* 25, no. 2: 135–51.

# Index

Abravanel, Isaac, 81, 92, 164n24
act, 4–5, 10–14, 21–2, 84, 101–1,
    143, 151n8. *See also* deed
activism, 11, 37, 57–9, 147;
    narrative, 6
aesthetics, 18, 22, 97, 144, 153n18
Agamben, Giorgio, 42
agency, 7, 12–15, 26, 43, 48, 52,
    57, 125, 135, 170n14; spatial
    distribution of, 105. *See also* act;
    border; frontier; sovereignty
AIDS, 29–33, 40–2, 44–7, 51–5,
    58, 62–3; epidemic, 37–9,
    155n10, 155n11. *See also* pan-
    demic; Sida
Aizenberg, Edna, 163n18
aletheia, 19
alterity, 13–14, 26, 42, 153n18.
    *See also* identity; selfhood
amnesia, 8, 100. *See also*
    memory; oblivion
Arenas, Reinaldo, 47
Arendt, Hannah, 177n5
Arfuch, Leonor, 13
Aristodemou, Maria, 6
Aristotle, 9, 152n14, 161n10;
    *Aristotle on Memory and*

*Recollection*, 70, 161n10;
    *Nicomachean Ethics*, 9; *Poetics*,
    152n14. *See also* Bloch, David
Attias, David, 159n3
Auden, W.H., 144
*audi alteram partem*, 15, 27
authority, 7, 13, 21–2, 31, 38, 104,
    107–8, 110, 117–20, 174n36
autonomy, 15, 168n4; individual,
    115. *See also* sovereignty

Badiou, Alain, 142–3; *In Praise
    of Love*, 142
Bakhtin, Mikhail, 13–15, 98;
    *Problems of Dostoevsky's
    Poetics*, 13–15; *Towards a
    Philosophy of the Act*, 25. *See
    also* dialogism
Balbuena, Monique, 77, 95,
    163n19, 165n28
Bañuelos, Juan, 35
Baudelaire, Charles, 23–5
Beiner, Ronald, 177n5
Benjamin, Mara, 118
Berardi, Franco "Bifo," 150n5
Berlant, Lauren, 13, 41, 57, 104–5,
    116, 167n1; "Intimacy," 13;

"Sex in Public," 104–5, 116; "Slow Death," 57–8. *See also* Warner, Michael

Bernstein, Paula, 167n2

Bersani, Leo, 37–8; "Is the Rectum a Grave?," 38

Bertrand, Aloysius, 24

Bianchi, Emanuella, 16–17

binary, 4, 17, 116, 168n4. *See also* sensuality

Bloch, David, 161n10

body, 28, 41, 45, 55, 58–9, 67, 86, 93–4, 109–10, 116–17, 124, 128–9, 136–40, 146, 167n2, 174n36; infirm, 32; politic, 32, 43; social, 13

Bohórquez, Abigael, 27, 29–33, 34–7, 41–5, 49, 52, 62–3; *Fe de bautismo*, 34; *Poesida*, 27, 29–33, 35–6, 39–40, 43, 49, 51, 55, 58, 59

border, 104; US/Mexico, 27, 34, 36, 45. *See also* frontier

Borovaya, Olga, 162n14

Breuning, LeRoy, 153n18

Bunis, David, 68–9, 74–5, 80–1, 83, 85–7, 111, 159n2, 159n3, 163n16, 23

Burt, E.S., 25

Butler, Judith, 58

Cassani, Alessia, 78–9

Castillo, Anna, 170n11

Castro, Américo, 149n4

Catelli, Nora, 142

Celan, Paul, 81, 92

Chodorow, Nancy, 112–13

Christakis, Nicholas, 33

citizenship, 38, 114, 153n17

Cixous, Hélène, 136

class, 32, 38, 42, 51, 111, 113, 114, 117, 125

closeness, 10–11, 23, 56, 105–6, 117, 127, 139, 145–7. *See also* intimacy; radical proximity; togetherness

Cohen, Julia, 162n12, 162n13

Cohen, Marcel, 77, 164n27

community, 3, 7, 76, 91, 110

consonance, 17–18, 105

Corral, Fortino, 35, 43

Cover, Robert, 5, 7

Dalton, Harlon L., 155n10

daughter, 28, 30, 90, 93–4, 106, 107–8, 111–13, 114–18, 119–20, 125–8, 130–4, 139–40, 168n4, 170n13, 170n14. *See also* mother

de la Cadena, Omar, 36, 155n8

deed, 11–12, 25, 37. *See also* act

Deleuze, Gilles, 95, 98. *See also* Guattari, Félix; minor literature

Derrida, Jacques, 150n6

desire, 20, 31–3, 63, 89–91, 108, 110–13, 115–17, 125–6, 128–31, 134, 139–40, 146; homoerotic 35, 128, 131; sexuality, 128. *See also* closeness; intimacy; resistance

dialogism, 13–15, 35

dialogue, 14, 18, 36, 82, 84, 139; inner, 15. *See also* dialogism

diaspora, 69, 98–9, 122–3, 126; diasporic context, 71, 77, 90, 161n5; Sephardic, 27, 81, 159n2. *See also* exile; Jews

diglossia, 67, 71

dissonance, 17–19, 35, 97, 105

Dolven, Jeff, 21–2

Domínguez, Efrén Ortiz, 35
Dowling, Emma, 114

elegy/elegiac, 28, 36, 45, 49, 53,
    78, 93, 94, 97, 107, 124–5,
    128, 168. *See also* mourning
empathy, 11, 62, 89
enladinar, 71, 80, 159n3. *See also*
    Jewish languages
Enlightenment, 21, 71, 73
epistemic event, 101
epistemic resistance, 65; struggles,
    27, 65, 142
equity, 3, 104. *See also* fairness
erotic attunement, 117
eroticism, 110, 133, 136, 138;
    auto-, 108, 128–30, 134, 136,
    138; homo-, 108, 128, 134;
    incest, 108, 112, 114, 134,
    170n10; queer, 108; self-, 129.
    *See also* desire; sensuality; sex
ethics, 9–12, 21, 45, 104,
    110, 123, 141. *See also*
    injustice; justice
ethnicity, 8, 76, 83, 113, 114
ethos, 20, 113, 120; morality 22–3,
    114; pedagogical, 101. *See also*
    ethics
Evans, Mary, 107
exile, 17, 35, 47, 99, 122, 126, 138,
    159n2. *See also* diaspora
exodus, 81, 121. *See also* exile
exophony, 78, 96
exotopy, 96, 98; outside-
    situatedness, 80, 98
expulsion, 68–9, 71, 92, 97, 159n2;
    Edict of, 97, 164n24. *See also*
    diaspora; exile
extimacy, 12, 20, 89, 93. *See also*
    intimacy; radical proximity

fairness, 4, 5, 9, 20–2, 85, 105–8,
    119, 122, 149n1, 152n15.
    *See also* equity
feminism, 6–7, 16, 28, 107,
    112–14, 134, 140, 142, 168n4,
    170n13, 170n14; Jewish, 69,
    111–12, 122–3, 137
Ferré, Rosario, 126
Fischlin, Daniel, 16
Frank, Jill, 19–20
Freedman, Jonathan, 16
freedom, 52, 63, 84, 118, 121
Fresco, David, 64, 74, 101
Freud, Sigmund, 107, 112–14,
    122, 134, 170n10
frontier, 4–5, 12, 17, 36, 45,
    105, 108, 116, 119, 126,
    132, 140, 147, 177n4,
    178n8; existential, 119;
    obliteration of, 116; of
    the law, 17. *See also* agency;
    border; limit

Gabbay, Cynthia, 82, 101
Garapon, Antoine, 26
García Lorca, Federico, 48–9
Gelman, Juan, 76, 78, 163n19
gender, 29–30, 32, 38, 42, 76,
    95, 117, 118–19, 125;
    asymmetry, 114, 134; gap, 69
Gervitz, Gloria, 28, 106–7;
    109–10, 125, 134, 138, 146,
    170n7; *Migraciones*, 28, 106,
    108–12, 117, 118, 124–5,
    128, 131–3, 169n5
Giménez Cacho, Julia, 109
Graubard, Stephen, 32–3
Guattari, Félix, 95, 98. *See also*
    Deleuze, Gilles
gynaeodicy, 111

## Index

Hades, 48, 127
Halberstam, Jack, 42–3
harmony, 3, 94, 105, 152n12;
    atonal music, 17–18, 105;
    in music, 17–19; social,
    18–19, 24. *See also*
    consonance; dissonance
Hatty, James, 41
Hatty, Suzanne, 41
Hebrew Bible, 70, 122, 143
Herzfeld, Michael, 176n3
heteroglossia, 76, 122, 173n25.
    *See also* Jewish languages
heteronomy, 118
Holocaust, 28, 75, 77–8, 81, 89,
    92, 164n27, 165n28
Huerta, Efraín, 34
Huidobro, Vicente, 36
human rights, 6, 31, 47.
    *See also* sensuality

identity, 11–12, 15–16, 28, 76,
    78, 80–1, 89, 97, 112–14,
    134, 142, 153n18, 165n32,
    170n13. *See also* alterity;
    intimacy; relationality
ideology, 8, 31, 41, 65, 71–2, 75,
    78, 101, 141
illness, 29–33, 38, 74. *See also*
    AIDS; pandemic; Sida
imagination, 8, 38, 61–2, 70,
    90, 139, 146–7, 161n10;
    dialogic, 13–15; literary, 7, 22;
    social, 65
inequality, 10–11, 107, 114, 117.
    *See also* injustice; justice
injustice, 5, 8, 10–11, 25–6,
    29, 32, 43, 51–2, 83, 107, 114,
    147, 151n8; epistemic, 65.
    *See also* inequality; justice

institution, 10–11, 23, 42, 84; of
    intimacy, 113, 134, 143, 167n3,
    176n3; legal, 5, 7, 19–21·
intimacy, 4–5, 10–15, 16–18,
    27–8, 82, 84, 86, 89, 93, 100–1,
    103–8, 113, 116–18, 124, 133,
    134, 139–45, 149n1, 150n7,
    151n10, 155n6, 167–8n3,
    176n3, 177n4; breach of, 7, 28,
    101, 134; *intime*, 15; maternal,
    107, 140; sexual, 55. *See also*
    closeness; extimacy; radical
    proximity; togetherness
intimate, 10, 12–14, 26–8, 30,
    32, 42, 45, 65, 69, 71, 79, 81–2,
    84, 95, 104, 107, 108, 122, 133,
    142, 176–7n3; bond, 12;
    dialogue, 122; form of respect,
    151n9; lyric setting, 10;
    motherhood, 134; practices,
    168n3; public sphere, 30, 177n4;
    relationship, 100, 108; space
    of the self, 26; territory of the,
    176n3; word, 14
Irigaray, Luce, 115–16, 171n14

Jakobsen, Janet R., 149n2
Jewish languages, 122; Judeo-
    Spanish, 8, 27, 81, 84, 163n18;
    Ladino, 68–70, 75, 80, 97,
    161n8, 161n9, 163n23. *See also*
    Judezmo; Yiddish
Jewish literature, 68–70, 73–5,
    76–80, 95–7, 159n3, 163n23
Jews, 16, 71–5, 88, 95, 122, 149n2;
    Ashkenazi, 76; Ashkenazim, 75;
    Iberian, 64, 68–9, 97; normative,
    122, 165n32; Sephardic, 28, 64,
    69, 71, 74, 78–9, 81–2, 100;
    Sephardim, 27, 70–1, 73–6,

78–9, 99, 159n2, 163n16, 165n28. *See also* diaspora

Johnston, David, 20, 152n15

Jones, Gail, 8–9

Juan de la Cruz, San, 96–8

Judezmo, 8–9, 27–8, 64–8, 71–6, 77–9, 80–2, 90–2, 97, 99–101, 159n2, 159n3, 161n5, 162n11, 163n16; afterlife of a language, 65, 102; Djidio/Djudio, 75; Djudeo-Espanyol, 79; Espanyol muestro, 75; Haketia, 27, 75; Judeo-Español, 75; Spanyolit, 27. *See also* Jewish languages

Julien, François, 15; *L'intime* 15

jurisprudence, 6. *See also* law

justice, 3–4, 8–12, 16, 19–23, 25–7, 28, 33, 74–5, 100–1, 104, 106, 111, 114, 117–19, 122, 140, 143, 146; epistemic, 65; poetic, 7–8, 21–2, 42, 62–3; social, 7, 27, 29, 62, 149n2, 150n5; theory of, 5, 152n12, 152n15. *See also* injustice

Kafka, Franz, 95, 98

Karageorgou-Bastea, Christina, 35, 172n18

Kullavanijaya, Pranee, 13

language, 27, 64–80, 84–7, 89, 91, 94–6, 98–101, 106, 113, 117, 120, 122–3, 125–7, 133, 134, 139, 143, 146, 150n5, 150n7, 159n1, 159n2, 159–60n3, 160n4, 161n5, 161n9, 162n11, 162n13, 163n16, 163n17, 163n18, 163n19, 163n20, 164n25, 164n26, 164n27, 165n28, 169n6, 174n36;

aesthetic use of, 67, 85, 98, 143; of desire 139; excess of, 127, 150n5; foreign, 167n40; holy tongue, 68–9, 122; mother tongue, 67, 73, 99, 111, 126; native linguistic competence, 67, 99–100, 102; poetic, 9, 150n5; post-vernacular, 67

Lares, Ismael, 36

Latin-American literature, 35, 51, 78, 82, 141

law, 5–9, 17, 22–5, 85, 112, 118–19, 137–8, 143–5, 151n11, 176n3; lawmaker 7, 61–2. *See also* jurisprudence; limit; legality; legitimacy; nomos

legality, 6, 8, 20–1, 118. *See also* law

legitimacy, 9–10, 23–24, 121

León, Denise, 77

Lethe, 109; river, 111, 127, 132. *See also* aletheia

liability, 5, 11, 151n8

limit, 4, 7, 9, 11–12, 17, 21, 25, 31, 52, 85, 93, 104–6, 111–12, 116, 118, 120, 129, 131, 132, 150n5, 151n10, 151–2n11, 153n19, 173n23, 173n25, 174n32, 175n42; of death, 63; of expressivity, 95; of incest, 134; of intimacy, 108, 124; *límite*, 132; of self, 145; of sociability, 52; spatial limitations, 95–6. *See also* law; prohibition

Lipking, Lawrence, 153n18

Lockhart, Darrell, 76, 78–9, 163n17

love, 28, 44–5, 47, 61, 83, 97–8, 142–5, 151n9, 152n16, 177n5; law of, 144–5 lyricism, 8, 45, 77, 86; lyric poetry, 8–9, 15, 19–20, 25, 26, 31, 141; lyric self, 37, 45, 48–51, 108, 121, 139, 174n36; self and other, 30, 32, 63. *See also* poetry

Machado, Antonio, 49
MacKinnon, Catharine, 133
Manrique, Jorge, 52
Marcus, Barbara, 170n14
Marder, Elissa, 23–4, 125–6
Martí, José, 94, 176n2
Matitiahu, Margalit, 76–7
matrix, 94, 106, 108, 136
Mbembe, Achille, 45. *See also* politics: necropolitics
Medina, José, 9, 65, 97; *The Epistemology of Resistance*, 65
Mei, Todd, 6, 149n3
Mejía, Luz María, 109
memory, 8–9, 12, 14, 25, 32, 38, 40, 43, 58, 70, 76, 93, 100, 101, 105, 108, 110–11, 122–3, 129, 134, 161n10, 167n2, 168n4, 170n6, 171n16, 172n19, 173n26, 173n28; poetic, 101. *See also* amnesia; oblivion
Mexican literature, 34–6, 71, 76, 78, 82
minor literature, 78, 95. *See also* Deleuze, Gilles; Guattari, Félix
modernity, 55, 70–1, 142; early, 64, 149n4
monologue, 35, 88; dramatic, 36. *See also* dialogue
Monroe, Jonathan, 153n18
Moody-Adams, Michele, 6–7; *Making Space for Justice*, 6–7
Morales, Dionicio, 35

Moscona, Myriam, 8–9, 27–8, 70–1, 75, 78–82, 99–101, 162n11; *Ansina*, 8–10, 27, 65–7, 70–1, 75, 78–82, 85–9, 98–102; *Tela de sevoya*, 75, 79
mother, 6, 28, 49–50, 77, 93–4, 106–8, 110–14, 115–19, 124–8, 131–4, 138–40, 167n2, 168n4; attachment to, 107, 112, 126, 131, 134, 168n4; authority of, 108, 117, 174n36; grief for, 124; law of the mother, 137–8; mothering, 107, 112, 115; tongue, 67, 73, 99, 111, 126. *See also* daughter; elegy/elegiac
mourning, 93–4, 127–30, 168n4. *See also* elegy/elegiac
Munguía Zatarain, Martha Elena, 35
Muñoz, José Esteban, 42–3, 55
Murdoch, Iris, 99, 167n40, 177n6; *The Sovereignty of Good*, 167n40
Murray, Michelle, 170n12
music, 17–19, 47; atonal, 17–18, 105. *See also* consonance; dissonance; harmony

Nehamas, Alexander, 22–3
Neruda, Pablo, 49–51
Nice, Vivian, 107; *Mothers and Daughters*, 107
Nicoïdski, Clarisse, 76–7
Nissán, Rosa, 76
nomos, 5. *See also* law
Nussbaum, Martha, 7, 61–2

oblivion, 16, 32, 108–9, 111, 132, 139

orality, 35, 64–5, 67, 69–70, 75–6, 80–1, 84, 163n23

Ottoman Empire, 71–5, 100, 159n3, 162n12, 162n13

outcast, 29, 32, 36, 47, 49, 58, 71. *See also* pariah

pandemic, 33, 37–9, 45–6. *See also* AIDS; Sida

pariah, 27, 38, 47, 49, 70. *See also* outcast

parity, 8, 10, 13, 15, 19, 78, 105, 111, 167n1. *See also* fairness; justice

Paz, Octavio, 34

Pellicer, Carlos, 34

Pentateuch, 68

performance, 33, 42–3, 176n3

perspectivism, 6, 149n4

phagocytosis, 128

Plaskow, Judith, 122

Plato, 6, 19–20, 24, 152n12, 152n14, 152n16

poetry, 4–5, 7–10, 19, 23–7, 29–30, 61–2, 67, 85, 91, 121, 135, 141, 143, 145, 150n5, 152n14, 153n18; Latin-American, 44, 78, 82, 141; lyric, 8–9, 15, 19–20, 25, 26, 31, 141; Mexican, 35–6, 78, 82; mystical, 31, 97. *See also* lyricism

polis, 5–6, 16–17, 19, 22, 24–5, 134; Kallipolis, 19

politics, 11–13, 25, 28, 42, 47, 82–5, 113–14, 141–3, 165n28; biopolitics, 42; global, 47; necropolitics, 45

power, 13, 45, 105, 108, 113, 115, 117–19, 133, 167n1. *See also* authority; law

praxis, 10, 21, 104, 146

prohibition, 85, 112, 125, 131, 173n23, 174n36, 175n39, 175n42; of incest, 170n10

prose poem, 24–5, 77, 85–6, 109, 153n18. *See also* lyricism; poetry

Pythia, 109, 111, 132–3, 139, 174n33, 175n37

queer, 16, 27–8, 42–3, 48–9, 51–6, 136; failure, 9, 42–3; sociability, 32–3, 49. *See also* desire; eroticism

race, 8, 29, 35, 38, 42, 51, 83, 97, 111, 113–14, 117, 125, 141–2

racism, 35, 37. *See also* race

radical proximity, 4–5, 9–10, 12, 14, 16, 26, 28, 31, 69, 94, 101, 104, 106, 124, 139–40, 145–7, 149n1, 150n7, 151n9, 167n1. *See also* closeness; intimacy; togetherness

Rawls, John, 5, 10, 15, 152n12, 152n15, 176n3

receptacle, 16–17, 106, 117; chōra, 16–17. *See also* polis

reciprocity, 5, 11, 20-1, 152n15; balanced, 20; unbalanced 20

relationality, 9–12, 65, 106, 114, 118–19, 124, 133, 148, 149n1; relational sociability, 9, 30, 65, 105–7; relations of asymmetry, 8, 105. *See also* identity

representation, 3, 17, 84, 90; artistic, 143; literary, 86, 120. *See also* imagination

reproduction, 28, 129; of motherhood, 113, 115, 118, 134, 139, 146, 170n14

# Index

resistance, 13, 25, 35, 42–3, 65, 136, 141, 150n5

responsibility, 10–12, 26–7, 62, 114, 118, 147, 150n6, 151n9. *See also* justice

retribution, 20. *See also* justice

Rich, Adrienne, 114

Richards, Marvin, 153n18

Richardson, Henry, 151n9

Ricoeur, Paul, 143

*Roe v. Wade*, 28

Rosenberg, Charles E., 38–9

Rowe, Noel, 8, 9

Rymer, Thomas, 21

Salinas, Pedro, 172n21

Salminen, Tapani, 159n2

Scarry, Elaine, 22, 150n7, 152n16

Schafer, Mark, 109, 111, 120

Schoenberg, Arnold, 17–19, 105

Schopenhauer, Arthur, 151n11

Schwarzwald, Ora, 161n9

Sefamí, Jacobo, 78, 95, 110, 163n17

self-estrangement, 97

selfhood, 5, 28, 42, 107, 151n11, 170n14

sensuality, 51–2, 117, 121, 129, 134; as human right, 31. *See also* eroticism

sex, 52, 104; heteronormative, 42–3, 55; masturbatory, 128–9, 136–7; queer, 28, 49, 59, 136; sexual exuberance, 134; sexuality, 31, 41, 55, 108, 115, 138–9, 168n4, 170n14; unsafe, 30. *See also* binary; eroticism

Shoah. *See* Holocaust

Sida, 30, 39–40, 50, 53, 55. *See also* AIDS

silence, 9, 12, 27–8, 52, 65, 86, 101–2, 103, 120, 126–7, 135; silencing other kinds of knowledge, 65

simulacrum, 102

slow death, 57

sociability, 4–5, 9–10, 52, 94, 133, 149n1; democratic, 65; queer, 32–3, 49; relational, 9, 30, 65, 105–7

solidarity, 20, 47, 124–5

Sontag, Susan, 38; *Illness as Metaphor*, 38

sovereignty, 15, 42–3, 118. *See also* agency

Spanish, 31, 46, 67–8, 76, 78, 80–2, 92, 98, 99, 127, 163n18; Castilian, 64, 74, 77, 97, 99. *See also* diglossia; language

sphere: domestic, 67–8, 124; private, 90; public, 17, 30, 38, 73, 107, 141, 176n3

Spitzer, Leo, 149n4

state, 25, 84, 141, 143; of injustice, 32; State of Israel, 64, 90

Supreme Court, 5, 28

togetherness, 4, 10, 12, 20, 91, 113, 127, 129, 134, 146–7, 149n1. *See also* closeness; intimacy; radical proximity

Tomain, Joseph, 6

tongue, 86, 101, 127–8, 134, 136, 139–40; mother tongue, 67, 73, 99, 111, 126. *See also* language

Torah, 68, 85, 122–3

Traina, Cristina, 117

Trigo, Benigno, 126, 172n23, 175n39

*Trilce*, 31, 154n5

utopia, 8, 33, 42–4, 62–3

Vallejo, César, 30–1, 44, 146–7
value, 20, 60, 150n5; civic, 29
Vega, Garcilaso de la, 172n21
Vidal Sephiha, Haïm, 161n7
virtue, 19, 21, 22, 147, 152n16;
epistemic, 97; social, 5, 27; of
virtues, 104

Walker, Michelle Boulous, 170n14
Warner, Michael, 104–5, 116,
167n1
Watney, Simon, 37–8, 156n15;
*Policing Desire*, 37–8

Whitman, Walt, 25, 48–9, 61–2,
153n17
Winnicott, Donald, 103, 113–14;
"Hate in the Counter-
Transference," 113–14

Yates, Frances, 161n10
Yiddish, 110, 122, 173n25. *See also*
Jewish languages
Young, Iris Marion, 10–11, 151n8
Yousef, Nancy, 5, 11–12, 103,
106, 155n6

Zelizer, Viviana E., 167n3
Zirker, Angelika, 21